John Franklin Crowell

Logical Process of social Development

A theoretical Foundation for Education policy from the Standpoint of Sociology

John Franklin Crowell

Logical Process of social Development

A theoretical Foundation for Education policy from the Standpoint of Sociology

ISBN/EAN: 9783337073787

Printed in Europe, USA, Canada, Australia, Japan

Cover: Foto ©ninafisch / pixelio.de

More available books at **www.hansebooks.com**

THE

LOGICAL PROCESS

OF

SOCIAL DEVELOPMENT

*A Theoretical Foundation for Educational Policy
from the Standpoint of Sociology*

BY

JOHN FRANKLIN CROWELL, Ph.D., L.H.D.

*Sometime Larned Scholar in Philosophy, Yale University
Sometime University Fellow in Sociology, Columbia University
Late President of Trinity College, North Carolina*

NEW YORK
HENRY HOLT AND COMPANY
1898

PREFACE.

THE social process in its logical character is here regarded as *the process of the selective survival of types of personality*. This process of course takes place under the natural conditions of personal association and through the historical tendencies of the social organization. The development of the social population is thus systematically realized by man's membership in typical groups capable of being coordinated in the common pursuit of a more or less conscious social policy.

Social policy requires us to recognize two primary factors—the natural conditions and the historical conceptions by which aggregates of men in organized association are influenced. The purpose here is to study the conceptual life of social aggregates as historically organized in order to arrive at some statement of the logical modes and the forms of their reckoning as communities and peoples.

The study of the logical process by which social aggregates are guided in their development at once raises the following questions:

1. Is there any class of conceptions by which a

community conscious of its conditions, its functions, its character and aims really reasons out the
process of its development ?

2. If there are such conceptions, on what conditions natural to human association and in what
forms known to human thought may these conceptions be regarded as the working standards of
the social process ?

3. And if these conditions and operative norms
of personal association are determinable, by what
axiomatic sequences or scale of convictions known
to human history must we conceive of the social
population as attaining to the successive stages of
its development ?

4. And if such developmental axioms are historically definable, on the assumption of what sociological hypothesis can these differentiating axioms
and those integrating conditions of natural association be coordinated so as to give us the fundamental law of the process of social development ?

5. And, finally, if such a law can be inferred from
social phenomena, by what sociological methods
must we proceed in order to give to this conclusion
the warrant of scientific demonstration and at the
same time lay the foundation for a social policy
whose complemental aspects are the employment
and education of the individual through association into the solidarity of the ideal ?

These questions indicate the attitude entertained
for a decade toward sociology in the hope of finding there a more satisfactory basis of educational
policy. Neither the Positivist idea of humanity as

the universal aim of education nor the Herbartian conception of the ideal personality as the norm of educational effort seemed to me to have mastered the facts which sociology has been forcing upon our attention. Particularly were they defective in not recognizing sufficiently what sociology had suggested but did not develop, namely, the fact of the self-conscious community and its selective function in fashioning personality in accordance with its own typical standards. On this account it seemed to me that the whole superstructure of educational organization was built too largely without foundation in associative reality. To what that is fundamental and ultimate in social thought do the facts lead back ? To what line of policy would we naturally and historically be obliged to conform if we proceed on this basis ?

These aspects of the subject engaged my attention first as a graduate student in philosophy in Yale University, after having made a summer's investigation into the employment of children in American industries (Andover Review, Vol. 4, July, 1885). Subsequently as President of Trinity College, North Carolina, active relations with college and commonwealth forced upon my attention from another point of view the necessity of reconstructing the theoretical foundations of educational policy in the light of social conditions generally. My part in the conduct of an educational investigation in New York City under the Tenement House Commission of 1894 revealed the municipal aspect of the same general problem. Finally as Fellow of

Sociology in Columbia University I began to put
in shape the conclusions to which this official experience had led me, only again to be interrupted
by two professional engagements—a course of lectures on Railroad Problems in the graduate depart-
ment of Columbia University and two years of
teaching economics and sociology in Smith College, Massachusetts. Both of these engagements,
however, materially helped to widen the scope and
emphasize the importance of the problem to be
solved.

This problem in process of solution became twofold in its character. First, to determine in a theoretical outline the nature and logical method of
the social process; and, secondly, on the foundation of these results, to determine the normal educational policy for the community. As it now
stands, this volume is offered as one way of working out the first of these problems—that of arriving
at such an interpretation of the logical process of
social development as will serve for a conceptual
outline of social policy in which education may
take its normal part in national progress. In a sub-
sequent volume on the social principles of educational policy it is my purpose to make concrete application of these conceptions to actual conditions.
But in the present volume it is only intended to lay
bare the sociological foundations in the form of
abstract conceptions with which a theoretically
sound and a normally progressive educational policy must reckon. This basis it is believed is given
us in the sociological conceptions, that, between·

the limits of animality and ideality, it is the social
process that really educates us by the selective evolution of types of personality; that these types of
personality begin with the organic and normally
prevail by being social, thence through the potentially normal or sociological type they tend to reach
the ideal; that this progression is attained by the
individuation of organic man with the potentially
normal type ; that educational policy finds its
standard, not solely in the ethical culture of the
individual will, nor in the universal ideal of the
race, but in the social type of personality that
normally tends to prevail at that time and place in
the *direction* of the ideal in which the community
finds its solidarity.

No bibliography has been added because the
sociological writings of Spencer, Ward, Giddings,
Mayo-Smith, Patten, Small, Vincent, Ross, Nash
and Fairbank, in English, are all available. The
bibliography in Giddings' Principles of Sociology
is extensive and recent enough as a reference list
for the purposes of this volume. On logical method
most use has been made of Lotze's Logic translated
by Bosanquet, together with Mill's Logic, especially the sixth book, in which we have the first
classic attempt after Comte to formulate a logic of
the social sciences prior to the evolutionary era of
thought beginning with 1859. Within more recent
years we are especially indebted to Tarde and
Durkheim of France, Simmel of Germany, and
Baldwin of Princeton, with others worthy of special
mention for positive contributions to sociological

method.   For current discussions I have relied
mostly upon two American journals, The Annals
of the American Academy of Political and Social
Science (Philadelphia) and the Journal of Sociology (Chicago).

I am much indebted for helpful suggestion, criticism and encouragement to my friend and former
teacher, Professor Giddings, of Columbia University.

J. F. C.

New York City, January, 1898.

TABLE OF CONTENTS.

ix

BOOK I.

THE SOCIETARY PROCESS.

THE LOGICAL PROCESS

OF

SOCIAL DEVELOPMENT.

CHAPTER I.

INTRODUCTION : SOCIOLOGICAL THEORY.

THIS book is a theoretical attempt to introduce orderly arrangement into the study of the phenomena of social life by the rigid application of a single logical hypothesis—the selective survival of sociological types.

In this fundamental law of the social process the governing principle is found which defines the relation of personality to social development. By the application of this principle to the interpretation of personality in relation to nature and to civilization a theoretical foundation is laid for educational policy centering in the type of personality as the product of human association.

Before proceeding to make formal analysis of social phenomena it is well to sketch in relief the comprehensive outline of the subject before us. Sociology is both a scientific and a logical body of knowledge. It is scientific in taking account of the concrete social conditions sensibly apprehended by

3

us. It is logical in abstracting from these concrete conditions those working forms of thought by which theoretical procedure is made possible in any science. Likewise is it natural and historical· in its character as knowledge. Sociology in its theoretical aspects, often called social theory, is a pure science of society. A pure science gives expression to the results of comparison exclusively.* Sociological theory, which is properly contrasted with all systematic social sciences, makes comparisons between the set of facts given us in sensible experience as social beings and the necessary truths or norms of our subjective life regarded as fixed features of the inner life of the race. We thus compare natural aspects of association and historic qualities of social organization. The essential results of this comparison are a third set of rational propositions concerning the social life of man, which it is our business here to elaborate.

These rational propositions systematically arranged and illustrated give us the principles which constitute the pure science of society. These principles are of course abstract, but none the less principles of social reality; and, having as valid a reality as the phenomena from which they are inferred, they can be merged into no social science less general than that which gives them birth, without entailing confusion of method and wastefulness of effort. But out of sociological principles, properly elaborated from analysis of the phe-

* James, Psychology, Vol. II., p. 641.

nomena of society and synthesis of these fundamental results, there must necessarily arise that
clear-sighted grasp of methods and aims in a systematic treatment of the facts of human association, which will bring helpfulness to every kindred
branch of social research, harmony among all disposed to find the truth that in them lies and pre-
dictive service of the greatest value to an otherwise
haphazard and eclectic social policy of civilized
communities. The pure science of society is
therefore necessary as a preliminary step to the
scientific mastery of the materials of a systematic
sociology as well as for the conscious mastery by
society of its own destiny. To the pure science of
society, or sociological theory, Tarde gave the
name of Social Logic—a proper designation so far
as sociological theory is the attempt to determine
the logical processes especially appropriate for the
investigation of social phenomena.

Sociology, in its systematic aspects, is directly
concerned with the concrete materials of social existence. With the logical methods and aims developed by the study of the conceptual elements
of social phenomena as given in theory, the sociologist now proceeds to a systematic analysis, classification and coordination of the facts which enter
into association. Hence sociological theory is the
logical aspect and systematic sociology is the scientific aspect of the subject of sociology. The one
furnishes the theoretical method which enables
the other to control materials: together they develop a sociological science.

Sociological theory is primarily concerned with four main aspects of its subject. They are respectively associative conceptions, normative axioms, developmental laws and interpretative methods. Otherwise expressed they are

1. The Conditioning Forms and the Abiding Relations, under which we group those observable phenomena which belong to the collective experience of personalities in human association. This part of the subject requires an analysis of what is conveniently termed the Societary Process. From this analysis we arrive at the theoretical conditions perceived to be necessary and the theoretical relations conceived to be universal as the structural postulates of the selective survival of types. A social type presumes certain conditions and relations.

2. The Sociological Axioms or functional sanctions which are theoretically normal to both the thought and things of social reality. These axiomatic criteria comprise deductions made from the comparison of the concrete conditions and the conceptual relations peculiar to the societary process. A social type survives by respecting certain social sanctions.

3. The Sociological Laws, or those fundamental principles by which we explain the human relations as social facts persisting under the orderly succession of social events. These laws comprise (1) an hypothetical induction under which the natural conditions and the historical forces recognized in sociological theory are brought into a self-consistent

synthesis; and (2) a series of deductions from this induction corresponding to the established forms and the active relations of men with one another in the social process. Social types develop by virtue of this reaction resulting from change.

4. The Sociological Method, or modes of sociological procedure, by which, in accordance with the laws or principles previously elaborated, we make theoretical preparation for descriptive exposition, practical investigation, and administrative criticism of the course of social life in any or all of its aspects, in their bearing upon the type of personality that normally tends to prevail. Social types are our instrument of logical interpretation.

In this purely theoretical enquiry little attempt has been made at illustration of statement. Some degree of familiarity with the data of sociology is taken for granted. But, owing to the commonly confused idea as to what sociology at heart really is concerned with, and fearing lest the reader may at times find difficulty in connecting the more abstract phases of this analysis with concrete social fact, certain elemental assumptions, or view-points, as to things essentially social are put in formal statement.

It is avowedly assumed, to begin with, that the personal units which compose the collective bodies of men, with which our subject is primarily concerned, are each normally endowed with what for want of a better name we must call a social sense. This is the personal capacity, partly instinctive and partly intelligent, by reason of which every person

in associative existence may be relied upon to exercise certain social preferences, involving reciprocal relations with his own kind, and of avoiding
reciprocal relations with other kinds of beings. ·

1. The first of these assumptions is that man prefers to survive by living in association with a kindred type of being. Man is capable of entering
into truly conscious community of life with others
like himself; he is capable of consciously distinguishing one kind from other kinds, and from other
beings of a different kind.*

This we may call the social impulse, or survival
by a sort of selective coherence with the serviceable objects of associative choice.   Up to a certain
limit man prefers subjection in association to freedom in isolation.   This primary preference may be
called sociality, sociability, fellowship.

2. The next assumption is that, so far as the conditions of existence permit, man not only tends to
associate himself with those particular types of personality which are like himself in kind, but he re-
sists any associative relation which tends to subordinate him to an inferior rather than to develop
him toward a superior type.   Among different
types of personality he is capable of distinguishing
not only between a tendency toward the superior
and subordinate or inferior, but also of utilizing
means toward the end deemed superior, and of
disengaging himself, in thought if not in fact, from
one and of realizing or endeavoring to realize the
other type of being.

* James, Psychology, Vol. II., pp. 430, 431,

This personal capacity we may call social intelligence, or development by a sort of selective synthesis of the means to the ends conceived of as superior.

This selective survival of types of personal attainment through the agency of synthetic adaptation is an equally fundamental social fact. But this aspect of man's social sense is reflective.

3. This fundamental fact of the survival of types by selecting kindred degrees of personal attainment in the social process leads us to the point of view from which it is desired to proceed, namely, that sociology is preeminently concerned with types of personality. The real member of society is consciously participating in tendencies among typical groups. Not with social man disassociated from individual man is sociology concerned, but with that only real personality in which the individual and the social are complemental and correspond as the two terms of a fractionally expressed ratio correspond. The relative efficiency of these personal beings in keeping up with such groupal tendency determines the social type with which each member of the community affiliates. In this aspect social man appears as an organic factor.

4. The reciprocal association of persons typically grouped together in social tendencies requires a fourth assumption—that these social tendencies have a capacity to set out before themselves singly and severally more or less conscious ends or aims conceived as normally necessary for their self-reali-

zation. In this aspect social man evinces a potential capacity.

There are, therefore, four forms of coexistence under which social man associates in typical groups with his fellows :

Persons may be *typically alike,* in which case we should have a *homogeneous type.* Typal community of kind is the simplest ground of coexistence in association. The personal quality is like enough to actualize association. Here we have the factor of *Fellowship* in society, or the simple impulse to act in concert with some one else.

Persons may be *typically unlike,* in which case we should have *heterogeneous types.* Typal conflict of kind is the second form of coexistence in association, resulting in conquest, toleration or extinction as a means of removing the typal contradiction. The typal quality is too unlike voluntarily to permit of associative adaptation. Here we have the factor of *Struggle* in society.

Persons may be *organically reciprocal,* in which case we should have *complemental types* or complementarity of kinds as the ground of coexistent association, such as exists between the sexes. Here we have the factor of *Sex* in society, and all institutions arising from sex.

Persons may be *potentially continuous,* in which case we should have *hereditary types* or perpetuation of kind as the normal ground of coexistence of kind, such as exists in the relation of parent and offspring. Here we have the factor of *Development* in society.

If we accept the facts of fellowship or sociality, struggle, sex and development as the points of view from which to study the social process, then the field at once opens to us the four following propositions :

1. That the types of personality in human association give us the logical conceptions which are required to explain the grouping of men as given in the social process.

2. That the elaboration of these types of personality is effected by the struggle with the objective factors of natural association on the one hand and with the subjective factors of social organization on the other, enabling us to arrive at those axiomatic judgments which govern the normal tendencies in the development of man in society.

3. That the comparison of these data of types of personality and the axiomatic tendencies enables us to give tentative statement at least to the principles which govern the process of social development—a process which is essentially organic because it constitutes an organized system of reciprocal functions necessary to live together in society.

4. That the formulation of these principles of development and their application to social policy must be helpful in enabling the community to organize its interests and its efforts in the service of the type that normally tends to prevail in the direction of the social ideal.

CHAPTER II.

WE enter now·upon the proposed analysis of the process of social development to define those necessary and universal conceptions which the scientific interpretation of society requires for its uses.

Our analysis is intended to show that this development has a twofold aspect. First, that the process of association is an object of scientific observation as well as any other part of the cosmic process. The social process, as an objectively known part of the cosmic process, comprises both the physical and the psychical aspects of human association. Association is a fact of nature.

Our analysis is also intended to show that the associative activities of man by virtue of his being human are therefore imbued with conscious or intuitive qualities of thought, and consequently tend to evolve a corresponding conceptual process peculiarly social and definable as such in the course of social development. This conceptual process being the logical phase of the social process includes all conceptions, judgments, laws and logical .

12

methods of social interpretation. We have, for
purposes of distinction, designated this conceptual
or logical process by the term, the *Sociological
Process*. These two aspects of the associative development thus formally set apart are comprehensively spoken of as the Societary Process. Our
enquiry is concerned synthetically with the judgments of the Sociological Process about the Social
Process.

This distinction by which the Societary Process
of development is first differentiated into its cosmic
aspect and then into its self-conscious aspect is
necessitated by our growing insight into the nature of associative reality. The more we penetrate
into the facts of association—physical and psychical—the more certain are we that there is within
the associative movements of men a logical process
by regard for whose conceptual norms the development of the race is realized and by which alone it is
possible to be reduced to rational interpretation.

Nor is this inconsistent with scientific procedure
elsewhere. Every domain of phenomena has a
language and a law peculiar to itself, whose normal
conceptions are not normal to other spheres of development. The same is true of the associative
aspect of human life. It is neither purely psychical; nor is it purely physical; it is both and yet
it is neither in its normal quality which makes the
associative to have a law and a life that can be
called emphatically its own.

The basis of this distinction lies in the fact that
the phenomena of association are unique in the

nature and the method of their development. We have therefore to designate that differentiating mark or quality by which the social is to be recognized both in the individual and in the race—in the actual social life and in the theoretical thought about that life.

This distinguishing quality among all other logical qualities that enter into the experience of the individual and the race is the consciousness of the *typical*. The type of personality is the all-pervading logical conception on the assumption of whose validity a universal law can be shown to prevail throughout social existence. It is the logical quality by which any human being is to be recognized as social. It is the key to all forms of association. It therefore not only enables us to designate and differentiate the social from all else as a *fact* to be determined, but it furthermore is the logical form in which we must find the *law* of the development of social man and the systems of relations under which he lives.

The type in its objective sense, as a part of the social process, is a representative example of a class or group. We constantly think in this way. It is that conception by which, when one of a kind presents itself, we at once by a process of inference call up the group to which it belongs. We regard such an one as typically at equilibrium with that group. This is the social type—the individual member that stands for a class. It is the norm of imitation, the occasion of reaction, the impulse to cooperate, the incentive to realization.

The type in its theoretical or sociological sense is a conceptual object potentially normal and logically necessary to the social development of the coherent life of a group of kindred beings. The sociological type is that ejective norm of association which two or more persons construct out of the qualities which they mutually recognize in each other when they meet. It is not the persons, but a working inference for personal association; it is an ejective self around which they both rally if homogeneous, or for which each fights or flees if heterogeneous. As the potential norm of associative relations, it enables man to reason socially in advance of his experience.

In the development of society the sociological type of man or the potentially normal type, as we shall call it, is the principle of suggestion by which all associative activity is guided. The relation of the social type, in equilibrium with the group, to the sociological type, which defines the potentially normal relation of the community to the condition of existence, is that of a series of tentative adjustments of the members of a group for survival's sake to a series of potentially more normal equilibria. This adjustment of personality to the social type and of the social type to the potentially normal or sociological type is occasioned by the change of circumstances of association. The process of progressive adjustment to typical standards, from the actual to the potential, is the essence of social development.

Our analysis therefore shows that this series of

conceptions, which pervade the social process, takes the form of social types and sociological types, between which there is the most vital and fundamental connection known to social evolution. That connection is called social selection. It is a necessary capacity in the survival of aggregates. It is the selective synthesis which exists as the developmental bond between any social type and its corresponding sociological or theoretically more normal type. Social aggregates select the type that is and that tends to be as the conceptual requisite of continuous survival. This constitutes the gist of the Typological Series—the social type or representative man, the sociological or potentially normal man, and the selective relation between them.

Does this conception of the developmental process in human association as an evolution of social types comport with social facts and the theoretical convictions we generally hold about the life of the race ?

With this problem before us we turn to the analyses of human association. Possibly the most available form under which to think comprehensively of the phenomena of association in the present temper of critical inquiry is that of an evolutionary process unfolding from within. The observed behavior of human beings in mutual association with their kind under cosmic conditions of existence is what may be permanently regarded as the associative process. Is it possible to give this process intelligible interpretation in terms of such ideas as growth, development, evolution—ideas which seem to be the most helpful instruments of expression of the laws of knowable reality now at the service of the progressive portions of mankind ?

Will the conception of development of types of social man fit into these processes ? The answer here offered to this question is substantially an affirmative one: Types are logical forms into which the phenomena of social aggregation may be analyzed. The prevailing attitudes of men toward such categories of social conduct give the synthetic judgments theoretically normal to the life of society. These judgments are constantly being revised and in their formative state express the trend of social suggestion in the thoughts, feelings and purposes of a people. These tendential judgments are sociological types the selection of which by the typical groups for the sake of survival in association is the law of societary evolution. By suggestive selection society has evolved all the essential forms of social organization. The principles of personal association are but necessary deductions (postulates) of this fundamental law; and the axioms of social development are the successive forms which selective association takes under necessary conditions which change with the stages of social evolution.

In confirmation of this analysis of the developmental process we study the societary process from its two main points of view.

First, we examine its actual content by observing the persons who enter into its associative composition, singling them out one from another on the ground of likeness and unlikeness of quality and relationships, following in our thoughts one by one those who seem to us in some substantial and convincing way to represent the rest of the members similarly characterized. By so doing—and this is the way that practical life proceeds—we should come to regard what is true of a representative example as being true of all persons of that class in like conditions. But an example of a class is a type. In other words, what is habitually observed to be true of a representative member of a class or group of like kind is, in every-day life, logically accepted as predicable of all who are really believed to be included within that group or class of persons similarly conditioned and sustaining similar relations. Such a one is confidently regarded as typical and put under that category until he proves himself to be misplaced. We act, we feel, we think by the constant aid of the typical. It is evident then that any attempt at sociological interpretation which starts from the concrete point of view of the particular social object—the personal member of society—must sooner or later inevitably formulate his social judgments in terms of social types of personality as a logical necessity of experience.

Secondly, the other point of view from which the societary process may be analyzed is the conceptual—that which primarily concerns itself with finding out and formulating such judgments as are

held to be universally true of social man. Now
that the reflective powers of man are developed
to the point of sustained analytic effort upon subjects social, we start from this point of view by regarding the whole genus of man as the comprehensive subject of study. Under this procedure
our analysis would have to be firstly anthropological, limited in its scope only by the differentia that
bar mankind out of the non-human realm of animality; secondly, we should have to mark the distinguishing features physical and psychical of the
separate groups of human beings found upon the
earth in associative relations, thus discovering that
the most enduring classes into which mankind is
divisible on the basis of likeness are the several
races, examples of which have been diffused over
the surface of the globe. Yet no one man has
seen one one-hundredth of the beings whom he
reasons about most confidently.

But whether we consider social man from the
anthropological or the ethnological view-points,
the mind recording the observations and making
the generalizations takes much the same method
of keeping in coherent order the content presented
to it: the examples critically observed are only a
part of the total of the kind under consideration
about which general propositions can be valid;
but these examples have been so near like others
known to exist, and believed to exist if not known
by observation, that here too an example or a series
of examples has been taken as confidently to represent the great race-groups or the peoples that make

up the earth's aggregate of population. What has been learned of some of the most representative members of races and peoples of mankind has been taken as substantially true, either by observation of fact or inference therefrom, of races and peoples as a whole. That is to say, the examples of groups of human beings which show the most enduring marks of differentiation and of continuity have been taken as typical of the most complex aggregates among whom they have been observed to belong. So that from the generic point of view our observations of man with a view to reflection lead us early to the necessity of formulating our ideas in the form of organic types as modes of representing the facts of human existence both known and inferred. And whether we study civilizations and culture eras or generic man and ethnical groups, we are logically obliged to bring before our minds the concrete types of human personality which fit into the social fabric among whose remains we have sought for some indication of what the peoples were. Whether we begin with the observation of the experience of two or more members of a community of which we are a part, or with the most comprehensive survey of the organic character of man as a type of animal life, the result seems to be the same—that of resorting to the typical forms of judgments respecting social man to explain his evolution.

If this conclusion be tenable, then we have at last found the key to the crux both as to method of analysis and the synthesis of social phenomena.

These two points of view—the actual and the generic or theoretical—represent two different conceptions of critical analysis. The one is that of a natural science, the other that of the philosophy of history. They mark the limits of the developmental process. The former concerns itself primarily with the actual facts, conditions and organic products of the societary process. It shows us that social development begins with organic types. The latter measures the societary movement with respect to its conformity to or departure from an end or goal. It shows us that social development ends with ideal types. Unless sociology is prepared to turn over its tasks to either of these two views of social analysis, it must seek a solvent of this difficulty. According to the view taken in this inquiry, it is neither necessary to reduce all social phenomena to measurable causes as in physics or chemistry, nor to define for every aspect of social reality its place in the ultimate ends of the societary process, before we dare to formulate the law of society's life. On the contrary, we effect the reconciliation of both of these analyses if we can but trace the law of the societary movement in the selective survival of the social types actually realized and the selective development thereof toward sociological or potentially normal types of personality. The societary process therefore is neither to be viewed as a purely natural science in the sense of being physical, nor is it a purely mental or moral science in the sense of being a march of mind purposefully directed and fully conscious of its ongoing and its ideal ends; but it is a *typological process* in which types of personality as typically organic beings gradually become typically social and develop through the potential type into or toward the ideal. Thus arise four grades of types of personality—the organic, the social, the sociological and the ideal type—from the union of the factors of nature and history in human evolution.

The typical is therefore conceived of in association as the norm of survival and development, valid both to the particular person in society and to the race as a whole. It connects the individual experience and the universal judgments of man under a category in which the selective tendencies of the developmental process find their synthetic expression.

The societary process may thus properly be described as a typological series, that being its normal characteristic; in this form, both the concrete and the universal aspects of association find their norm of valuation. In its natural character the developmental process is that complex ongoing of personal life in systematic association which, from the aspect of our every-day experience, reveals to us man's modes of selective survival among his own kind. But, from the point of view of his conceptual character as a race, the developmental process exhibits those universal marks which characterize humanity in its prolonged effort at selective survival of certain qualities of character. But both of these aspects are conjoined under a third category—the typical, in which the particular and universal aspects of socialization are united under the selective synthesis of progression in the types of personality—organic, social, sociological and ideal—in human association. The individual and the universal in man meet in the typical.

More simply expressed the societary process is a process of selection of the means and ends of survival by typical groups of different degrees of development. Among the essential tendencies at work in the systematic association of human beings the selective evolution of the typical in personality is the only normal quality which the testimony of nature and of the history of the associative consciousness is willing to respect as the common criterion of social valuation.

The following scheme exhibits the societary process from the two essential aspects of the particular and the universal (A, B) whose reconciliation in the formal expression of a type-developing process is here described. The scheme also exhibits roughly the several essential aspects (a, b, c, d) arising out of the two phases of the societary process (A, B), by which in the history of social interpretation it has been sought to make the life of society intelligible. Aa_1, Aa_2, Ab_3, Ab_4 are the concrete aspects from the point of view of individual behaviour in natural association.

In social organization, Bc_1, Bc_2, Bd_3 and Bd_4 are the conceptual aspects from the universal point of view of the behavior of man as a race, that is, as humanity. Each of these aspects (A, B) *appears* to

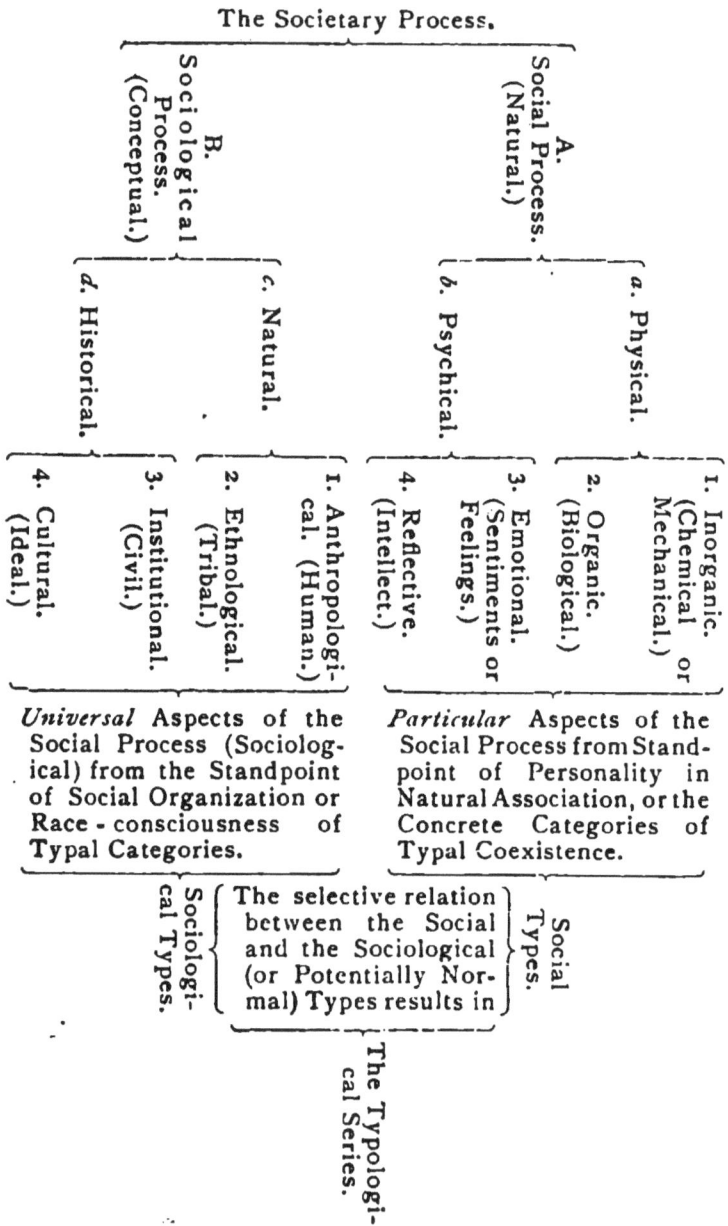

The Societary Process.

A. Social Process. (Natural.)
- b. Psychical.
  - 4. Reflective. (Intellect.)
  - 3. Emotional. (Sentiments or Feelings.)
- a. Physical.
  - 2. Organic. (Biological.)
  - 1. Inorganic. (Chemical or Mechanical.)

B. Sociological Process. (Conceptual.)
- d. Historical.
  - 4. Cultural. (Ideal.)
  - 3. Institutional. (Civil.)
- c. Natural.
  - 2. Ethnological. (Tribal.)
  - 1. Anthropological. (Human.)

Universal Aspects of the Social Process (Sociological) from the Standpoint of Social Organization or Race - consciousness of Typal Categories.

Particular Aspects of the Social Process from Standpoint of Personality in Natural Association, or the Concrete Categories of Typal Coexistence.

Sociological Types. { The selective relation between the Social and the Sociological (or Potentially Normal) Types results in } Social Types.

The Typological Series.

be sufficient in itself to explain the societary process. Both have something of the forces of nature
and of the motives that belong to civilization in
them; but neither of them has ever been able to
justify itself in the sight of the other, as an adequate
presentation of the societary process taken in the
threefold aspects of its particular or individual, its
universal, and its typical development. The theoretical presentation of the phenomena of society
has always found its main difficulty at this juncture.
But with the union of the particular and the universal, of the individual and of society under the conception of the typical; and with the connection of
these differences in degrees of development of the
typical by the selective impulse to survive in association, we come to the standpoint from which the
facts of society can be seen logically arranged in a
successive series of types that are naturally and historically true to fact.

The developmental process has thus far been
represented as a grouping of the phenomena of
association under a series of typical standards of
social organization.

Exhibited in this light, we see that what actually
goes on in the individual and what tends to find
realization in the universal human both find their
equilibrium in the logically valid conception, the
normal type of personality. This is the fundamentally sociological conception. The typological process must be regarded as combining its two essential aspects. The particular and the universal must
become one in a truly fundamental process logically

satisfying the requirements of both natural association and the historical movement of humanity
toward the universal. The selective evolution of
the typically normal adequately takes account of
the essential qualities of both processes in the same
fundamental principle.

The nature of the societary process may be
further elucidated by the study of the component
factors in each of these aspects of development in
order to define the *limits* of the developmental
series. The series begins in organic types and ends
in ideal types, but its central feature is the relation
of the social type already developed with the potentially normal types.

If as a naturalist we then consider the development of society from the aspect of natural association, we note, first, that on certain physical conditions (climate) man as an organic being prevails
and propagates his own kind. He develops as food
and feelings permit. The social process, for one
large portion of mankind and for nearly all of primitive mankind no doubt, must have been and is now
to be regarded as a natural process—natural in the
sense of being largely dominated by forces little
higher in the scale of tendencies than that of the
superior non-human animals. That is to say, that
the major forces in their existence are those employed in satisfying the demands of the animal part
of their human nature. These are subsistence and
sex. One cannot look long upon the great bulk of
mankind, with all its aspirations that differentiate
it from the lower animals, and balk this conclusion

—that for the greater portion of man's career upon the earth and for the greater portion of the persons now alive upon its face the social process is still predominantly a natural process of organic survival. The weak physical types fail to survive and are eliminated. The strong guide the race. So far, then, as the social process is dominated by natural forces, by which its tendencies are limited and its types of personality evolved, we cannot go far wrong in saying that the social process is a selective process whose types survive by virtue of their efficiency in providing for the natural requisites of social existence. The social process is rightly regarded, therefore, from the point of view of nature as a process of the survival of *organic* types by natural selection of associative relations. Natural selection defines the minimum limit of typal development in society. The organic type of personality is the basis of the typological series. Hence physical culture of the organic type of personality is the natural basis of education.

The process of race-development, on the other hand, is a process of selective development towards the *ideal* type as the *maximum* limit of development in society. Its secret lies in a subjective solidarity. In this aspect of the societary process we recognize the spiritual motives seeking expression in the course of history. The upper level of the societary process is leavened with the genius of history; on the lower level, the natural forces, in which scientific analysis finds its field of operation in the study of the formative forces, make for the survival of

organic types. Between these two we must look
for the series of potentially normal types of personality in which the authority of the conceivably attainable in selective association gradually becomes
less and less devoted to survival and more and more
given to development—less and less controlled by
natural forces and more and more filled with the
conscious spirit of history—until the normal type,
as the controlling characteristic of the societary
process, is found to be the selective standard func-
tioning as the socializing organon of human development. If ideas rule the world, the idea of the
typical rules the social world, and the idea of the
potentially attainable rules the progressive portions
of the race.

Within the limits of the organic type of man and
the ideal type of man lies the realm of social development. We may, from these opposite directions,
approach still nearer in defining the typological
process. In what typical forms do these two aspects of our evolution—the organic and the ideal—
find their developmental transition? There are
certain self-evident relations which characterize
social life as known to us. These are the necessary
categories which neither let man be a beast nor
consent to his being an angel. His life must be
typical in order to be social. Natural association
imposes four categorical principles upon man as a
member of society.

We shall call these *The Typal Categories of Personal Coexistence*, or the typical norms of natural
association.

The social process thus regarded is a personal process. As indicated in the previous chapter these categories normal to personal association are: (1) typal community as seen in fellowship, (2) typal conflict as seen in struggle, (3) typal complementarity as seen in sex, and (4) typal perpetuation as seen in child-growth. To follow a leader, to fight a foe, to woo a woman, to rear a child are the categorical imperatives of human nature. Without these typal categories ruling association society itself must become extinct. And it is only by the authority of these imperatives of nature that nature puts into man's hands the means of development from the organic toward the ideal.

This being the case with the concrete social life as we recognize it, we now ask whether, from the side of our universal conceptions of man as humanity, the type is also the normal concept by which socialization has always proceeded. Here we see the typical in terms of categories of the race-consciousness.

We shall call these *The Typal Categories of Race-Consciousness*, or the typical norms of social organization throughout the race.

First among the universally valid judgments on the validity of which man lives and moves and has his being among his own kind and not with the beasts of the field like the Babylonian king or like the Cyclopean shepherd of Homeric story, is that of *the consciousness of typal kinship*. As Maine shows so well, kinship is the basis of ancient society. The presence of this quality in control of conduct in all known peoples of the ancient world is the evidence of the conception of the typical as the universal associative quality. This consciousness of kind, defined as that intuitive or instinctive capacity of the human species to identify itself with its own species and to distinguish itself from other species and from other typical groups of its own species, is as essential to sociology as sensation is to psychology.* We may call this the anthropological category of typal quality, or the universal consciousness of organic type, because it integrates the generic human type from the non-human by association. Man universally knows himself as walled off from the beast below him. The race punishes corruption of kinds and nature helps heartily thereat. My kind my kingdom is, is not only naturally true but also universally necessary, for the evolution of the race toward the solidarity of the ideal type.

The second category of universal validity in our thought of the race is the *consciousness of typal conditions*. The race everywhere reckons with environment. The type is the norm of adaptation to environment. The consciousness of the necessity of adjustment to changes and of the fact of the existence or non-existence, the fitness or the unfitness, the utility or inutility of such adjustment is certainly among the primary data of the developmental process of the race. This consciousness of conditions normal to survival includes subjective as well as objective conditions of typal equilibrium.

* Giddings, Principles of Sociology, Bk. I., Ch. I., pp. 17–19.

Without this conscious control over itself in the interest of the typical aggregate, communities could not escape elimination. This second category common to man as a race may be called the ethnological category or the ethnical consciousness of type, because upon it is conditioned the differentiation of mankind into ethnic groups. The tribe was the fighting machine in social organization then as class is now. In specific groups this is *the tribal consciousness.* It sets limits to the scope of adaptation to attain to its typal ideal.

The third category universal to the race is *the consciousness of typal relations.* This is the category of social order in organized life. There is in typical groups that consciousness not only of their own typical quality and their conditions but also of their superior or inferior degree of development with respect to other types in the institutional organizations of society. This consciousness of relations of typical groups in the social system is universal and as valid in the process of development of man as it is universal. Hence another sociological category in the race-consciousness is that awareness on the part of a community or a class not only of its own typal standard, to which all of its members are habitually sensitive, but also the consciousness of their being related to other typal standards, such as prevail within differentiated classes of the community. To be aware of class-membership is to belong to a type of which one is conscious.* To be conscious

* Wines, Genesis of the Social Classes, Charities Review, Apr., 1897.

of equilibrium with both the class-type and the community-type is the third typal category. This appears in all composite social organizations. We may call this the *civic consciousness of type*, because it is that quality of the social consciousness which enables a tribalized community to pass into the civilized organization of society.

The fourth category of the race-consciousness is *consciousness of typal possibilities*. This capacity organizes society around its ideals. This datum of the social consciousness is cultural in its quality and mode of expression. The speculative capacity of the social consciousness normally sets in prospective relief before the peoples of all times, types of potential attainment. Potentiality is a quality of humanity. It is evident in human invention, in the rhapsody of the bard, the wisdom of the magi, the foresight of the seer, or the warnings and promises of the prophet or the precepts of the priest. The artist, the idealist and the interpreter of the new truth all reflect it. There are potential norms of realization to which every social process tends, leading the types of life away from the actual toward the possible, or seeking to merge the potential into the ideal—the maximum limit of associative development. The representations of this potential quality of the human consciousness is seen in the universal effort to control social tendencies by cultural expression—linguistic, moral, intellectual and aesthetic. Each seeks to give fuller expression to human nature in typical forms. In this aspect of the developmental process the community first

comes to itself—to a social self-consciousness of
the potentially normal type as the organon of social
action and the seat of social authority.

We may therefore call this the potential consciousness or the social self-consciousness—the
categorical imperative of the developmental process
—which has become increasingly potent as a factor
in the evolution of the more progressive communities of mankind.

There are, consequently, four and only four typal
categories under which the race-consciousness
gives expression to its sociological judgments.
They are the organic, the ethnical, the civil and the
potential or cultural consciousness of type. There
are likewise four and only four typal categories
under which personal association expresses its socially necessary conditions of existence. These are
community, conflict, complementarity and continuity of type.

What form therefore must the process of social
development inevitably take, if both in its necessary
conditions of natural association and also in the universal forms of social organization of the race-consciousness the norm of social valuation is the typically social? There would seem to be but one inference available, namely, that the developmental
process of human association is an evolution of
types of personality.

Is the process of human association a *series* of
types, actual and potential, necessary and universal?
Can these categories be each arranged in a developmental series of terms in each term of which a com-

mon quality persists and in each successive term of which a differentiating mark appears to give it its place in a progressive order of complexity?

The answer from these data seems self-evident, that the categories of associative authority have the typical quality as the constant quality demanded of man as a member of society, and that each successive term in this series of categories is characterized by some differentiating property which makes it logically and actually the next term in the series on the ground both of its likeness in quality and its increasing diversity in degree. The same is true of the categories of race-consciousness—they, like the categories of the association of individuals, have all the requisites of a series whose unity is in the typical *quality* as the secret of social development, and whose increasing complexity is the outcome of the varying *conditions* under which typal development takes place. The typical guides both the individual and the race in associative choice.

Putting these results together diagrammatically in Fig. 1 we may illustrate the relations of each of the series of categories to the resultant series arising from them. In this third series we have the typically normal forms under which the process of social development appears.

The societary process is everywhere pervaded with typal practice. From its lowest form of instinctive reaction up through the wide domain in nature, in which consciousness of kind gives us the natural test of sociality, to the highest type of personality of which social selection is capable, all.

societary phenomena are seemingly capable of satisfactory interpretation in terms of typical qualities
and relationships. From the natural or organic
type, as a basis of development, we rise to the consciousness of the typical as the test in social group-

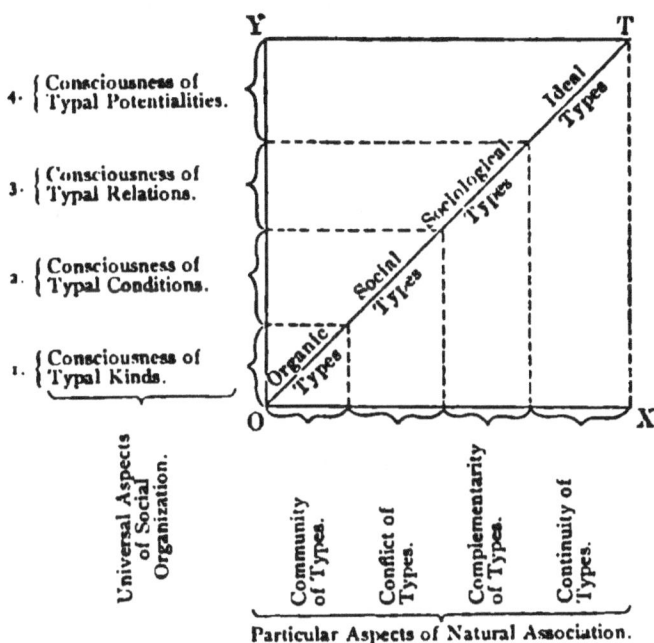

FIG. I.

ing into aggregates. Man is no longer simply an
organic object whose relations are defined by instinct. As soon as society rises to the level of
recognizing the type of personality as a datum of
conceptual utility in social selection, the type becomes itself part of the conscious agency available
for the evolution of newer types of personality after
a purposeful pattern. Under selection by the
purely natural process the type of personality is the

product mainly of nature's sealed orders; the social consciousness of man is aware of the surviving worth of nature's types, but not as yet equally aware of the developmental value of the typal judgment as a subjective principle fashioning the course of society into conformity to a consciously perfected norm. The process of the universal social in history becomes dominant whenever the social consciousness has learned to use its conceptual machinery to penetrate to the limits of the ideal, as the goal of social attainment. By the action and reaction between the actual types in nature and the ideal in the process of history, the community has learned to poise its social tendencies in natural association and the universal tendencies in the social judgment of the race in the same normal process of socialization. Thus the trend of development begins in the organic, proceeds by being typically social and is progressively realizable in the type of personality that normally tends to prevail. Thence it learns to follow the lead of the ideal.

Any attempt at the representation of the societary process in any form less fundamental than that of a typological succession is beset with difficulties out of which there seems to be no way that does not involve contradictions more serious than those that may be solved. Any attempt at social interpretation must see in the social process considered as natural, that the developmental forces are those taken up with organic reproduction and adjustment of type to the requisites of survival. And, at the same time it must appear that the

generic motives of history, or the universal process
regarded as a race-process, are essentially a striving
after conscious realization of an ideal type. Without uniting these two in one interpretation the
student of society is more than apt to miss the
meaning of the societary process by seeking the
law of social evolution in environment. Nor can
we explain association by some particular quality
or set of qualities in the individual person or in the
race which characterizes the life of the species.
Neither the universally ideal, as for example in
ethics, nor the organic, as in the individual, is alone
adequate. To treat the social process from the
point of view of personality in particular as a
mechanical, an organic, an emotional or sentimental, or a reflective process or as any complex
of these, as has been done a thousand times, affords
us no comprehensive solution of the demand for
some sociological organon that will make society
understandable. All of these representations are
contributions of detail in a comprehensive whole,
but are not in themselves anything more than partial representations of a greater whole whose center
is not revealed. The same is true of those efforts
which take into consideration only the generic aspects of the sociological process, such as the anthropological, the ethnological, the institutional and the
cultural analyses of society. They are, as Letourneau frankly recognizes, but necessary approaches
toward a complete interpretation of the process of
human life. But neither the ideal goal nor the
organic genesis is the sole key to the develop-

mental process. Each marks the limit of the societary process, but neither alone gives the law to man's development. That law has to be found in the union of the particular and the universal in the typical. We must know why and how types of men develop in society.

It is this feeling after some point of reconciliation between the generic and the specific aspects of the tendencies recognized as germane to human association that has led the sociologists to ask and to help to answer the question, What possible form of expression can be found in which both of these characteristic aspects of the societary movement may find their equilibrium?

The answer is that the developmental process of human society is a series of typal equilibria between the necessary conditions of personal association and the universal categories of the race-consciousness, both of which tendencies find their equilibrium in the types of personality actual and potential that normally tend to prevail. The law of development must take the form of a type-producing tendency.

It is now necessary to explain the functions of these two products of the societary process—the social types and the sociological types. These are really the primary features in the process by which types of personality are evolved. With organic types of personality given us by birth as a natural process, the formative process of creating character by association begins. To associate is to be educated; that is, to be made social by relations with one's kind. But in order to remain social a group must constantly readapt itself to what is normal. What is normal to-day is abnormal to-morrow. Hence the process of keeping the type normal requires it to respect the potential as well as the actual. This makes *the social type the subject of a tendency or process from the actual to the potential type.* The potentially normal type is the sociological type. It always lies in the direction of the ideal possibilities of the species.

CHAPTER III.

THE sources of sociology are nature and history. Nature and history are conceived of as coordinate factors in social evolution, the joint product of which two factors working together in the same process is to be seen in the progressive unfolding of types of personality. It is necessary, therefore, to describe the characteristic features of this process both from its natural and its historical points of view.

Starting from the side of natural society—the social process regarded primarily as a natural process—we find in the words of a trustworthy authority that " most naturalists now regard the type as nothing but that normal which is most perfectly fitted to the environment, and they hold that it is kept true through the extinction of aberrant individuals by selection." *

The scientific view of natural processes in the organic world is full of the evidence that, as Romanes puts it somewhere, nature cares relatively little for the individual, for the specific member of the genus, and relatively much for the type which

* W. K. Brooks, Pop. Sci. Monthly, Feb., 1896, p. 481.

is best fitted to prevail. Nature puts an immense premium on the preservation of the better type; and better means the more or less social; so that, once having found association of kind by typal equilibrium to be the better way to secure survival, she invests her all in society. The aggregation of organic beings of like organic type produces the social type.

The social type therefore becomes not only the method but the measure of social progress. This function is exemplified by the limits it sets to struggle in any established group. Not only in the animal world does progress go hand in hand with the subordination of the individual to social ends; but, in the corresponding progress in the historic world, in the sexual relations, in the family, the tribe, the city, the nation and the race, "Competition and survival of the fittest are never wholly eliminated, but reappear on each new plane to work out the preponderance of the higher, *i.e.*, more integrated and associated type." * "The type," says Martineau, "from a still higher plane of social interpretation, is a permanent standard, a pre-existing and imperishable idea, towards which, as to a model conception, all single births imperfectly strive." †

It is this preference in nature as well as in history for the social medium or *milieu* as a means for the survival of the organic man that gives us those characteristic elements of the most enduring per-

* Geddes, Evolution of Sex, pp 311, 312.
† Types of Ethical Theory, Vol. I., Introd., 1886.

sistence. From past ages they present themselves to us in the form of existing physical types in the variety of human beings that cover the greater portion of the surface of the earth. Each great climatic division of the globe has its native type, the product of nature's processes. Territory and types of mankind have the most intimate relation in the selective process of natural association.*

Looked at from its internal organization the social process is broken up into the variety of races in which we actually find them. This ethnical organization gives a still more concise meaning to the typical. Man is not only a type in the animal kingdom, a species of the genus animal, but also a member of racial groups. "The type," says Keane, "stands apart from all general terms in ethnological nomenclature. It is not a race, a tribe or a family, or any concrete division whatsoever; but is rather in the nature of an abstraction, a model or pattern to which all divisions are referable. Originally meaning a mould or matrix, or rather a casting from a mould, it is taken as a summary of all the characters assumed to be proper to a given class or group. Thus type becomes the standard by which we measure the relative position of individuals in a group. But in practice no individual exists, or ever did exist, who is entirely conformable to any given standard. Hence type necessarily resolves itself into a question of averages; individuals possessing most of the characteristics to

* W. Z. Ripley, Geography and Sociology, Polit. Sci. Quarterly, Vol. X., No. 4.

a group are said to be typical members of that group, and even this only in a relative sense. They approximate nearer than other members to the ideal, but none absolutely reach it." *

A comparative study of what Ratzel calls the natural races, to find among them the characteristics which would enable us to locate any specimen of mankind, would lead us to look for at least three kinds of typical qualities—the organic, the emotional and the reflective. On the basis of these we could form some estimate of the social efficiency of the races as a whole. And this is just what we observe in the study of the groups of mankind from the point of view of social efficiency: different races possess very different combinations both in degree and quality of these typical characteristics. Therefore in the competition among races they prove themselves to have very different degrees of social value. In some, to follow the facts collated by Letourneau,† the relationships are simple, the social feeling sluggish and relatively subordinate to the animal impulses; the capacity to think and act together, to utilize the powers of nature and the attainments of other peoples in social organization is consequently confined to the simpler acts of life. Some, as low as the Fuegian horde in which the children are named after the place in which they are born, exhibit a sociality not much higher than the ant,‡ the beaver or the bee. In other types, in

* Keane, Ethnology, p. 12.
† Letourneau, Sociology, I., Chap. I.
‡ Lubbock, Scientific Lectures, Lect. IV.: On the Habits of Ants.

which these natural qualities have a more favorable combination for survival by association, the capacity for social organization has enabled them not only to extend their conquest over nature and the so-called natural peoples, but still more signally to tame themselves into that capacity of spirit, that talent for social aggregation and cooperation, which has made them the masters of purposeful policy and the arbiters of the quality of civilization that should prevail.

For our purposes it is sufficient to think of racial elements as a class of factors that are present in the constitution of the social type so far as nature has a hand in the process. The place of the races in history is that which the efficiency of the social type determines for them. Owing to the great differences in their social efficiency as compared with other races the different races within themselves have played very different parts in the development of social types. In the black races we look in vain for any of the highly complex forms of social organization as the receptacle and guardian of cultured civilization. Here the end of the social organization is primarily that of survival of the natural type with but subordinate regard for development. The selective resources are at their lowest and the variety of social types is naturally limited. In the yellow races there is a greater variety of social types developed to a particular plane, and then apparently brought to rest by the restraints of the social organization. It is generally speaking only among the white races that we find social organ-

ization used systematically as a scaffolding to con-
serve the culture of the past, to control the resources of nature and to combine the two factors of
nature and history in the service of the selective
survival of progressive types of personality.

While it is to be taken for granted that race is
the tap-root of typal quality in social survival, a
rough comparison of the different races from the
social point of view shows us, as Ward has insisted,
that the true order of development in social efficiency of man to man is from the non-psychic to the
psychic.* We come to see that the more efficient
social types are the more highly developed psychical types. Mind plays the major rôle in the development of human society. The ratio of the animal
to the ideal type determines the progressive unfolding of social capacity and so, too, the multiplication
of variety of social types of personality. We have
therefore to look primarily to those races in which
physical or organic types are controlled by the
psychic factors of collective life—the emotional and
the reflective energies yoked together in type-
developing socialization. Where these factors are to
be found and measured, there we have material for
scientific analysis. These are the greatest socializing forces; the ratio of the physical and the psychical rules social relationships and thus determines
the tendencies at work in the production of social
types. Only among the more advanced races do
we find development of psychical qualities to that
degree of fulness which makes possible a theory

* Ward, Psychic Factors of Civilization, Ch. XVIII.

of social valuation based on types of personality. On this account sociological interpretation of values is at once retrospective, introspective, and prospective, by being concerned above all things else with the present tendencies between the organic and the ideal types of social man.

Postponing for the present anything but the mere mention of Mill's masterly discussion of social types in the development of the social sciences, in which we have for the first (1843) a substantially sound analysis of the logical quality of the societary process, we now come to note the next great advance upon the ethnological doctrine of social types, in Bagehot's *Physics and Politics.* With the growth of enlightenment in the popular consciousness, the races cease to be regarded as the most concrete form of the societary experiment: the nation takes its place and becomes thereby the area within which the social types come into view as the result of societary activity. The physical and the spiritual or psychical elements mingle by the aid of linguistic instrumentalities and organizing institutions, to the extent of developing in the social consciousness the sense of a superiority of attainment in social type common enough to be within the potential realization of the entire people. This is the national type of social character.

Bagehot formulated this fact in the following proposition which he proceeded to interpret by means of natural selection: " Within every particular nation the type or types of character then and there most attractive tend to prevail; and the most attractive, though with exceptions, is what we call the best character."

Since the suggestive effort of Bagehot at the analysis of the typical character of the societary products, scattered efforts have been made at its treatment apart from the view which is strictly ethnological. Most inductive analysis has been enumerations of aggregates or kindred groups by the method of statistical inquiry, or still more generally by the analogical method; and much honest effort has been spent upon the problem of defining man's relation to nature, or rather to discovering 'man's place in nature,' as if he were simply to be placed with reference solely to the animal world to be understood sociologically. But all this has not, however, been in vain. It has laid bare the natural aspects of sociological theory: the study of the human organism in its relation to the rest of nature, its organic constitution and its analogical relationships to society, its differentiation from the animal world and its divergence into varieties of race-types: all these results help us to define the outline of the limits within which the social process as a natural fact really goes on, and leaves us free to raise the question thus narrowed down, as to what the dominant aspect of the social process within these limits really is. If then the social process in the light of the natural history of society teaches us, as it really seems to, that to survive is to be socially typical and to be untypical is to court extinction precisely to that extent; then, we are reasonably safe in concluding that the social

process, so far as it is natural, is in fact a process
bent upon the production and perpetuation of the
social types that normally tend to prevail.

The study of the lives of people as social aggregates affords ample evidence of this. Franklin was
a typical American of his time. Types of personality appear conspicuously in the personages upon
whom social functions devolve or whom custom
has trained to follow a groove generation after
generation. The former we see in the diplomat,
the latter in the peasant. More obscurely but not
less really social types are definable in all groups or
classes of like kinds of persons. There is the typical
childhood, the typical old age, the typical parent,
the typical teacher. Yet the type and the group are
to be distinguished. The social type is a set of
social qualities or characters belonging to a class as
a whole and substantially found in each of its members. The more perfectly developed members are
imitated by the less developed. While the group is
variable in its composition and continuity, the type
is more constant and continuous. Though the
social type is more difficult to define to one's mind,
when once defined it has the force of a datum of
the scientific consciousness for which there can be
no substitute in sociological interpretation. The
social type is a logical necessity to the student of
society. The typical group is the social group at
equilibrium with its environment.

The social type is the logical key to those like
kinds of persons living together in groups of all
degrees of sociability. It is the instinctive regard for

the social type, thus developed in the sense of membership, that determines what sort of social existence lies within one's capacity to enjoy or endure. One's belonging to a social type is the first proof of his tolerability. Sociology has nothing to do with any human being except as he is or has been a member of a collective kind, and being or having been such, it has everything to do with him that in any way gives him a social value.

To every kindred group of persons having systematic relations between or among its members there is a typical criterion by which we may unlock the secret of its survival and development. As a matter of fact in our every-day experience we classify the stranger we meet upon the street, if we have been in the habit of taking critical account of faces, forms and manners as well as associations. The trained detectives pigeon-hole suspicious persons with a fatefulness that mystifies most of us; and there is that instinctive insight of women into the typical qualities of men which divines the type of social nature to which they are found to belong. Association is unthinkable without the typical as its mode of valuation.

Ampler illustration might be made of the way in which we really group the whole social population according to the typical qualities which we recognize as characteristic. But it is sufficient to point out that in the main social life is tolerable only with or in vital proximity to our own social type to which by nature or attainment we belong. The size, the composition, the organization and the progress or decay of every social aggregate is to be explained by the type in which it finds its coherence.

Assuming that the social type is the logical key to the social process composed of aggregates of whatever kind, the problem to be worked out is to define these social types, show what part they play in the natural and historical processes of social life, and thus reveal their connection with the fundamental hypothesis of selective survival. We shall have to show how this logical norm of social worth arises, varies, survives through a period and develops or dies out, and why all this takes place. To make this clear we shall have to define more fully the relation of the social type to socialization.

The actual social process is that process of typal development of personality lying between the physical mechanism of the inorganic world on the one side and the psychical limit of the spiritual world of the social ideal, on the other side. Between these limits lies the path of the evolution of social types. The types of social life are therefore characterized in their nature and development by the characteristics of these conditions. The typical members of a family, class, profession or community must be (1) *physical* in relation with the order of physical nature by which they are conditioned. They must (2) be *organic* by which successive survival is secured. They must (3) be *emotional* by which they are impelled to those satisfactions which alone meet their desires as social beings and bring them into equilibrium with the kind in which their reciprocal relations reside.* (4) They must be *reflective.*†

These are all aspects of the actual social process, or socialization, regarded as the type-producing process.

Socialization we regard as selective experimentation. The organized aggregates of mankind are forced to feel after the conceivably better solution of the problems that are normal to personal nature‡ in society. The social type makes socialization selective. Selection is inevitable, conditioned as human society is by a physical situation to which it has to adapt itself and the spiritual ideal with which it is haunted. The method of socialization requires the selective survival of groups by normal adaptation to a social situation. This is the systematic method in the production of efficient types. Among the so-called natural races of mankind the social types thus developed are largely the product of what we may roughly regard as natural forces; that is, selective *survival* is largely by natural selection or typal survival by elimination. Among the peoples known to human history the social type becomes more emphatically a purposeful end of social policy, to the extent even of controlling the resources of cultural civilizations.§ That is to say, where the community is aware of the kind

---

* Ward, Psychic Factors: Part I., "Subjective Factors." (Ch. IX.)

† Ward, Psychic Factors: Part II., "Objective Factors."

‡ Stephen, Science of Ethics, Ch. II., Secs. 34-42.

§ Ratzel, The History of Mankind, Secs. 3-4. Huxley, Evolution and Ethics, V., pp. 202-206.

or type of character it wishes to realize, selection is mainly social or that of typal development toward perfection.

The best conceivable attainment—the ideal type —at any period of any people's history or growth is a question of fact, and the types of excellence can only be compared by some standard of social serviceableness.*　The central fact to be looked for in our analysis of social conditions is the type of personality resulting therefrom.　Educational, industrial and political policies must pass this test of effect on social type.　Every such type is an actual solution which the social process presents to scientific thought.　Every such solution resulting from the composite process of socialization takes the form of social types.　Every type is what nature and history make him.　History feeds the flame of personality on the ever-burning altar of humanity; nature nourishes the bodily form endowed with wants.　Both pour their resources with varying degrees of fulness into the process of social selection, giving to us the progressive creation of social types of all varieties of efficient worth.

Within the limits of the organic and the ideal, and with respect to them, the social type is an imitable object.　Any typical person who is imitated is to that extent a *power*.　As the subject of imitation in the social aggregate in which it is to the manor born, he may serve as an objective ideal often exercising creative control of untold potency over the lives of entire groups, such as the family

* Simcox, Natural Law, VII.

and the school. The social type must not therefore be conceived of as merely the product of a physical or a biological process wrought out by an infinite series of impacts; it is not simply an object cast upon the shores of the social world by the currents of nature and the storms of civilization. Whatever else the types of personality which we recognize in human association alone may prove to be, each of them is at least the center of an educative activity and the source of those selective energies with which men are endowed. · The truest social type exhibits energies by which the trend of social evolution has been more or less consciously determined at every step. The truly typical personality is the magnet by which the associative capacity of man has been completely differentiated from all else that is known in the world of scientific investigation. It is this socializing genius that requires for man a unique treatment under a category which is peculiarly his own. Typical man, whether savagely natural or preeminently historical in his developmental estate, has as the distinctive property of his nature that selective secret of survival and development by which with one hand he exploits the formative order of the world about him and with the other lights up his path of progress to the next best estate by the civilizing genius of history within him. He is the criterion of his own kind, class and condition. But his power over his own kind is always measured by the degree to which he is typical.

The social type is, furthermore, the *norm of social adaptation.* Normality is the requisite degree of adaptability to conditions of existence at a given time and place. With change in conditions the once normal ceases to be so, except by virtue of selective adaptation to type, by the selection of the next best estate, as the situation in which social survival is more fully normal. A very large proportion of every social class lives not by the bread of the earth alone, but by the word of the social type that proceeds from the selective sense that resides in that class. The socially normal type of man is the seat of selected authority more fundamental than any law or institution by which the path of safe existence is hedged about. The type thus actively present, whether in person or in the mind and the method of the group of persons, is the epitomized content of past and present requisites of survival and the basis of future development.

Not only is the type of personality the center around which social groups of kindred natures are organically built up; not only is it the chief factor in normalizing personality in association; but it is evidently an agency of development, in every social group in which the degrees of attainment exhibit differentiations that excite men to effort. Socialization requires subordination to superior types, as a condition of development. Where adaptation to physical conditions has gone hand in hand with consciousness of superior possibilities of social ascendency, we have the social type acting as *an agency of assimilation* of the lower or less developed toward the higher types. The child that aspires to the role of citizenship, the immigrant to whom the atmosphere of his adopted people is a stimulus, as well as the colony that steadily converges its energies to the realization of a freer and more forceful type of civic character—these are all alike led by the types of attainment on which each has set its hope. But comprehending them all, as the ægis of their chosen fields of effort, the national type of character causes the variety of types it comprehends to converge toward an end which has an existence no less real because it is typical of what men tend to be. Uniform laws, uniform conditions and institutions promote this result. The capillarity of the modern municipality, by which the urban movement of population is called into activity, is a process of social typification. Reaction from the rural type and selection of the urban type as the norm of association is the preeminent feature of this socializing process. Within the city the process of assimilation is largely effected by institutional agencies. The club, school, church, factory, theatre, press, all mould men to type. The same is true especially of the assimilation of the foreigner to the American type of civic character. But in all cases of social assimilation the existing social type acts as a lodestone to the extent to which it has become an attainable norm of adaptation, if only in a few given examples to become the object of imitation by others, who learn through it how to be socially normal.

Finally, the type of personality must be regarded as a *constructive cause* of social realization. The truly typical characterized to our minds unifies and crystallizes our typical qualities. In this advanced sense the social type becomes creative of effort in the direction of the ideal. The story of the heroic impels the child to organize its fellows for enterprise. Out of the qualities which characterize men and women of the past we are continually constructing logically valid types of personality towards which we bend our energies and fashion our lives in the faith that the types we hold before us may be incarnated into our better selves. If the artist objectifies for us on canvas or in marble the type of personality we have vaguely outlined to our consciousness, we recognize at once the type which we have striven to realize. Thus the artistic expression of the social type is made the means of an effective formation of character—a causal power in social consolidation of those who share in the kinship of the deeper life. The creative types of personality stand highest in the price-current of social valuation.

We may sum up the results of this analysis in the following propositions:

1. That the group of personalities similar enough to come under the same social type affords to nature and history an area of characterization by which their specific effects upon persons can be conserved and made part of the social process to be assimilated into the life of the community.

2. That the development of variety of social types arising from this receptivity of the social process depends equally upon the appropriability

of the psychical and the physical elements by the social organization.

3. That the essential elements of typal worth are (a) adaptation to the ways of nature, (b) appropriation of the truth of history and tradition, and (c) selective anticipation of the assimilative tendencies of the social process.

4. That the social value of any particular person has to be practically estimated by conformity to the type of personal efficiency to which his capacities have assigned him in the divided labor of social organization; and secondly, by the capacity to share in the realization of the theoretically normal type of personality to which the life of the community tends as a whole. That is, he must be typically social in his own particular situation and he must share in the realization of the type towards which the social organization tends.

In the next chapter we shall see how this tendency toward the potentially normal type is realized by the social type, thus making socialization developmental in its character. Thus far it has been groupal, the social type being a representative member of the homogeneous group.

CHAPTER IV.

SOCIOLOGICAL TYPES.

A SOCIOLOGICAL type is either a potentially normal type of personality or a theoretically superior type of social organization projected as a goal of practice. It is one of four terms in the typological series: the generic type which is organic, the social type which is an example normal to a group, the sociological type which is a potentially normal type of personality or a type of social organization taken as a standard of equilibrium with a social tendency, and the ideal type in which all the typal tendencies are harmonized in a solidarity involving development. The selective connection unites them into a typological series. A social tendency is composed of the members of this series. The sociological type is a complex of potentials. Change compels the social process to move on or die out. Every social type normally constructs for itself at almost every step of its existence a sort of a series of sociological hypotheses on the strength of which it proceeds to normalize itself in the direction of the ideal, in the face of change which has disturbed its temporary equilibrium. The typical mother, father, or social leader always thinks of

possible needs of life. The contents of past experience are summed up in the social type. The presence of conscious possibilities gives us the potentially normal or the sociological type. The social
process also reckons with and regards the ideal.
Between the actual and the ideal lies the potential.
And this is the essence of the social process itself
so far as that process tends to be normal. The
potency to adaptation to a superior situation is
a quality of the typical person and of the community. This assumes that *if* the social type is
true to itself by acting on the basis of past experience (habit, heredity), in adapting itself to new
circumstances (suggestion), the individual as well
as the social aggregate must surrender itself substantially to the hypothesis which it has formed
out of these new potentialities in order to fulfill the
conditions of finding the new equilibrium upon
which its survival normally depends. That complex of potentialities, to which the social type must
attain to survive, is the sociological type.

This practice or power of suggestion of the conceivable facts which will potentially meet the want
of the newly required equilibrium for any social
organization or for any leading tendency therein,
may be called invention, suggestion, imagination,
mental construction, prediction, prophecy, faith or
the seeing of visions of the invisible. By whatever
name it be known, this *constructive anticipation of
the normally potential type* is real to both logic and
to life which science observes; because the process
of scientific thinking is none other than this process

—the application of past experience to the new conditions that arise, by the projection of the observed order of events into the future. The social spirit speculates on what had better be done next. The social process answers this question by giving in the sociological type the next term potentially normal enough to meet the anticipated requisites of survival. Development arises from this very act of realization.

The transition from the actual social type to the potentially normal type becomes therefore the logically normal tendency of the social process. Development of the community consists in the selective connection between the actual and the potentially more normal life of the typical groups.

The type towards which the social process tends is the sociological type—the theoretically normal type which tends to prevail in response to the impulse in social man which impels him to seek to realize the more normal rather than to be content with a less normal condition of existence. The social type is the type actually required for personal survival in any simple social situation; but the sociological type is the type toward which the actual social type must tend in order to develop out of the actual into a conceivably superior, that is, toward an ideal social situation. At every step of social development this speculative sense of the socially superior as a realizable social end is present.* We may therefore with strictest accuracy put this series of successive social and sociological types together

* Ward, Psychic Factors, Ch. XXXIV.

and regard this phase of the societary process as
the essence of the developmental process. The essential function of the sociological type is to provide selective continuity of social thought from the
actual to the theoretically normal by a series of adjustments between the social situation that is and
the potential social situation that tends to become
actual in the direction of the ideal. Hence the sociological type is the tendential index foreshadowing,
in a vague yet to the trained social sense in an effective way, the tendency and the direction to change
in the life of society. The selective continuity,
which renders development possible, from one situation to a theoretically better one, involves a series
of functional and conditional changes to enable the
social type to reach the sociological type. What
is loses its right of way to what had better be.

This distinction between types social and sociological rests on a strictly scientific distinction
which comparative sociology has made it necessary
to admit into sociological theory. The distinction
is that which we make between survival and development as substantial aspects of human association.
Any association in whose policy survival controls
the end of concourse with one another necessarily
evolves social types by natural selection. The
method of natural selection is survival by elimination of the non-typical. But any association in
which human beings coexist systematically with
their kind for purposes of betterment must deal
largely with the potential in human nature. That
is, every association in which problems of better-

ment are permitted to be preeminent over the mere matter of survival, will necessarily project mental pictures of possible states of social existence. Compared with the existing states in which survival is simply secured, these are deemed worth while for men in social concert to strive to attain to for themselves and their kind. This potentially better ' commonwealth ' of social existence, is theoretically the better of the two, just because it is regarded as containing the very characteristics and conditions which would cause the existing type to pass over into the realization of the conceivably superior type of personal existence. This projected type is the sociological type. Its conceptual reality makes development of social type possible; its absence limits human association to survival. It is a vague thing, but it is fatal to society to be wanting in it. In the natural races of mankind the social type is the criterion of social value, because there survival is practically the whole aim of association and consequently all change is withstood so far as it is possible to do so. That is the only logical policy. Among the civilized races, on the contrary, development is the principal or at least a prominent thing and the transition from the actual to the potentially superior type of social being by change of conditions more favorable thereto is not only encouraged, but the capacity to serve society in safely effecting these successive transitions in the right direction is the civilized test of sociological value.

When this conception of the sociological type is

SOCIOLOGICAL TYPES. 63

once grasped the student of society may regard himself as having in hand the speculative conception by which the social mind reasons out its future. No parliamentary discussion ever takes place without taking into account the effect of any measure on the type that normally tends to prevail. We must look for it at the point where the separate currents of social effort tend to meet. It is always in advance of us. It gives us the truly scientific standpoint by anticipating the real cause of development.

At the risk, therefore, of being prolix, a more detailed definition of the sociological type in its essential functions is deemed important. We have thus far spoken mainly of actual social types resulting from the objective social process. Living together in one place tends to make people more and more alike in type. Such types are those which the practised eye may, after a little deductive experience, see for itself on every page of history, in every living community, under every social relationship and in every one we meet. What is sensibly observed is, however, only an individual member of the kindred group—a typical member of an old and well-established family, a typical representative of the capitalist or of the aristocratic class, a typical American woman, a typical Southern gentleman of the old school, a typical representative of the Hebrew race, or a typical son of green Erin's Isle. The logical reality, the center or core of the aggregate of which these are respectively the typical examples, is the social type. The logically real social type serves as the commonly conceived standard by which each member is connoted to the group to which he belongs.

The social type has its theoretical importance rather in what it does than in what it is. It is the logical symbol of the objectively known aggregate. What it does is this: it serves as the representative unit of comparison by which to guide the mind in the scientific analysis of social phenomena, in the comparison of social movements, in the enumeration of social objects and their arrangement into classes and kinds, and finally in the formation of social judgments about people as they are and are to be found.

Our description of social types as objective centers of characterization in which the natural forces and the historical motives effecting the evolution of personality found actual expression in typical characters, was simply intended to make clear to the mind occupied with social thought that the social type is to be regarded as a characteristic member of a group in possession of a given social situation. It failed to make clear to the mind in search of a method of treating the more refractory phenomena of progression, by what conceivable way the once normal product could pass out of any given situation which has now changed and of which it was the exponent, into another conceivably more normal social situation in the ordinary course of socialization. It fell short of furnishing us with an intermediate term between the actual and the ideal, towards which social development normally tends.

This datum of the social consciousness we find in the sociological type. It is a logical necessity of human evolution.

Here as elsewhere we start in our quest from things as they are to find what they tend to become. Any existing social types may be regarded as determined by past social tendencies.* And what is true of any one is true of all social tendencies which have a type-determining importance in a given social condition of things. We must know the position and the possibilities involved.

The problem then is to find, for the right grasp of the societary processes, a guiding standard or progressive point of view going before and giving precision of aim to the tendential forces, so that these various type-developing tendencies may find the focus to which they are capable of converging, lest the creative energies of the movement fail to effect that characterization of types which is its normal function and the typal tendency pervading civilization be lost, as it were, like a stream in the desert.

From what we know of socialization we are sure that it cannot be a blind, aimless movement. Neither the course of nature to which society is bound nor the quality of history from which we get its subjective meaning allows us thus to conceive of society. Yet we are not scientifically justi-

---

* Paulhan, Les caractères, II., Liv. II.

fied in assuming that a teleological authority is thrust into the process of typification from outside of society itself, other than that which comes to existing society from appropriating the contents of past civilization and from utilizing with a wiser foresight and firmer control the environing conditions of social living. Nevertheless, no society which has come to self-consciousness doubts that this alembic of social experimentation, into which the powers natural and historical pour and out of which new types of social worth come into being amongst its people, is presided over by some fundamental principle under which the actualized types of to-day become part of the goods of history and nature to-morrow, only to be assimilated into the making of the types of the future.

The logical form under which we may conceive of the socially becoming must be a tendency-controlling criterion capable of giving constructive character to the elements of the developmental process. It must be a hypothetically valid norm towards which the variant aspects of socialization tend in order to enter into the realization of potentially truer types of personal worth. Social order moves, whether in progressive or decadent civilizations. Is there any theoretically definable type towards whose focus the concurrent ongoing we call society sends its several active tendencies—industrial, religious, political, æsthetic—for characterization? And, if so, how are we to recognize in sociological theory the principle that rules in this interesting nexus of typification?

This guiding norm which gives *organic character* to the complex tendencies of socialization is the sociological type. If, however, the sociological type be the selective criterion in which the variety of social types and tendencies of all grades and degrees of actual development must find their co-ordination as a requisite of a potentially completer development; to which of these two—the social or the sociological type—are we to look for a working standard of social valuation ? The social type being the practically normal type, at home with the social aggregate, to which its members give adherence; and the sociological type being the potentially normal type that tends to prevail, we have two essential points of view from which the products of socialization may be estimated: we may judge of the societary process either in terms of the practically normal type of man as we see and know him at his work in the relations of actual life. This is the concrete social man. Or we may measure social value by the extent to which the societary process tends to promote the growth in personality of those more or less purposeful anticipations which the progressive community and developing personalities consciously or habitually formulate for their own development. This is the potentially superior or sociological man. The reaction of this type upon the aggregate then develops the social organization. Which of these two—the social or the sociological man—is entitled to exercise sovereignty over socialization?

If we now recur for a moment to the concluding

summary under the description of the Social Types, it will be seen that these two norms of social worth are not really competing but complemental norms in the same process. The real problem then is not which is the type containing the law of social valuation, but how to balance the claims of both which are alike indispensable in the formation of social judgments. Our answer must be found in a more specific presentation of the distinct functions of the sociological type and its relations with the social type—its complement—in socialization.

1. *The Sociological Type is Synthetic: as such it defines the limits of typal survival.* Social man has hedged himself in from the forces of nature in which the unrestrained struggle for existence goes on. In this state of existence one of his chief characteristics is his susceptibility to suggestion, for the facilitation of which he has developed a great many symbols of communication by which common grounds of conduct are the more readily established. Centers of social interests are recognized, by reference to which all changes are to be judged. To these interests the typically social man is normally loyal. But the different groups of interest arising within the same community, thus shut out from nature and her selective methods, make it necessary that some degree of differences should be tolerated. But just how much toleration of one type by another is required for survival in the same society is a question of policy peculiar to the social organization. The logical necessity arising out of this situation is a type of social organization which

tends to adjust itself so as to be generic enough to
insure unity of organization and yet allow variety
of typal adaptation in the social groups within that
organization sufficient to tip the scales of policy
in favor of developmental potentialities. This requisite of the societary process is found in the sociological type—the right and the faith to risk the
next best step.

This synthetic outcome of the social characteristics and conditions to the mind of social man becomes a necessity of every relation he enjoys.
Imitative suggestion having reached its limits of
expansion or rather intension of type, variation
from type sets in by way of reaction. But reaction
toward what? The conceivably superior, the theoretically more normal or sociological type. Only
a few are thus affected at first, then a few more,
then the social lump is leavened. To limit the
range of typal reaction the sociological type becomes the vital necessity of any state of human
society. It sums up the possibly better terms on
which men may live together.

The sociological type thus becomes the theoretically normal standard of social valuation by determining what kinds of actions, relations and interests
shall be regarded as compatible with the progressive life of the community. It gauges the amount
of struggle which may be admitted and it thereby
puts limits to the degree of cooperation deemed
requisite for the development of the various types
of social nature without prejudicing the unity and
continuity of civic well-being for which social or-

ganization exists. A community which so controls
and constrains the rivalry among its social types as
to lower their level of social efficiency to that of its
weaker types of personality, as injudicious charities
tend to do, thereby subordinates its more normal to
its less normal type, and puts itself in a fair way to
become decadent rather than developmental, or at
best to be subordinated or absorbed by some competing community, the tendency of whose social
life is toward a superior type of personality and
thus toward a more efficient type of social organization. Wherever this subordination of the sociological type, which represents the normal trend of
the societary process, is effected by putting an
actual social type in its place, whose developmental
possibilities are practically exhausted, the result is
not a synthesis of social tendencies from the actual
through the typically normal toward the ideal, but
a recoil from the direction of the ideal resulting in
an arrest of development. The whole scheme of
social control which Hobbes worked out is exposed
to this criticism. An atrophied survival is the inevitable outcome, because normal development is
theoretically impossible. The limitation of struggle tends to become extreme.

2. *The Sociological Type is Selective: it indicates
the logically normal adjustment of all specific tendencies of social development within the same social organization.* In its synthetic capacity the sociological
type serves as an indicator of the area within which
unity of type must dominate the group. There
struggle was limited. But in its selective capacity

it must have respect unto the requisites of survival of variant types and conditions of social existence. Here struggle must be organized and equated among classes. Speaking of the well-known facts about animal communities Dr. Arthur Mitchell remarks that "through the general cooperation they seem to give to the weaker members of the community a better chance of survival than they would have if each individual were battling for itself." Now it is just this purposeful—not instinctive—capacity of selectively projecting or suggesting a system of association with a greater number of better chances of survival in it, that puts and keeps the civilized societies of men upon the track of development. But the winning of the potential chance is always at the price of struggle—selective struggle. The roaming horde at some time in the past must have begun to select for itself that set of better chances which led to the better organization of its divergent impulses. The brute-communities never body forth any such a complex of attainable chances as are woven together by the social consciousness of human societies in the sociological type. So in the modern city and the contemporary nation we have the same normal criterion admitting an infinitely greater variety of social tendencies through which provision is made for that multiplicity of methods of adaptation to conditions. Thus is made possible an ever-increasing realization of the aims of the component social tendencies. Only the trend must be under the selective control of this governing principle of a potentially normal type taken for granted by the competing and co-operating tendencies within the sanction of the social sense. The several tendencies work by sociological types as several builders work by architect's plans. All types that develop at all must find their *raison d'être* therein. Tendencies that ignore the sociological type, to that extent become abnormal in degree and consequently the social type resulting therefrom is abnormal. The selective relation of the social types, at all times of divergent tendencies, to the sociological lies in the line of the normally superior assimilation. Different classes and conditions are unequally prepared to participate in the tendency that leads on to a superior adaptation; but the sociological type none the less indicates the direction in which selection by the actual types to realize the potentially superior type of existence must be exercised. For any social type, therefore, the direction of its development from a given social condition is indicated by finding the minimum and the maximum limits within which any movement toward the sociological type would result in a potentially more normal adaptation to the conditions of existence. This gives us the limits and the line of development.

3. *The Sociological Type is Systematic: it provides the societary process with a principle of superiority and subordination in groupal competition and coopera-tion.* This function arises where there are several social types existing at the same time representing different tendencies and yet each is aware of the common conditions on which any tendency may

develop into attainment of its specific end. Here arises the necessity of coordinating the different social types under such established relations of interdependence as to provide a system of superiority and subordination among themselves. Otherwise the competition of types comes into play to such an extent as to result in the possible subversion of social order and the cutting off of all except the most efficient types from survival or development. This conflict, if not arrested by some mutually acceptable system of relationships implying a control in the interest of some sociological type, imperils the dominance of the moral purpose for whose pursuit society has been called into existence and for the sake of which civilization persists. The sociological type furnishes us with this principle of superiority and subordination to which the developmental grades of social types in the same organization have to be coordinated. The higher social functions have to be coordinated with the lower. But among themselves there must be a reciprocal service centering in the sociological type. On their respective planes of typal capacity all have to be assimilated to that ruling end—the sociological type of attainment which is potentially within the reach of all types. Otherwise the higher types must have no inducements to development as the lower types despair of self-realization; but the theoretically normal type calls into activity all possible social types which that type of social organization is capable of developing.

4. *The Sociological Type is Purposive: it gives*

purposive character to the societary process. As such it is the focalizing nexus through which the aims of the great classes of the social population effect the transition from the actual types of attainment toward the progressive realization of the social ideals. The feeling of solidarity recognized in the harmonizing of communities and social classes under a comprehensive self-consistent unity, has in the history of peoples constantly brought them under the sway of some informing impulse, some energizing insight, some controlling consciousness, some conquering conviction. The psychical capacity of a community, a nation or a class to construct a sociological situation into which the half-awakened social forces and aspirations can be directed and therein find the superior sphere of development, is not possible except by the social spirit building for itself some such tentative outlook or conceptual model as the sociological type, from whose height it can see visions of the potentialities of the societary process. The history of prophetic types in the growth of great religions illustrates this. No great typal attainment has ever been achieved by person or people without the use of this intermediating framework by which its possibility was first demonstrated to the minds of men. The synthetic, selective, systematic and purposive projection of types is the sociological key to those otherwise mysterious transitions in which masses of humanity have been lifted out of an old civilization by the irresistible virility of a new power in human his-tory.

The preceding chapters will permit of the following summary of the nature, the limits, the method and the conditions of realization of the process of social development.

The nature of the process of social development is fundamentally typical both in the individual and the aggregate. In the objective course of social events regarded as part of the cosmic process and called The Social Process of natural association, and in the conceptual course of social reasoning in the race-consciousness, called The Sociological Process of social organization, we have found two related series or successions of controlling norms by which the particular and the universal aspects of human association are coordinated under a common typological series as the ruling conceptions in the course of social development.

The scope of this process of typological development lies between the minimum limits of the organic types of personality, whose survival is conditioned upon the inorganic order of nature, and the maximum limits of typal potentialities as set by the conscious apprehension of the race-ideals as types of social solidarity. Personal force and social organization create the type through association. Within these limits there arise what are on the whole the leading conceptions in sociological science—namely, the social types which govern the life of the groupal aggregates; and, secondly, the social tendencies whose origin is in the actual social types as centers of social aggregation. These tendencies seek their self-realization by the impulse toward potentially more normal types and by the control of the sociological conceptions in the direction of the ideal. The whole social organization is therefore under the immediate guidance of the potentially normal type of personality in which each social tendency conceivably finds its solidarity.

The method of finding the tendential equilibrium both for typical personality and for the social tendency, as well as for the community composed of such tendencies is a process of selection. The equilibrium of personality is to be found in the social group to whose typical standard his personal capacity enables him to conform. The equilibrium of the social tendency in turn is to be found by the adjustment of that tendency to the functions of the social organization it is capable of performing and at the same time by adjustment to the convictions of the community. The community itself is only at equilibrium in the recognition of the type of personality toward which its organized activities normally tend to prevail. The function of the sociological type in selection is therefore that of guiding the social tendencies to self-normalization in keeping at once with both the natural requisites of personal survival in association and with the conceptual demands of the race-convictions as revealed in the prevailing degree of culture. The typal equilibrium of the community is found by the selection of that potentially normal type of personality in which the convictions of the community and the conditions of its natural existence tend to balance.

themselves in social policy. This is true of house-hold, of class, of village, of city, and of nation, to all of which the process of typal selection is the constructive principle of social development.

The conditions under which this process of social development is made possible are to be found by a study of association in its essential connections with and dependence upon nature, and by an equally necessary study of the sociological concepts whose content is given in human history. From the relation of the process to nature we get the conditions under which the successive types of personality in the developmental series are evolved. From history we get the categories of the social consciousness. By the union of the two—the conditions in nature and the content of history—we are enabled to combine both the static conditions and the dynamic tendencies of social man into a single developmental process—the evolution of organic man through successive stages of typal equilibria toward the ideal type of personal realization attainable only in associative life through purposeful organization.

BOOK II.

THE SOCIOLOGICAL POSTULATES.

CHAPTER V.

FUNCTIONALLY defined, the sociological type proved to be that reasoned datum of the social consciousness through whose control was effected the unification of the conditions of individual life with the universal tendencies expressed in the convictions of history.

The process of human association therefore requires us to define these necessary conditions and the universal tendencies out of whose juncture this typal resultant arises in all the range of development between the organic and the ideal.

Logically stated, the problem is to define the Sociological Postulates of the evolution of types of personality.

1. What are the necessary conditions in actual association for the development of objective types of personality? What conforming conditions must a member of society observe for the production of this result?

2. What are the universal tendencies or abiding relations of personality to the community for development by sociological types of personality? What normal connections must govern social organiza-

tion in the forms of the social class, the family, the community, the nation, in order to reach this result of development among its members by being true to the typical?

These necessary conditions to which the social aggregate must conform, as also must the individual, are the postulates of typal development. They are (1) The Social Situation, (2) The Social Interests, (3) The Social System and (4) The Social Mind. These are the logical conditions without which we can give no formal explanation of social development.

The corresponding universal tendencies to be postulated for typal development, are (1) Typal Integration, (2) Typal Differentiation, (3) Typal Assimilation and (4) Typal Solidarity. Without these we cannot explain the processes involved in social organization.

Within each of these conditions the principle corresponding thereto prevails. The social situation integrates, the social interests differentiate, the social system assimilates and the social mind consolidates. The selective survival of social man is by the method of development from the actual toward the potentially normal type of personality, but always by virtue of such tendency as the conditions require.

Typal integration is the subordination of personality to the social type in any given social situation or simple social state. The societary process is a process in which the social causes—natural forces and psychical motives—impel the members of the community to typal survival and development, or typal succession from the less to the conceivably more favorable situation. In order to proceed with a strictly scientific analysis of this process we shall have to define to our minds a simple situation, or condition of things, or 'state of society' as Mill calls it.* Within this situation social causes may be conceived of as operating upon personality in association; from this causal area for the time being all other influences must be regarded as excluded on the assumption of their relatively insignificant part in the moulding of the personal organism into the typical member. Such a formal situation we designate the Social Situation.

We have then also to picture to ourselves the requisites of that transitional movement by which any social type of character or of organization, as already realized in a given situation, passes over into a more highly developed type of personality or organization between the actual and the ideal, through the selective synthesis of the sociological type. The social situation is the starting-point of a social tendency.

The answer given is substantially as follows: Typal progression or socialization takes place by the logical process of constructing, out of the contents of the psychical experience of society aided by the knowledge and the use of the factors of natural environment, a conceivably more normal social situation into which the social type known to our

* Mill, Logic, Bk. VI., Ch. X., § 2.

observation is theoretically capable of entering. This projected social state is the logical reality necessary for the realization of the sociological type. Within this process conceived of as a series of social states, situations or types of attainment occupied by typical groups of persons in and upon whom the causal factors of associative life play, we must look for the stages in the evolution of social man. According to this view the process of developmental typification is to be looked upon as a series of coordinations of the individual and the universal in successive types social and sociological. The coordination occurs in the social aggregates wherein the animal and the ideal are integrated in the typical. This gives us the social type in any given social situation. The sociological type the social sense contrives and constructs as a potential habitat for the social type to enter into successively, and towards which the social forces and motives impel the group or some of its members to proceed. The potentially superior or sociological situation in each case of transition deeply intersects the actual or social situation. The transition is effected by the social type as rapidly and as certainly as it is capable of selectively appropriating the normalizing elements of objective nature and the idealizing elements of spiritual history. This is the essence of the social tendency—the selective transition from the social to the sociological type.

The social situation, concretely defined in terms of social causation, is the area of typal characterization within which the product of the societary proc-

ess is a substantially homogeneous type of personality. This is the case in the family, in particular.
This area of characterization has to be marked off
in theory as it is in fact from the cosmic process
of which it is none the less a part; so that the causal
factors peculiar to the societary movement may be
the more readily recognized in the definition of the
social situation and the series of social situations
which make up the social tendency. This is clearly
stated by Professor Huxley: "Men in society,"
he says, "are undoubtedly subject to the cosmic
process. As among other animals, multiplication
goes on without cessation, and involves severe competition for the means of support. The struggle
for existence tends to eliminate those less fitted to
adapt themselves to the circumstances of their existence. The strongest, the most self-assertive,
tend to tread down the weaker. But the influence
of the cosmic process on the evolution of society
is the greater the more rudimentary its civilization.
Social progress means a checking of the cosmic
process at every step and the substitution for it, of
another which may be called the ethical process;
the end of which is not the survival of those who
may happen to be the fittest in the respect of the
whole of the conditions which obtain but of those
who are ethically the best." * The same authority
continues, "Society differs from nature in having a
definite moral object; whence it comes about that
the course shaped by the ethical man—the member

---

* Evolution and Ethics, p. 81.

of society or citizen—necessarily seems counter to that which the non-ethical man—the primitive savage or man as a mere member of the animal kingdom—tends to adopt. The latter fights out the struggle for existence to the bitter end, like any other animal; the former devotes his best energies to the object of setting limits to the struggle." *

On the side toward nature and nature's methods of survival the social situation is delimited by the systematic association of personalities in domestic, municipal, national and other groups, within which the prevailing effort entailed by the cosmic relationship is to discount conflict by which the social type has become integrated and differentiated and to put a premium on cooperative characterization of personality in conformity with one of several varieties of homogeneous social types. The rate and the extent of this process of typal characterization depend very largely on the *relative* importance which the prevailing type of personality in command of the social situation puts upon the procreative functions of personality and the productive control of natural resources; if the energies of personality be too procreative for the survival of the social type out of the productive resources at command, the process of desocialization begins within the social situation and the very end of social organization tends to be defeated by creating the conditions of struggle within the limits of society formed for the purpose of putting limits to the struggle. The level

* Huxley, Evolution and Ethics, p. 203.

of the social type drops in the scale of the race-consciousness. It is an alternative between fewer and better men, or more and worse men as a matter of social policy.

Desocialization may take the form of the conflict of classes, each of which occupies a social situation of its own, primarily of its own making. Or it may be effected by the systematic repression of the affective motives* of which legalized infanticide was the primitive and ancient method, and irresponsible systems of providing for foundlings a modern expedient. The typal potentialities of a given social situation are therefore directly conditioned on the existing ratio of procreative to the productive energies of the community. If the present time and place—the social situation—are such as to exhaust the resources of a class to preserve its equilibrium with its environment there is no adequate proportion of effort available for anticipating or realizing a potentially more normal situation among competing classes. Hence the possibilities of a class depend upon the ratio of the social type to the sociological type, between which the units of social efficiency are distributed, in any social situation or any community made up of any number of typical groups. And what is true of the community is equally true of any particular type in that community. Any particular type of personality with respect to whose energies the procreative claims outbid the productive claims, tends thereby to neutral-

---

* Letourneau, Sociology, Vol. I., Bk. III., Ch. V.

ize the advantages of association against nature. As the quantity grows the quality declines beyond a definite limit. This introduces the cult of struggle—homeopathically it may be, but no less surely —whose effect and process is the relatively more general individualization of the membership of society. This typological ratio is one of the chief social factors in the formation and maintenance of social classes. The defensive effort is akin to that of the whole society against nature. Social classes above the lowest retain the advantage of an acquired social situation, occupied by a homogeneous type, by limiting the excessive spread of the competitive cult to the social classes in which it had its procreative origin. Hence there are as many typal areas of characterization as there are social levels of homogeneous class-life or of standards of associative tastes and tolerance.

So much for the social situation as it is related to nature. On the side of the social situation toward which history tends, on the other hand, and in which personality receives progressive characterization, there arises another and counterpoising tendency—the opposite of desocialization by conflict. In any social situation in which the type of personality represents the superiority of the productive over the procreative powers, there the tendency is decidedly to socialize the type of personality in the direction of the sociological type by which the cult of concord is maintainable. Classes are assimilated toward a superior type of social organization. In spite of all that has been written by

way of gainsaying the essential conceptions of the
Malthusian analysis of the social process, it remains
true tendentially at least for any given social situation, that for that situation these two typal tendencies—the socialization of the individual toward superiority of type and the individualization of society to the extent of irresponsibility to type—may
be so related to each other in point of relative subordination of the socializing to the individualizing
tendency as to force the whole social situation held
by a once superior type down to the level of ineffi-
ciency where the type is dealt with by the method
of natural selection, that is, survival by elimination
of the inefficient types. The control of the tendency to typal integration in the simple social situation requires the subordination of personality to
the type of personality best fitted to prevail. And
the ratio of the procreative to the productive claims
upon the existing social type in command of a social situation determines which of these two tendencies shall be given priority of social control, the
organic or the ideal.* Sociological policy would of
course seek to keep the eyes of the self-conscious
group steadily set toward the theoretically normal
situation to which the social type through the soci-

* By procreative claims I mean of course that requisition
which the reproduction of the species makes upon the energies of social capacity; by productive claims I mean not
simply economic goods but also æsthetic creations, moral,
legal and all other social services by which society improves
its chances for survival and development of the types of life
it represents.

ological type is deemed reasonably capable of succeeding.

The tendency to typal integration within the
same social situation becomes the primary feature
of association, by this analysis of the societary process. The social tendency is that typal succession
of situations social and sociological by which when
men are sufficiently integrated to work together in
the social organization each type may seek the ends
that seem best. The key to the social situation is
the type of personality which normally prevails
therein; and the type of personality which prevails,
and is in actual possession of the situation, together
with the sociological type potentially realizable
by the social type, gives us the two necessary data
to determine the social tendency peculiar to any
social class or condition. We get the locus of the
process within the social situation by determining
two facts: the social type as it is and the sociological type—the potentially normal type which the
developing type tends to become. Each of these
has its separate coordinates in the necessary conditions and the universal relations accounting for its
realization. We must judge of a family, a class or
a people by what it normally seeks to attain to as
well as by what it actually is. The direction is vital.

The social situation, considered as one of the
theoretically necessary forms of the social process
in scientific analysis, within which the social type
finds itself tenanted, has three essential aspects or
characterizing factors. Our analysis reveals (1) the
type of personality in which the social aggregate

finds its unity or integrity; (2) the conditions of existence to which the social type must normalize itself in order to survive in the given situation; and (3) the sociological type, in which the social type of personality and the conceivably more normal conditions of existence tend to find their potentially more perfect equilibrium. The most simple example of the social situation as a sphere of typal development is the family,* in the course of its natural growth. Its business is the integration of members to a homogeneous type.

This being the nature of the social situation, what is its law or principle according to which typal integration goes on? We have a product here—the social type. How does the individual ever become typical and thus tend toward the universal ? If each necessary form of social activity has a correspondingly universal relation from which to regard the process, then we shall have to look in each necessary form of social order for a corresponding type-developing principle coordinating these aspects. The social situation, the social interests, the social system and the social mind have each a law of its own.

The sociological law, or, as we prefer to call it, the sociological principle, dominating the social situation in the developmental process is called the *Principle of Typal Integration*, and may be stated as follows: In every simple social situation the principle governing typal integration requires that *the*

* The Politics of Aristotle, Bk. I., Chs. I.–III. (Welldon).

individual member of the social aggregate shall be subordinated to the type of personality which tends toward the maximum equilibrium of personality with the conditions of existence. That is, the normal family, class, community or nation is one which tends toward the potentially more normal type of attainment of which the social aggregate is capable.

The principle of typal integration by subordination of personality to the homogeneous type which the social sense deems worthy of survival, is one of the fundamental principles of social reasoning. For this there is no lack of confirmation in the facts of social existence. The best illustration of the principle in practice is to be found in the study of primitive tribal life, the functions of the family in social evolution, and the fortunes of the several social classes. Under these conditions it is more natural because easier to conform to a homogeneous type. The few who resist the natural inertia suffer punishment or social pressure to conform. For the purpose of participation in this process men originally must have remained in society after type-controlling maternity lost power over its offspring. For this end man stays in society. And, when once within the social situation which secures for him survival by imitation of organic type to which he is capable of conforming as the price of his life, it is impossible but that contact, tolerance, communication and cooperation should develop and diffuse a sense of a typical criterion in which the social aggregate finds its logical equilibrium. The tendency in personality to regard this typical center of social equilibrium as the essential of survival, is the subjective process of typification. The principle of typal subordination in the interest of homogeneity is the principle governing the social process within the social situation. It is no less developmental than necessary for survival, since it disciplines the individual organism into cooperation with the moral standard called the social type.

By far the largest proportion of the phenomena of early societies which relate to genealogical organization of society can be explained satisfactorily only on the assumption that the social type was the actual and the sociological type the potentially normal law of these communities. With them, in the early stages of social development unity of type overshadowed all else. The machinery of religion was utilized to maintain that as the requisite of survival. Systems of consanguinity changed from matriarchal to patriarchal or reverted from one to the other in obedience to the requisites of typal survival by more normal adaptation to that tendency which gave increased potency of typal continuity. While this homogeneity of type was the primary social aim, typal integration was the supreme tendency to which personality had to yield himself.

In the complex structure of modern society a member may owe allegiance to several social situations at the same time. A child owes primary allegiance to domestic authority and his survival and development depend on his conformity to the type it represents. Similarly the youth owes allegiance to the school as the situation in which he finds a transitional equilibrium. Likewise, the adult owes allegiance to the interests of his class in which his equilibrium lies. Finally, all owe allegiance to the type which the national organization of society seeks to realize for its members. But there is no confusion in typal allegiance, because these forms are successive and complemental.

CHAPTER VI.

SOCIAL INTERESTS: TYPAL DIFFERENTIATION.

THE developmental process presents another phenomenon which cannot be explained on the assumption of a society within which homogeneity of type is the transcendent fact and in which therefore the prevailing causal relation of personality to the community is typal integration.

The phenomenon in question is the existence of variety of types and divergent tendencies which somehow manage to disturb the simple social state in which the homogeneous type prevailed. This fact is observable in any complex community outside of the normal family of civilized life or the tribal life of savagery, though it is also present in subordinate phases there.

On what formal conditions can their appearance in the social process be explained ? What necessity drove society to this result ? We must assume that in the place of a homogeneity of type as the requisite of survival there has arisen a variety of social interests. These divided the population against itself and each personality according to its ratio of personal efficiency follows the bent of interests in the effort to attain to social equilibrium.

These centers of social interests become new centers of integration. The transition from the homogeneous to the heterogeneous types calls for a potentially more normal type of social organization. The dominant causal relation of personality to the community is now that of typal differentiation. Typal differentiation is the reaction within the social aggregate of a tendency whose object is the substitution of an adaptive variety of types for a traditional homogeneity of type.

This first stage of socialization required such relations of the social population to one another as to cause the energies of the people to be primarily occupied with the development of a sovereign sense of membership. All other impulses and inclinations within the social organism were systematically subordinated to this overmastering spirit of the highly socialized community. This lasted as long as fellowship was the main want of the community. The early life of the race, and the communistic communities to some extent even now, have to look to the socializing of the individual. Life is the cornerstone of liberty in society. Consequently unity of social type by conformity thereto extends continuously through long ages, tyrannizing over the whole archaic organization.* The farther back we go, or the farther apart we go from the social types of modern achievement, the more dominant becomes the dictum of conformity to unity of type in the minutest and in the most comprehensive as-

* Hearn, The Aryan Household, Introduction, pp. 4-9.

pects of association. Changes in social organization, such as had to be made, were made in the interest real or fictitious of survival by conservation of social type. The same is true of the basal relations of society at all times—integration of type is fundamental.

The second aspect of the developing process appears when the reaction of personality from conformity sets in as a divergent tendency seeking social survival not by conservation of type but rather by deviation from type. A new norm of social relationship has to be provided. At this juncture in the process the problem is to make intelligible the rise of variety in social types; and the social process has to be tested by its capacity to produce effective varieties of types of personality and of social organization in any given time and place. After a few more words of definition we shall see that the nature and constitution of personality is such, in its relation to what we call social interests, that both the natural and the historical factors in human nature conspire to develop *specific centers of social interests* within the social situation, and that in connection with these interests specific types of personality tend to arise and a complex type of social organization arises therewith.

The appearance of specific types of personality in the social situation calls into prominence a correspondingly distinct principle of development. In the simple social situation, the equilibrium between the actual member and the conditions of existence is theoretically expressed in the tendency to the integration of all to the same type. But here there was only one type to take into consideration. Subordination to this single type which tended normally to prevail was the simple requisite of survival and integration was the principle of development of the whole community in its earliest stages.

When, however, homogeneity of type begins to give place to heterogeneity of type the simple community becomes differentiated into several kinds of social interests or social centers, and each social interest tends to become the normal home of a homogeneous class. Then the equilibrium of each kindred group of members with its specific conditions, and of all competing groups constituting the now complex social organization, become matters of analytical determination. Social groups have to reckon with a type of personality and a type of social organization. That type of personality which held the situation under homogeneous conditions we shall call the traditional type. The new types of a more specific character we shall call the adaptive types because adaptation to new conditions is a necessity of association. We shall see that both of these classes conform to principles which their conditions of living require. The American-born workman adheres to traditional standards; the foreign-born faces new conditions without that traditional bias in adaptation to change. It is thus seen why the traditional type keeps on its course of conformity to the past as its guiding principle in both practice and precept. The new or divergent types seek survival not by the line of higher in-

tegration directly but by the method of normalization on the basis of social interests. This differentiation of variety of interests out of the common
general interests of the community has become a
more or less highly developed fact of the developing society. So that the next step in our analysis
of the societary process requires us to show how
the rise of variety of social interests affects the
developing process and to state the sociological
principle which is brought into prominence through
this change. How does this new feature or tendency affect the type of personality that normally
tends to prevail ?

'Social interests' is a none too satisfactory term
with which to denote those common considerations
which everywhere have part in causing 'birds of a
feather to flock together' and act in concert with
reference to the rest of the community. Nature
makes no two men over exactly the same pattern
and no two persons are situated in exactly the same
set of circumstances. The rise of social interests
comes with the apprehension of a special stake in
the social organization, on the part of a typical
group of persons. Our kindred, our class, our
community and its estimation of us are social interests, of each of which *the individual is the coefficient.*

How are social interests developed and established ? They are developed by integration of kindred characters and established by differentiation
from common interests. That is, the aggregate
comes to center around a type of personality to
which it more readily conforms than to the tradi-

tional type of personality. There tend thus to arise
secondary areas of integration within the community of complex interests. The secondary areas of
integration are the domains of the various social
interests. Social utility or efficiency secures their
separate existences. The social interests may
therefore be defined as those groups of goods which
bind the individual to the social organization for
survival and by which different degrees of typal
capacity are simultaneously developed among the
members of the same social system. Each degree
of development finds its home with social interests
in which its normal equilibrium with the requisites
of survival is more nearly realized than with any
other interests. The connection of personality
with this or that social interest, is the outcome of
what each personality has, what he is, and what his
wants are.

Personality has become what he is by conformity
to traditional type; this factor plus his impelling
desires are the two terms indicating to us what he
tends to become. The use of what he has determines his developmental tendency. When these
tendencies to satisfy desires have become established in what we might call vested interests such as
property or personal relations accredited by social
sanction expressed or implied, we may then say
that social interests have become established as features of the now differentiated activities of the
community. Social interests are therefore to the
social process simply conventionalized systems or
organs of satisfying personal wants, but wants

which personality only by living in society has found normal methods of satisfying. Social interests are functional phases of the more general social process. Their governing principle of development is that of the differentiation by the substitution of specific variety of activities for a generic form of activity. Each sphere of interests tends to perfect its peculiar type of character.

Professor Baldwin, from a somewhat different point of view, has worked out a similar conclusion: " In our search for a definition of the ' interests ' of the individual, in relation to his social environment, we find a certain outcome. *His wants are a function of the social situation as a whole.* The social influences which are working in upon him are potent to modify his wants, no less than are the innate tendencies of his personal nature to issue in such wants. The character which he shows actively at any time is due to these two factors in union. One of them is no more himself than the other. He is the outcome of " habit " and " suggestion," as psychology would say in its desire to express everything in single words. Social suggestion is the sum of the social influences which he takes in and incorporates in himself when he is in the receptive, imitative attitude to the alter; habit is the body of formed material, already cast in the mould of a self, which he brings up for self-assertion and aggression, when he stands at the other pole of the relation to the alter, and exhibits himself as a bully, a tyrant or at least a master of his own conduct. Of course, heredity or "endowment"

is on this side. And the social unit of desires as
far as the individual is taken as the measure of it, in
any society, is the individual's relatively fixed conduct, considered as reflecting the current social
mode of life." *

What is here affirmed of the individual's social
interests becomes a tendency in the case of an aggregate of such persons. In this respect suggestion
is a factor of differentiation just as invention is.
The set ways of self-assertion of such an aggregate
become the traditional bonds by which change of
type is prevented in contrast with the adaptive tendency toward typal differentiation. In the latter
social suggestion and in the former personal habit
are the dominating factors. In the impulse to differentiation social suggestion indicates the course
of activity; personal habit marks a limit to variation and so becomes a primary factor in the social
process.

The place of the problem of typal variation in
the growth of the community may be thus described. The two great problems of social man are
(1) respect for the limits of conformity to traditional type, and (2) a more normal adaptation to
the changes in the immediate conditions of existence, to which certain stimuli arouses us,† resulting
in differentiation of a potentially more normal
type.

The first of these problems—conformity to type
by subordination of the individual—is wrought out

---

* The Monist, Vol. 7, No. 3, pp. 351-352.
† Ward, Dynamic Sociology, Vol. II., p. 128.

by instinctive, intuitive, imitative and customary regard for the type of person recognized as entitled to control in the family, the class, the community and the nation. The principle under which this problem of typal evolution is wrought out is the subordination of all divergent tendencies to the undisputed supremacy of a single disposition to run no unnecessary risks in social relations.

The second of these problems—that of survival by adaptation which results in differentiation of varieties of types—may be stated as follows: Given a social situation in which the hitherto homogeneous type of population is breaking up into divergent tendencies by reason of the rise of different social interests; what is the process and the principle by which the different degrees of personal capacity, representing the variety of social interests, come to find their equilibrium ? What are the requisites of a more normal adjustment to the specific social situations ? How does each new variety of type, which the differentiation of social interests— the division of social labor—calls into existence, adapt itself to the requirements of self-preservation while it is unfolding its capacities, without subverting the authority of the homogeneous type in which the whole community must still find its social equilibrium ? The answer is that the social interests are functions of the social system or organization.

Social interests in which types of character are shapen may be personal (courtship, wedlock), economic (trade or profession), political (party, policy), or they may be ideal (convictions, aspirations).

The community puts metes and bounds to their pursuit, but regards their function as indispensable to growth. This growth involves divergence from the homogeneous type, adjustment with the social interests in which personal adaptivity finds its grade of equilibrium, and finally reintegration with the new type of social organization of the community. Once any divergent tendencies to adaptive efforts at more complete normalization have arisen, as when a family or a class breaks up, the features of the process here considered are the re-grouping of the once homogeneous aggregate into several different groups of interest, on the basis of homogeneous grades of personal efficiency. The social interests are the situation in which these respective grades of efficiency find their more normal equilibrium. This equilibrium of the members of the community with their normal interests will have been fully worked out only when the respective interests shall have evolved the types of personality constantly taken as representative of such interests. Men must know to what type they belong before the integration of interests becomes organic. But this part of the process, by which the differentiation of the population into groups is effected, is simply integration on a smaller scale than that within the simple social situation. But the social functions have multiplied with the change in structure. Each specific area occupied with any particular social interest becomes a new field of personal development within which the principle of subordination to type is the ruling impulse. By this process social interests are made organic parts of the social system. Burke says, with even more than his usual perspicuity, "To be attached to the subdivision, to love the little platoon we belong to in society, is the first principle, the germ, as it were, of public affection."*

The process of typal variation may be represented as a differentiating development from the generic type of social man through the identification of personality with social interests whose tendency is toward the ideal type of social man.

Let OY, OX represent the limits of the social situation, OY being the line on which the several grades of homogeneous personal efficiency in conformity to type are measured; and OX the line on which adaptive efficiency is measured, O being the point at which all members of the social situation conforming to the traditional type are equally in possession of the generic qualities of social man. Let I represent the ideal extent of typal attainment.

What would be the differentiating process from the generic or homogeneous type at O, in the effort of personality to realize a conceivably more normal or sociological type of attainment in the direction of I ?

It would depend upon the constitution of personality. That portion of the members of the social population having a relatively high ratio of adaptive efficiency would take the line OtI ; that portion having a relatively low ratio of adaptive efficiency would take the line Ot_2I ; and that portion having

---

* Quoted from Stephen, Science of Ethics, p. 191.

these two factors of personal constitution in about
equivalent quantities would take the line Ot_1I.
These three groups of relatively homogeneous
membership based upon conformative capacity as

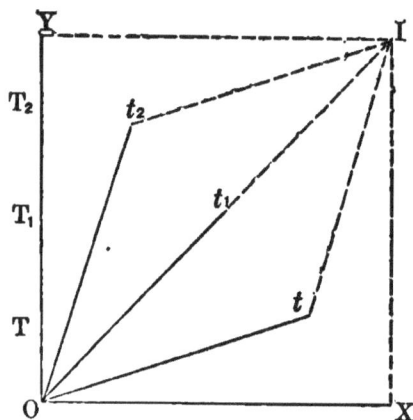

FIG. 2.

compared with adaptive efficiency would, before
typal variation on the basis of social interests began, be represented respectively by the positions T,
T_1, T_2 representing degrees of homogeneous typal
quality.

After the differentiating process begins, where
would each group of relatively homogeneous members find its typal equilibrium in connection with
its pursuit of its own social interests? Somewhere between the generic social man O and the
ideal social man I, that is, at the point of realization
of the sociological type at which the social qualities (typicality) are at equilibrium with the specific
social capacities (adaptivity) which each group of
social interests requires of the type normally at

equilibrium therein. That is, at t_2, t_1 and t. These are the points at which the new types tend to appear in obedience to the principle of typal integration by subordination of the individual member to the interests of the class to which he belongs. If any group of social interests, for example t, should degenerate in typal efficiency to the level of OX it would place its members on the very margin of the social situation in momentary peril of becoming food for natural selection. To be truly typical is to live out one's personal capacity in efficient identification with that group of social interests which will admit of one's being equally loyal to the demands of the organic and the ideal social man.

Society really reasons by social interests as soon as any group of interests becomes conscious of the differentiated functions which that group of interests must be relied upon to perform in that type of social organization.

Variation from type has its seat in personality and its relation to the social interests. Why conformity dominates the social process so long, and why variation comes so late in the history of human association, can only be fully understood in practice by the study of the facts of anthropology and ethnology. But whether we consider the changes of primitive and non-progressive peoples, or are concerned with the analysis of the contemporary processes of social differentiation, there is required a correct conception of the sociological function of personality to explain the principle of survival by variation.

1. The principle of differentiation is a process of substitution of a different type of personal unit as a measure of social value. The substitution of individuality for sociality as a superior means of social survival in changing conditions is a constant fact in social history. The release of the slave, the emancipation of the serf, the enlarged freedom of childhood and womanhood, all modify the nature of the personal unit by enlarging the individuality of each member. Personality is to be regarded as having in its constitution two effective elements which occupy its energies, namely, sociality and individuality. They are like the two kinds of matter in the brain, each performing a specific function in the service of survival, yet both complemental and delicately coordinated in their constitution. Sociality is the capacity for typal integration with other persons; it is the element in personality which provides for adherence to type; it is the quality without which the captive in war would be put to death rather than be enslaved by his conquerors. He who has it is a *socius;* he who is without it is a *hostis.*

Individuality is the adaptive capacity in the social efficiency of personality. While the element of sociality in any member of a group goes toward guaranteeing conformity to type, the element of individuality in personal constitution on the other hand determines the point in the process of typification at which the members of the requisite constitution will react; and why they do so is self-evident—because individuality has outgrown sociality to such an extent as to impel them to substitute the one for the other in order to survive in relations with their fellow-beings. This reaction is the parting of the ways in the social process at which unity of type is obliged to resist or to share with variety of type as a requisite of selective survival. A process of substitution begins.

The ancient, and still more the primitive and prehistoric polity, found social value primarily in sociality. The one thing needful was survival by loyalty to a single type. But when it came to be seen that individuality served indirectly, though not quite so inevitably, towards social survival of the aggregate, then this relatively unmarketable personal capacity became a source of surplus resources available for increasing the security of the community. The appearance of private property or personal estate illustrates this.* The limits of sociality under favorable conditions in any social situation were necessarily restricted, from the inability to hold in unity of social action a large mass of homogeneous members. But the reaction of personality from typal conformity, after being integrated thereto to the extent of its sociality and beyond, left available to the community all the resources of the undeveloped individuality. Personality is under the selective control of the sociological type to which differentiating interests impel it to aspire. It seeks a conceivably more normal satisfaction by adaptation to conditions

* The Politics of Aristotle, Bk. I., Chs. IV.–V.

more consistent with its interests and desires than conformity to a single social type requires. The community has lost nothing directly; the individual member has gained something directly, and through him the chances of survival are greatly enhanced for the whole social population. A new avenue of personal rivalry has been opened for human development. Life is no longer simply fellowship, but now includes conflict as a mode of development of man.

This change in the constitution of personality, in which society favors the individualization of its members, has the effect of substituting the indirect social qualities of personality for the direct social qualities in social valuation, and thus causing diversity of interests to arise in the community. There is room for more men because of this diversification of activities. Hence differentiation can go one step farther.

2. Differentiation of social interests insures the substitution of the *adaptive variety* of types of personality for the *traditional unity* of types.

Personality is so constituted as to require a scope of action which permits its adjustment to the changing conditions of existence. When these changes are so great as to affect the social aggregate to the extent of re-distributing the population in new relations to the national life, for example, we have the gradual elimination of the traditional types and the introduction of the types of efficiency which have been able to survive and effect their realizations under new conditions. The Industrial

Evolution in England disposed of the traditional type of ' country gentlemen '; the results of the civil war in the United States had the same effect upon the corresponding type in the South. Any such disappearance is proof of ineffective adaptivity to the changed social conditions; any surviving successor is for that reason, sociologically considered, the more effective type. Every trade, profession, industry or pursuit of a sufficiently extended history illustrates this process of the traditional type of personality representing that interest giving place to a new type effective enough to prevail in the changed conditions which successfully caused the older type to disappear altogether.

3. Social differentiation insures the substitution of potential typal tendencies representing complemental social interests in the place of actual tendencies involving conflicting social interests.

The most convenient illustration of this aspect of the principle of typal variation by the removal of the contradictory elements from the societary process by the substitution of complemental tendencies, is exhibited in the history of the relation of the church and state. Here the civic and the religious types represent permanent interests of society; these interests may embody such tendencies as to furnish the community with conflicting types, such as result in the division of the community against itself. But the potentially normal types resulting therefrom are not contradictory but complemental. The policy of adjustment of one set of type-producing social interests with another is one which belongs to the analysis of the function and form of the social order. But wherever such conflicts for the control of the social process arise there must be some want of adjustment on the part of existing social types with the conditions of existence and the possibilities of development.

While the interests of property, for example, occasion typal departure, the really causal factors in this process of differentiation are to be looked for in the subjective sense of contradiction. The logical incompatibility in the common consciousness lies between the social interests in substantial control of the given state of society and the sociological type insisting that superior interests shall prevail and asserting for personality the right to a completer self-realization in a potentially more normal group of social interests. This attitude lies at the root of the social question. The tendency to substitution of a variety of potentially more normal types for the existing type exhibits the principle according to which the youth of a community, for example, congested with incipient tendencies to variation from type, really distributes itself through the selective agency of social interests and, when thus distributed on the basis of the ratio of personal efficiency, the respective centers of social interests become thereby the seats of characterization of correspondingly specific types of personality. Members having an equivalent ratio of these two personal elements of social efficiency (sociality and individuality) constitute in the re-distribution the relatively homogeneous elements or groups of social interests which crystallize around more normal centers of aggregation in the population now undergoing reconstruction. Consequently we should look to these groups, likewise, for that degree of equilibrium which is capable of utilizing to the maximum the resources of personality. Hence differentiation of types increases the sum-total of the efficiency of the community.

This formal principle is universally valid in the social process within the conditions given and is capable of verification by appeal to the facts of the behavior of the aggregates which throw light on the causes and conditions of social departures from type. It is sufficient here to refer to the history and nature of the migratory movements of man, of the part which social fictions play in the evolutions of social life,* of the revolt of social classes and their established interests, of the differentiation of industries, ideas, institutions and ideals, all of which reveal the sociological principle of the differentiation of the type of personality through the agency of social interests whose growth reconstructs the social organization.

It seems obvious that beyond a definite limit of homogeneous typification in development of personality, as a member of a community, the divergence of the ratios of personal efficiency among the membership sets in motion differentiating tendencies of more or less variety in degree of development. Otherwise extinction or repression of social

* Lalor's Cyclopædia, " Fictions." Maine, Ancient Law, pp. 20–30.

variety is inevitable. Normally, however, under circumstances of divergence of type, personality has to seek adjustment to that particular tendency in which his particular degree of personal efficiency —individual and social—finds its equilibrium. Among all possible tendencies that may arise, only those can hope to survive which are called out by the organic functions of the differentiating activities of the community. In each organic tendency the membership must be substantially at equilibrium both with the conditions of existence and the conviction of the community. And the community itself can attain to progressive equilibrium only by such differentiation of functional tendencies as will enable it to utilize the various ratios of efficiency in its population for its own adjustment to the requisites of survival. Without differentiation of social interests the conditions of development in the homogeneous people would be wanting. By the differentiation of the social population into groups on the basis of functional efficiency, development not only in quality but in degree of attainment of personality is effected. Through the selective function of groups of social interests the type of social organization is invented or elaborated by which the various functional tendencies are coordinated into a coherent community; the agricultural population is differentiated into the industrial and agrarian types. Thence the commercial arises, giving new content to the social mind by outside communication. But every change in the types of personality that make up the community has been effected through this general process of differentiating a previous group into complemental groups of interests. While the same order is not always observed in the evolution of a people the differentiation is always from simple to complex interests. The organization of these interests calls into being the social system. Differentiation of types that are contradictory may prevent the organization of a systematic development. Complemental types make the social system all the stronger. Hence the intolerance of ideas that contradict the ideal interests of organized communities. Persecution has frequently been the best social policy. In education we have constantly to rule out contradictory factors to prevent premature or opposing tendencies in development. Differentiation regardless of normality of type must invariably be perverse. The countless varieties of voluntary associations are so many modes of defining, enjoying and preserving the social interests in which certain types of men and women are in their normal social *milieu.*

CHAPTER VII.

THE SOCIAL SYSTEM: TYPAL ASSIMILATION.

WE have hitherto regarded social interests as static conditions moulding the type of personal character. But they are with equal accuracy to be regarded as dynamic. As such they become social tendencies.

Among the necessary logical forms or conceptions by which man is guided and controlled in his social reasoning, two have thus far been defined which enter primarily into the question of 'social survival. By the first of these—the Social Situation —the requisites of survival were definitely set down as conformity to traditional type. By the second of these conceptions—the Social Interests—there arose, on the basis of a securely established degree of development by generations of efficient conformity, an impellant effort at personal re-adaptation, by seeking superior satisfaction of individual desires in groups of kindred levels of social interests. Within a fixed social system each divergent member identifies himself with that group to which birth and capacity lead him. From these conditions tendencies arise which call into play another necessary conception with which the social conduct of man has rationally to reckon. This is the tendency to differentiation of type-developing interests. The systematic relating of the several tendencies within the social process has to be effected. The now complex experiment has to be confined within recognized limits or lose its unity. This logical factor is the Social System, the best example of which is nationality or what Holland defines as a people*—a natural social unit far surpassing the State in its antiquity. The normal function of the social system is the assimilation of organic social tendencies into reciprocal relationships requisite for social development of the people as a whole.†

Under the assimilating relationships personality is free within the social tendency to which he belongs, but each tendency within which he is denizened is amenable to the type toward which the social population tends for individuation of its aspirations. Those ideals are the ultimate tests of the social system as a means of development of man.

Social assimilation is the individuation of social tendencies toward superiority in social organization. It has been seen that integration by subordination to type and differentiation of variety of type by adaptation to controlling social interests brought into play what seemed to be two competing sets of values, the traditional types of personality and the adaptive types of personality. During the period or process of the development of

* T. E. Holland, Jurisprudence, p. 40.
† Giddings, Principles of Sociology, Bk. II., Chs. III.-IV.

the adaptive types out of potential into effectual
value in the social situation, the traditional type
served as a historic basis for the process of substitution of the adaptive types. The necessity of seeking and finding a more complete social equilibrium
was entailed upon the societary process by change
of conditions of life. This was effected by social
selection bringing the divergent degrees of past
experience into adjustment with present conditions
under a new type of social organization.

Now however the problem arises of finding the
reciprocal relationships between these two classes
of tendencies, traditional and adaptive, the one of
which conforms to the principle of integration by
subordination and the other to that of differentiation by substitution. The structural agency by
which this is actually done in the social process is
the social system or that organization of institutional relationships by composition of the organic
social functions under a comprehensive social constitution. The social principle governing the process uniting the divergent tendencies in the evolution of the theoretically more normal type is Typal
Assimilation. Typal assimilation defines the reciprocal relations of the organic tendencies in the type
of constitution in control of the developmental
process.

The social system of assimilation has to deal with
tendencies. It is the third stage in the process of
the evolution of social man. Every simple situation, every social interest or tendency must take
this process into account. In this aspect of the

process the social order rises to supreme importance, as the means of systematizing the natural
tendencies in the direction of an ideal development.
The chief subjective factor in this development is
the growth of the social consciousness by which
the societary process has exercised over it a systematic control. This control involves the selection
by society of the tendencies normal to both organic
and socially ideal man. The result of this systematic control in the interests of superiority is the
assimilation of the several social types which social
interests develop into a potentially normal type of
character. This is the fundamental meaning in the
fact of nationality which works by the light of a
potentially normal type. Industry and education
adjust themselves to and react upon it. We appeal
to our future possibilities as peoples as well as to
our present powers in the effort to control social
tendencies in the direction of a desired type of national character.

The societary process is known to us as an orderly process. Whether we regard society as an
organic or a super-organic object, it is in either
case an organization of personalities existing under
the form of functional tendencies. It is consequently a relating of social types within such a complex of static and dynamic relationships as to combine the phenomena of *stability and change* in the
same associative system. Under this system human
society secures the life of both unity and variety of
social types in its composition. It secures unity of
type within the social situation; it secures variety of

type by the existence of specific social interests. The problem arising out of this is: By what means does the social process secure that orderly composition of the differentiated variety of interests, tendencies and types, while still resting upon its organic basis of typal unity and while these interests, tendencies and types each and all seek to find development within the systematic order of the community? How, too, shall we coordinate the past and the present in the effort to realize the possibilities of the future benefits of association?

From the natural point of view this is evidently a problem of coordinating actual social aggregates under some as yet unrealized but potentially obtainable type of social order. Having secured unity of type and variety of type as the orderly basis for further developments, the problem still remains that of the assimilation of the whole toward a conceivably superior system of social *development*.

Considered as a historic process social assimilation presents a problem of social individuation by absorption of foreign or as yet non-typical elements into the social composition. It is the mingling of races, peoples and blood in a newer type. In the analysis of these mingling elements we must look for the historical forces of development.

These two aspects of the same societary process —the natural and the historical—find their coordination in the social system. The function of social system in assimilation is twofold: It serves to preserve the existing social types within it by limiting conflict, and simultaneously to guide differentiating tendencies toward this conceivably superior type of social attainment toward which the social population tends. Social tendencies not susceptible to orderly guidance are either eliminated or restrained; at any rate, tendencies hostile to harmonious social assimilation of types neutralize to that extent the efficiency of the social system as an instrument of individuation. But tendencies which respect the ends of the social system are such as combine in their composition the loyalty to the existing type—which the social situation as a whole requires—with the devotion to the social freedom of development which social interests stimulate us to enjoy. Such a tendency is an orderly succession of social interests, seeking *self-realization by transitional stages* of development from the socially actual in the direction of the socially ideal by the guidance of the theoretically more normal type of organization in the social system. Assimilation is from the actual, through the vivid appreciation of the typically attainable, toward the ideal.

How does the social process impress upon persons and interests, upon tendencies and types the logical reality of the typically attainable as a norm of reckoning in social realization?

If we may glance at the natural process of typal individuation, working apart from history, we see that this process is one in which types are elaborated by elimination, unmothered by a kindly control of a sympathetic social order. As Stephen puts it, " We learn from the theory of evolution that as the individual organism is composed of mutually

dependent parts, and that its existence involves the
maintenance of a certain equilibrium, so each organism supports itself as a part in a more general
equilibrium, and that its constitution depends at
every moment upon a system of adaptation to the
whole system of the world. And this may be expressed by saying that every animal represents the
solution of a problem as well as a set of data for a
new problem. . . . A new state of things slowly
substitutes itself for the old, but in such a way that
each species is continuous with the preceding, and
has been slowly remoulded by an incessant series
of unconscious experiments conducted under the
constant condition that failure means extirpation.
Hence, though we cannot say that either the end
or the conditions are absolutely constant, and
though any full statement would have to be unend-
ingly complex in consequence, the whole process
is describable as a slow elaboration of types." *

In its systematic aspect, regarded as a historical
process, the assimilating process stands for the organized systemization of social interests and aims
within which this elaboration of types of character
and constitution takes place. Race, nation, classes
and family embody these features of organic structure in the building of the social system. It is not
simply a way of regarding one another nor is it a
mechanical structure. We may say that it represents the more stable relations and the more enduring attributes of systematic association. The social

* Leslie Stephen, Science of Ethics, Ch. II., pp. 79–81.

system is composed of a variety of states of society which tend to lose sight of the unity of social interests. It utilizes these as organs of assimilation. Hence it is in the most generic sense *institutional* in its nature and method. *It is by institutions that the logical reality of the conceivably attainable is impressed on us.* Organized into the social system they constitute the most comprehensive selective agency which social man can utilize in the service of the natural relationships that arise among his kind, in the effort at preservation or in striving after a consciously higher type of individuation. In short, a society has aims which it entertains; it has desires which dominate its constitution—desires and aims that are, up to a certain level, substantially common to all of its members, and beyond this aims and desires as diverse as the development of its membership will permit. The social system defines the conditions upon which these aims, these enduring relations, the persistent attributes of social man, may find expression in associative development. *The Social System is the institutional organization of the functional tendencies of society for the assimilation of actual varieties toward a potentially superior type of character and constitution.* " The first necessity of societies," says Letourneau,* " is that they shall endure, and they can only do so on the condition of providing satisfaction for primordial needs, which are the condition of life itself, and which imperatively dominate and regulate great social institu-

* Letourneau, The Evolution of Marriage, p. 2

tions." Such as these are the institution of property, the institution of marriage, the institution of government, and the institution of worship. All of these emphasize the typically attainable. All of these organs of the social system arise from the existence of certain preponderant forces to which man in society is ever seeking to give a conceivably more satisfying expression. And any systematic form of social expression has its corresponding type of personality towards which portions of the population are normally assimilated.

We may put this same truth, descriptive of the social organization, in another way by saying, as many sociologists do, that the social structure is the counterpart of the social functions. The greater the development of the primordial social functions of a people—the sense of fellowship, the economic powers, the political wants and religious life—the more complex and comprehensive must be the social system to which survival and development have required man to give institutional durability. By this means society at first naturally and, with its developmental advance, purposefully makes systematic provision for the reciprocal coordination of these social activities which it is necessary to take into account in the maintenance of a structural order for the realization of constructive aims and ideals of which the community is becoming increasingly conscious.

The growth of the social consciousness is a fact of social history. How it grows in grasp of the social process may now be seen. The social consciousness is the seat of control in the institutional organization of the social system. Its instruments of control are institutions and ideas. In practically all social history we find a more or less complex system of institutions surviving as instruments of attainment. As fast as history becomes purposeful the social system is ruled by ideas. Institutions become the selective agency for the conservation of actual goods, and ideas the instruments of the realization of superior ones. To the social consciousness the social system is a system of habits of association comprising a set of relations, properties, purposes and practices which persist by virtue of some degree of common appreciation of the conception of membership therein; and this appreciation is of such a kind as to impel others to desire to enjoy or attain to, what some of its members have come to enjoy. All social unrest has its root in the social consciousness or diffused sense of a type of attainment from which men are debarred but to which all are potentially entitled within a given social order. Communities and peoples reason constantly on this scale. The apprehension of social ends of this character and the utilization of the social order for their realization is practically exemplified in the cultural policies of the modern states.

The study of the social aims of modern societies reveals the most extensive play of the principle of assimilation towards a potential type of personality in a superior type of social system as the remoter goal of their existence. Social emancipa-

tions of all kinds are an answer to this faith. Such
actual aims may have their root in tradition, in the
conviction of duty lurking in a social remnant, or
in a popular faith in the ' manifest destiny ' of a
people to attain to a superior type of life and manhood; or it may originate in the conscious necessity of assimilating heterogeneous types of social
character into a homogeneous type of civic efficiency, as in the earlier and later growths of the
conception of citizenship in the United States. The
purposeful use of the social order in striving after a
superior type of national character may also arise
from antipathy between rival national sentiments,
as in the case of France and Germany; or it may
arise by the imposition of one social order upon
another, whereby the superior type substitutes a
more efficient type of control as in the English conquest of India. In all such cases the social system
is consciously made use of as the instrument of
assimilation of the elements of population into a
more efficient social system.

But while the social system may be efficient and
though the work of development is done through
the use of institutions we must not forget that the
logical goal of the developmental process at this
stage is individuation of the potentially superior
type of personality and not the social organization.
Chief among the aims and ends of the social organization are those great departments of life, the *political,* whose object according to Aristotle is the supreme associative good, the *religious,* the *industrial*
and the *æsthetic or cultural* aims, all of which are, so

to speak, *institutionalized* for the express purpose of embodying their several elements in the individuation of a potentially superior type of personality. Individuation is the product of the assimilative union of two or more tendencies in the production of a superior type—of the traditional type embodying past experience with the differential which adaptive variations to new conditions develops. It is integration, on the grandest scale yet possible, of all organizable elements of national life and is one step nearer to the ideal of the community than the social conditions permitted when social interests controlled the community each in its own behalf.

The social system of institutions tends to become static, and to find the equilibrium for the social process by quiet repression. This is either due to the dearth of ideating energies in the assimilative purposes of society or the hardening of the institutional habit to the extent of suspending the developmental process. In either case, the conservation of the established relations among existing interests becomes the burden of social endeavor rather than the development of the community toward a higher type of living. This type of character choosing between settled interests and social visions while in the control of the social order through institutional agencies of individuation may well be called *the assimilative or institutional type of personality.* It alone determines whether the social process shall proceed by evolution or revolution, or whether development shall perish altogether by

ceasing to assimilate the resources of society toward the ideal as the goal of association.

To this end of individuation every institution
contributes an essential element. If not, it is a
burden to the assimilating process, to that extent.
That is a false view of the social process, as well as
of social life and policy, which encourages the es-
chewing of any of the elements of social worth that
round out the symmetry of life. The political, religious, industrial or æsthetic elements are to some
extent lacking in all classes. The ignoring or un-
dervaluing of any of these in the scientific analysis
or in the constructive synthesis of popular policy is
evidence of defective coordination of institutions in
any social system. The function of institutions in
the social process is to get the elements of social
efficiency individuated in the type of personality
potentially realizable in the given social conditions.
The progressively normal type of personality is the
central aim of institutional effort.

The problem with which we started will now be
readily solvable. The traditional and the adaptive
types of personality, representing two main tendencies in the societary process, become more and
more complemental and less and less contradictory
as the societary process becomes more fully aware
of the potential aims comprising the social policy.
Neither of these types alone could hold the social
system to its true aim. But both stand for two
complemental factors in social evolution. The traditional type emphasizes the conceptual content of
history in its deepest sense. The adaptive type in-

sists upon the social system's meeting the demands of nature upon man in society. Culture and vocation here contend for the control of the social policy. This is evident in every system of education, which seeks to individuate into character the elements of culture historical and natural. It is the business of institutions to bring into appropriable form the constructive elements required to produce the type of personality, which shall find its development in the social order of life that tends to be. Taking the social types that are present, the principle of typal assimilation requires that, with the elements of power which nature and history can give to personality, the selective services of social institutions must be consecrated to the realization of that individuation most directly in line with the ideal. By the institutions of society we bridge the gap between the actual and the ideal types.

While therefore the social system seems from its more objective aspects to be an arena of contending tendencies not meant to make for peace, in reality, however, it is far truer that the social order in which the social consciousness has come to itself finds its equilibrium not within itself but above itself in the sociological type of personal attainment toward which man is really bending his efforts in normal life. A remoter but superior social aim removes the contradiction of the traditional and the adaptive tendencies into the future. But development is thereby made possible once more.

The potentially normal type is the peculiar trust of the institutional agencies by which the aims of the societary process are worked over and wrought into unity for presentation to the social conscious-ness. These institutions interpret the remoter type to the social population; and the response from any tendency or social interest in the direction of superiority depends largely (1) on the social situa-tion with which one is customarily at home, (2) the social interests which engage his endeavors and de-termine the conditions of his development, and (3) the social institutions with which he appropriates the resources of nature and civilization. These three points more than any other determine a man's relation to the sociological type and thus decide the question of superiority and subordination as a prin-ciple of the social process in all ages and conditions of human association. The social process is the friend of that aristocracy which utilizes the social system for the purpose of the individuation of the whole social population in the direction of the ideal.

Institutional agencies, under the selective con-trol of the consciously directed social system, con-serve the types of personality which each organic tendency has integrated and differentiated. By the institutions of law and of worship, of labor and of recreation, the social process assimilates the particu-lar classes and conditions toward that potential type in which the social system tends to find its equilib-rium. The individuation of the potential with the actual type gives us the superior social type. After the superior type of personality has become the more or less conscious norm of social guidance to developmental tendencies, survival is after all a somewhat secondary consideration. Then men must *develop* in order to survive in society. Such development could not take place without the assimilating services of separate institutions each of which is actively engaged in appropriating its peculiar portion of the content of nature and history to the service of superiority of type toward which the movements of society tend. All institutional specialization which increases the capacity of assimilation is in the interest of a higher level of efficiency of personality. Every new institution, as every new profession which has normally arisen to perform an organic social function, that is, to utilize conditions for the end of higher creations, must enable each member to appropriate a larger net portion of the resources of society for his own development. The augmentation of life, says Spencer, is the general function which all professional institutions serve.* And what is true in a general sense of the professional institutions is true in a special sense of every other class of social institutions into which Spencer elaborates his analysis of the societary process. They all serve the purpose of a potentially superior attainment for personality in the social system which has devised and developed them into use. This 'division of social labor,' as Durkheim calls it; this differentiation or specialization of institutions into ceremonial, political, ecclesiastical, industrial and professional, as Spencer classifies them, and this 'grouping of inventions'

¿* Spencer, Principles of Sociology, Vol. III., p. 180.

into institutional agencies, as Tarde defines the societary process, all have a common meaning at
bottom in the appropriation and the reincarnation
of the social resources, personal, natural and historical, in the typically superior personality.

Possibly all aristocracies have their origin in this
very utilization of the social resources in the interest of the superior type of personality by control of
the institutional machinery of the social order. So
far aristocratic history is a normal process in social
evolution but it is prone to make the class-type the
ultimate or ideal type. Arnold classifies aristocracies as aristocracies of blood, aristocracies of conquest or of colonies, and a third form arising from
these two forms. Each of these may and at times actually does control the social order in its own rather
than in the interest of the type in which the social
process normally tends to find its equilibrium. But
this does not invalidate the principle of superiority
of type, as the law of social assimilation; for if aristocratic classes utilized their control to bring the
several tendencies in the social system to a higher
consciousness of the potentially normal type, the
whole social population would normally tend likewise to be individuated. Where aristocratic control has cut off the ascendant efforts of other social
interests and forced other tendencies than those of
blood, and of conquests, back upon themselves,
there we have the fatal perversion of the normal
purpose of the social system. The ascendant assimilation of all social types toward a superior
individuation is arrested by severing reciprocal

relations of rights and duties among classes. " The guilt of all aristocracies has consisted not so much in their acquisition of power as in their perseverance in retaining it; so that what was innocent or even reasonable at the beginning, has become in later times atrocious injustice, as if a parent in his dotage should claim the same authority over his son in the vigor of manhood, which formerly in the maturity of his own faculties he had exercised naturally and profitably over the infancy of his child." *

The principle of assimilation toward superiority in ancient society is nowhere accredited with comprehensive application to all classes; it is almost everywhere marked by the arrest of the development of the lower types from entering into sympathy with the higher types. Typal solidarity becomes impossible. In marked contrast with this is the modern policy of loyalty to the lowly, on the part of the rest of the community, a policy in which the claims to ascendency of type are recognized in theory and avowedly acknowledged in practice as the grounds on which the social system justifies its existence.† The principle of helpfulness finds its more comprehensive expression among those modern peoples in whose social purpose the cultural content of civilization is systematically devoted to the development of more effective types of social worth. National efficiency requires that the type

* Thos. Arnold, Miscellaneous Works : The Social Progress of States, p. 312.
† Fowle, The Poor Laws, Ch. I.

of personality be nourished with all available means
to realize the ends which the common consciousness
controlling the social effort considers itself entitled
to attain to.   Modern nationality is, however, apparently, with few exceptions, prone to make the
social system the test of social worth rather than the
potentially normal type of personality by which the
institutional mechanism of society can alone be ef-
fectively utilized.*   The ancient city-state inclined
to find the criterion of worth in the single superior
social type with little provision for ascendency from
below.   The civic consciousness was as yet too
slightly developed.   After attaining to superiority
for one class, that class allied itself with that pre-
dominant set of social interests or so controlled the
social institutions as to shut out the many whom
they believed to be hopelessly beyond the reach of
development into 'the good life,' † or incapable of
the enjoyment of it if it were given to them.

  This principle of the assimilation of the elements
of social valuation into a superior individuation, by
means of the institutions which belong to the social
organization, is in the progressive portion of mankind endangered from two peculiar sources by the
ascendency of which the process of assimilation
may be arrested.   The first danger lies in there being a disproportionate increase in the size of the
social claims of the class devoted to the operation
of the institutional mechanism by which the resources of nature and the experience of history are

* Ingram, History of Political Economy, Ch. VII.
† The Politics of Aristotle, Bk. VI., Chs. I., VII., XI.

organized for the evolution of man. The other
danger consists in the rise of an aristocracy of vul-
garity—a fatal check to the ascendent potentialities
of individuation. This latter tendency is conspicuously jealous of the superior type of personality in
the community and therefore as intolerant as it
dare be. But such intolerance may nevertheless
only indicate that the superior types, which are in a
measure the creation of the social forces and forms
of the social order, exist by virtue of the evasion
of responsibilities to the less developed types of
personality between which two levels of attainment
there is closer interdependence required if assimilation is to take place. Consequently all authoritative types have to be valued by the use to which the
controlling social authorities put the institutional
agencies—whether the assimilation of the people
toward the normal individuation of type is accomplished by leveling the life of the multitude upward
through the creation of a keener consciousness of
the attainable type of life, or by leveling those master spirits downward which live for and in the ideal.
The system of social institutions performs the selective functions of appropriating universal convictions developed in social experience and then dif-
fuses this content of the race-consciousness to the
organic interests constituting the social system.
Thus the requisites of adaptation to conditions of
survival on the part of any portion of a people are
balanced with the demands of unity of all classes in
a potentially superior individuation of character.
The fatal disease is the lack of faith in the capacity

of some portion or some types of the population to appropriate the resources of nature and history for the realization of the potential type. This is a characteristic blunder of government toward inferior types of people. The strategic blunder is the selection of actual types rather than the potential types as the organon of association. Institutions are tools of social realization. The social population is unequally gifted with consciousness of its possibilities. The social class that administers the social system for any other end than that of the development of every social condition into conscious apprehension of that reciprocity of interests whose equilibrium is in the potentially attainable type, is committing that blunder. The tactical blunder of social development is the substitution of reform of objective conditions and relations for a well-poised developmental policy and purpose. Typal development not reform is the only normal law of social evolution. Reform is painful reaction against abnormal adjustment of men to conditions; development is progressive action in the direction of the potentially attainable. The function of a system of a social institution is not so much the reformation of actual conditions as it is the formation of social tendencies in harmony with potentially normal types of personality. To keep the social population in the current of conquest of nature and of civilization is the end of the social system.

Where conflict and rivalry rule between social orders, the assimilation of the social tendencies into superior individuation is quickened by the awakening of fresh forces in the popular life. The presence of a hostile neighbor transforms a people from a looser to a more compact type of organization; the shepherd people becomes military in its constitution; but the occasion being past, the military becomes industrial if the energies awakened can be potentialized, and the industrial becomes cultural.* Such transformations elaborate the potential type of individuation corresponding to the resources of the social population and the possibilities of the natural situation. In each successive stage the sociological type into which the expanding genius of a people finds realization becomes a more and more complex and universal individuation. The type in ascendency at successive stages emphasizes, in its tendency to individuation, the qualities of subordination or integration; then of differentiation and, following upon these, the superiority of type which assimilation enables the social system to attain to. Assimilation requires the organization of numbers with regard to their possibilities.

Personality has, under the most general conditions prevailing within the social order, a threefold adjustment to make by finding three different sets of equilibria to which to adjust itself in the social organization. These equilibria are (1) subordination to the type naturally assumed as the basis of the further development, (2) adjustment to the changing conditions which confront all social interests, and (3) assimilation with that individuating

* Spencer, Principles of Sociology, Vol. I., § 263.

tendency which is strong enough to re-combine order and change into a type of commanding superiority over conditions. Thus presented the sociological principle of assimilation governing the social order may be formulated as follows:

Within the same social system that institutional type of social attainment normally tends to become ascendent whose quality is generic enough to evoke developmental effort on the part of the traditional types, attractive enough to be deemed worth realizing by the adaptive types, and remote enough to limit collateral conflicts among competing tendencies seeking a higher equilibrium. But it must not be so remote as to weaken the consciousness of sympathetic interdependence among the leading social types upon the conceivably superior type of individuation. In other words, the social organization must be so adjusted to the aims recognized as superior in the social process as to give the ascendency to that tendency which most completely co-ordinates all other systematic tendencies in itself in the work of assimilation. But it must exploit none in the interest of any aim except the assimilation of the social population as a whole, in all tolerable degrees of development, toward the potentially normal type in which all organic interests tend to find their equilibrium.

This view regards the social system as the framework of an experiment leading to the discovery and realization of every enjoyment normal to social man. It is social organization for the sake of man, not man for the sake of social organization, that needs to be urged in social practice. It is a means to an end, which end is a *progressive* type of personality. That end can be achieved only by the subordination of the social system to the sovereignty of the social mind.

CHAPTER VIII.

THE SOCIAL MIND: TYPAL SOLIDARITY.

THE fourth logical conception which must necessarily be taken for granted for the realization of the potentialities of the social process is the Social Mind.

The reciprocal relations of classes, conditions and functions which the social system contains are largely impressed upon the social interests from without. This is effected by the institutional pressure exercised by the dominant majority or in the competition of dominant interests, controlling the social order through one form of authority or another. Thus systematic assimilation is not always, and possibly not generally, a purely voluntary process of associative evolution. It is nearly always the result of several opposing tendencies coming to a compromise. But it is still a necessary condition of development, and, when development has been suspended, of survival. The consciousness, among the ruling tendencies, of active or latent qualities or conditions incompatible with the potential type which the social system normally tends to individuate is the characteristic antinomy of this aspect of social evolution.

How can this the last sociological antinomy be dissolved ? The logical conception of the social mind meets this requisite. The external or institutional control of the tendency to individuation inevitably reaches its limits and gives way to a subjective solidarity of voluntarily associated groups of activities. The community coheres finally by consciousness of typal solidarity. This sense of solidarity among men lodges with each tendency an appreciation of those organic functions of the social order for which that tendency is normally fitted, and of which it is of course the most capable master. The consciousness of the community's convictions—the social mind as the actively organizing condition of association—so reacts upon each as to consolidate all tendencies into a complex but a concordant equilibrium among themselves in progressive ascendency toward the potentially attainable ideal. Under such conditions conflict is ultimately unnecessary as a developmental factor. The increasing consciousness of the ideal becomes the developmental lodestone. The striving toward the ideal removes the contradiction.

The essential relation by which each typal tendency is governed in its conduct toward every other tendency, class or condition, is that of membership in a social solidarity. The conditions of the development of all such tendencies under the potentially normal type from the institutional to the ideal stage of development are alone found in the social mind governing these active groups by the law of typal solidarity.

To Professor Giddings is apparently due the credit of first using in a systematic analysis of social phenomena the term " the social mind," * as one of the products of association which in turn becomes a structural factor of formative efficiency in its re-action upon personality. As originally defined by him the social mind meant that " common con-sciousness of associated men " which gives a com-munity organic character—a consciousness of its own quality of unity—and is in its more generic sense true also of the race. Later it is more con-cretely defined as " a convenient name for a *concert* of the feeling, the thought, and the will of associ-ated individuals." † Intermediate between these two conceptions lies that which defines the social mind as neither so concrete nor so generic as the others, but regards it as a resultant of the union of " the mental and moral elements of society," giving us a derivative or secondary product of associative evolution.‡

The nearest approach to this seems to have been made on the part of those earlier writers who sought to define the popular feeling or national sentiments as the coherent quality of associative consciousness. This class of writers, among them Mill and Schäffle,§ are primarily analytic in their

* Outlines of Lectures on Sociology, §§ 50–53. Columbia College Lectures, 1891.

† Theory of Socialization, p. 25. New York, 1897.

‡ Giddings, Principles of Sociology, Bk. II., Ch. II., p. 132. New York, 1896.

§ Schäffle, Bau und Leben, I., Vierter Haupt.

results and define the synthesis of the collective consciousness in universal or generic terms, applicable as a rule only to the larger forms of associative organization.

The difficulty of defining the conceptual organon of the collective life in a single synthesis which is neither given in terms of the individual consciousness nor in universal terms applicable to all kinds of association, is by no means slight. Ward comprehends the results of his analysis in the synthetic term "the mind," comprising the feelings as the dynamic and the intellect or intuitional form as the directive or structural aspect of the socializing mind—the main factor in associative evolution.* Patten's analysis of the conceptual content is gathered under the categories of knowledge and belief as a kind of "collective conviction." † In another still more concrete form we have Nash's historical elaboration of the synthesis of the collective life of personalities under "the social conscience." ‡ "The real unity of each group consists in the common mental life which it gradually acquires."§ "All individuals in society are arranged about centers of authority, which are related to each other, in a series of progressive subordination."‖

It would seem that this attempt to find a satis-

---

* Psychic Factors, p. 3. Boston, 1893.

† Theory of Social Forces, Chs. III., V. Philadelphia, 1896.

‡ Nash, Genesis of the Social Conscience. New York, 1897.

§ Fairbank, Introduction to Sociology, p. 85. New York, 1896.

‖ Small and Vincent, Introduction to the Study of Society, p. 330. New York, 1894.

factory expression under which to connote the most comprehensive solidarity, which any association is conscious of as its own, is provided in " the social mind." Every integrated aggregate and only such an aggregate of persons, has a mind of its own. And the really essential thing in the definition of that mind is the fact of integration of which the community is aware.

The social mind is here used as that integration of social experience common to the differentiated typal cults and convictions which have become organized into the settled attitudes of the associative consciousness. The different degrees of subjective development in the classes of a people or a community exhibit a common set of feelings and beliefs which comprise the undebatable decisions or choices of its life. These are part of the accretions out of the past. Once integrated, they give structural form to the flow of human feelings and thus control the emotions in the interests of reflective action. That is, they are selective, positively and negatively, in respect to the type that is actually or potentially normal to this organization of the social judgment. The social mind is definable therefore as that structural organization of the conceptions of past experience and present dispositions of any typically integrated community by which the community is enabled to exercise conscious control over its organic typal tendencies and to select the systematic order and the potential ends of its development. *The social mind is the typal consciousness of any integrated community of persons.*

The social mind is a necessary form of organic unity and continuity of the process of selective development. Without postulating its reality we cannot logically account for the solidarity of otherwise conflicting interests nor for the continuous belief the community entertains in potential realizations of the universal ideal. The continuous unity of the social consciousness lies in the selective connection which unites the two poles of the developmental process—the actual social types to which conduct practically conforms for survival and the potential type to which the progressive community believes itself entitled to develop. The social mind combines present interests with possible opportunities.

There are therefore from the standpoint of personality as many aspects of the social mind as there are integrated communities having a typal consciousness of their own. In the simple social situation the typal consciousness insists upon conformity to type by which association was made largely a personal reproduction of outward acts or inward attitudes—a mechanical method of survival to which personality yields itself of necessity. Persons are here more like monads hugging with a sort of chemical polarity the single type which the community enunciates. Such often is membership in the family. In the complex social situation of differentiated tendencies each tendency is an integration of like ratios of personal efficiency around a single social interest. Each organic social tendency has therefore a social mind of its own as soon as it has an integrated typal consciousness of equilibrium within itself and with the larger community without. This is the case with the three or four great social classes and of any other derivative classes.* In the compound social situation, such as the modern state, in which these tendential integrations are coordinated reciprocally into a social system, we have a still more comprehensive typal consciousness in the popular conviction. More comprehensive is the concert of Christian nations. This is the most comprehensive form of the actual social mind. The potential social mind appears in the form of the consciousness of the social ideal—the perfect type of social attainment on the part of the members of the community.

Not only from the side of personal connection with the community in all its forms but also from the standpoint of the race-consciousness of typal control the social mind is strictly necessary in the effort to determine the ends of human development in society.

The quality of the social mind in any thoroughly integrated community of kinship is *categorical*, that is, it is typical in what it requires of personality in its relations with other personalities. It drives the Mormon beyond the fold of civilization, because he insists upon associative relations which the social mind has long since eliminated from its list of selective integrations, but it keeps the expelled community intact. This intolerance of the untypical is some-

* Wines, Charities Review, April, 1897, pp. 1-2.

thing just as real as the sanctions under which the traditionally typical survives and develops. Both are aspects of the selective function of the social mind in its effort to keep personality and the tendencies of the community in line with the type that normally tends to prevail. In this aspect of the social mind it admits of no argument. Within the social circle in which community of type is established the least that the social mind requires of any one is to conform to the type then and there existing. The most that it can require is that he develop with the community, at the rate at which its more progressive tendencies move toward the ideal type.

The attitude of the social mind is *critical* toward all that is differentiated from it in typal community, but tolerant to all that is typically common with it. We know how any proposal from outside of a community, a class or a country strikes the thoughts and feelings of a people. Diplomacy is the art of not arousing the social mind. Each aspect of the social mind weighs the proposal with regard to its effect upon its conditions of survival and development, that is, its actual and potential capacity to maintain or strengthen its typal equilibrium. It is so of every piece of legislation, every political platform and in fact of every proposed or possible change in circumstances which brings new factors into the problem of social selection of conditions of existence.

The method of the social mind is *constructive* through the assimilation of the differential elements of social value, which the several tendencies produce, with the social type to which the community is practically integrated. What is integrated and what is differentiated is thus selectively individuated by the social process under the control of the typal consciousness. But such individuation of the integral type common to the whole community with the differential elements of typal value can only be effected through the projection of a potential type in which both factors find their realization and by the capacity of the social mind to control the typal tendencies to that remoter end.

The control of the typal tendencies of all degrees of development with reference to some remoter end is effected in the case of more or less integrated communities of great differentiating fertility, by means of social ideals. Social ideals are the creative forces in the social mind and with the desires constitute the strongest motive forces in human evolution.

The ultimate motive of the social mind is *creative*, through the reactionary effect of social ideals upon the social process of development. It is this reflex effect of the ideal of the social consciousness upon the several tendencies of the community and upon the community as a whole that reveals the relation of typal solidarity. The social ideal represents to the social consciousness the maximum potentiality of the social process. No experience in human association is more real than the consciousness of the impossibility of attaining to a given achievement under given conditions of existence.

Under such conditions the performance of certain functions is out of the question. The principle of typal superiority laid emphasis on functional efficiency as a *sine qua non* of typal attainment. If that efficiency be confessedly deficient attainment is impossible. As fast as this condition of things becomes general the social order, if not permitted to react, begins to number the days of its own survival. This reaction from the actual situation normally takes the direction of the ideal. The social consciousness enlarges the scope of the experiment, discounts the actual, puts a premium valuation upon the possibly perfect and makes up its mind to try again under more favorable circumstances. The social ideal is the most perfect set of conditions which man dares to propose for himself. It is ideal because it contains the essential characteristics of what he can conceive of as belonging to the perfect character of its kind. " To this insight into possibilities." says a noted authority, " there loom up uses and adaptations, transformations and combinations in a long series stretching into the infinite behind each finite real thing. The bodily eyes see the real object, but cannot see the infinite trails; for they are invisible except to the inward eyes of the mind. What we call directive power on the part of man, his combining and organizing power, all rests on this power to see beyond the real things before the senses to the ideal possibilities invisible to the brute. The more clearly man sees these ideals. the more perfectly he can construct for himself another set of conditions than those in which he finds himself." *

The characteristic of the social ideal consists in the pre-eminent emphasis which it puts upon some single principle according to which all tendential values within the social order as a whole are to be unified in a supreme good. The community like children outgrows its clothes. The simple social situation of the family order of life rises in the course of a generation to a condition in which the subordination of personality to the parental authority there in force proves inadequate. The social interests, such as property and power, while once necessary to satisfy the varying tastes and impulses of men have to yield to the outside authority of a superior type of social life as soon as the domestic ideal is outgrown and property fails to satisfy personality. But the realization of that result exhibits the limitation under which ideal ends admitted of attainment in the social system. Assimilation prepares us for the vision of the ideal.

We now come to recognize that these social ends institutionalized as the valid ends of social tendencies, as the objective ends of social effort after an escape from subordination to superiority of type by alliance with social interests, are only temporarily or tentatively capable of guiding the societary process in the pathway of human realization. The tendency on the part of all institutional systems is sooner or later to regard these agencies as social

---

* W. T. Harris, Education, Vol. XII., No. 4, p. 204.

ends in themselves and to sacrifice the types of personality to this monopolization of social method. History itself is full of illustration of governmental institutions sacrificing the social type to an exaggerated sense of its own function in the social process; the same is true of ecclesiastical institutions as the guardians of the moral codes of the people; not less in any sense is the history of industrial institutions replete with the tragedy of cultural aspirations, and even cultural institutions have a record of forgetting " the rock from which they were hewn " by separating themselves from the sympathetic effort involved in the solution of the problems of the common people. It is natural that institutional agencies should magnify their social jurisdictions; and it is historically evident that they do so. But whenever the social consciousness arrives at the point of discovering the logical incompatibility between the normal type of attainment to which it conceives itself entitled on the one hand and the institutional system comprising the social order on the other, then the realization of social solidarity has to be removed from the realm of the institutional or methodical to the ideal as the only form of social authority under which integration, differentiation, and individuation are capable of finding scope for development. The social order is too objective, too rigid, too systematic to give to all conditions of people that fluidity of self-expression which enables them to find their fullest development. Under given conditions the social system is weighed and found wanting as the controlling

instrument of typal evolution. Thence the appeal
is to the ideal: the question arises, under what conceivable conditions could typal evolution find its
most perfect expression in the social process ? The
task is the construction and diffusion of the most
serviceable social ideal within the apprehension of
all social classes. In the long-established community of differentiated interests ideals are often new-
born traditions of better days.

The relation of typal solidarity is that of reciprocal consciousness, on the part of the several social
classes, of the social ideal as the potential goal of
their development. The solidarity sought for is
rarely secured without pressure but is never realized by pressure of organization alone. It is realized by mutuality of obligation to an ideal endeavor. Art helps to give current expression to
that appreciation of the social ideal which is necessary in the social mind before action in that direction consciously takes place. But the capacity to
respond in action is equally necessary to solidarity.
And this prevents the sociality of a social ideal from
overshadowing the individuality of man even in the
ideal type of personality. Hence the effect of ideals
upon the community is both integrating and individuating. A conclusion of Marshall on the integrating effects of art emphasizes the former process. " The art instinct deals with the attraction
of others to ourselves, unconsciously indeed, but
none the less certainly for all that; in fact, it deals
with the overthrow of isolation and with the growth
of sociality and sympathy. And, although I can-

not agree with Guyau that the production of sympathy towards life is the end of artistic endeavor, I think we may surely say that the function of art in the development of man is social consolidation." * But solidarity is equally an individuating process. Each of the three typal tendencies—the traditional, the adaptive and the institutional—has constructed ideals and sought to impose its own ideal on all other tendencies. " There is a force at work throughout creation," says Carpenter, referring to Lamark's theory of Exfoliation, " ever urging each type onward into new and newer forms. This force appears first in consciousness in the form of *desire.* Within each shape of life sleep wants without number, from the lowest and simplest to the most complex and ideal. As each new desire or ideal is evolved, it brings the creature into conflict with its surroundings, then, gaining its satisfaction, externalizes itself in the structure of the creature, and leaves the way open for the birth of a new ideal." †

The chief service of the social mind in furnishing creative ideals lies therefore in the fact that it furnishes us with tentative standards by which to discover and remove the inharmonious elements of contradiction from among the typal tendencies of the social process. The social population susceptible to its impress, conscious of its reality and responsive to its beckonings raises harmony of typal

* A. R. Marshall, Aesthetic Principles, pp. 81–2, including note p. 82.
† Edward Carpenter, Civilization, pp. 52–53.

tendencies to the dignity of a first principle in social evolution. Calvin's struggle in Geneva, and Cromwell's struggle with the Cavalier conception of social system were efforts to reduce to harmony all social tendencies by the imposition of a particular social ideal. But the individuation of this superior type toward which the societary process presumably tends must regulate its rate and method of procedure by the absence or presence of incongruous qualities in the community with respect to the social ideal. One social tendency in the same social order must not seek ideal realizations too remote for the appreciation of other tendencies. The harmonization of these tendencies in the same commanding effort must rest on the social sense of the nobility and the beauty of freely belonging to and having a responsible part in the movement towards the ideal. This is the essence of solidarity.

In the foregoing analysis we have followed two coordinate lines of inquiry relative to the phenomena of human association.

First, we have considered personality in objective association with his kind. This continuous procedure we have designated the social process and have represented it as comprising four necessary conditions within which social types appear to us to have their being. These conditions are the *social situation* within which integrity of type is secured, the *social interests* within which the differentiated variety of types arises, the *social system* by which the too complex variety of typal tendencies is brought into coordination, and finally the *social mind* within which the social motives find progressive harmonization in the social ideals for the otherwise discordant tendencies of the social organization.

Secondly, we have considered personal association as presenting to us a sociological process—a process in terms of what man in association normally tends to become on the basis of the actual. These theoretical tendencies we have sought to formulate in such a way as to give expression to the universal tendencies in human association. Hence we designate them the Typal Principles. The four typal principles are *typal integration, typal differentiation, typal assimilation* and *typal solidarity.*

Each of these four principles expresses a universal relation or causal connection between personality and the social process and between any integrated group or tendency and the community as a whole. These principles are therefore the causal relations which sociology, like every other body of knowledge, finds it necessary to formulate.

For example, the principle of typal integration gives us the causal principle controlling the social process within the simple social situation (family) where personality subordinates itself or is subordinated to the type that tends to prevail, *because* such subordination is the natural mode of survival.

The principle of typal differentiation appears when the social situation is broken up by differentiated social interests (classes), requiring that the specific types be substituted for the single type as the requisite of survival by conformity to changed conditions. This adjustment of personality to the social process is a self-evident requisite.

The principle of typal assimilation defines the relation between the social tendencies, in which personality is at equilibrium, when that social order has become conscious of the potential type of personality whose realization its institutional agencies tend to accomplish.

The principle of solidarity gives us the causal connection between the self-conscious classes, interests or tendencies in social organization and the social ideal (humanity, the kingdom of God, Utopias). The common experience of every type which has become conscious of its essential relations and rank in the social order suggests that the social order is not sufficiently swayed by any authority which can unify its several tendential aims. Social action becomes wasteful, inharmonious, incapable of evoking the social forces to its support.* For the sake of social efficiency these neutralizing contradictions must be removed. A self-conscious community finds itself projecting a social existence ' wherein dwelleth righteousness.' The conception of a sociological state—a theoretically normal state —with conditions in which personality may find the fullest possible expression of physical, ethical, economic and æsthetic potentialities, not only furnishes the social mind with a final canon of constructive criticism of the actual but evokes those impellant emotions which bring out the elements of leader-

* Ward, Psychic Factors of Civilization, Ch. XVI.

ship and loyalty in the social population. So far as this grasp of the ideal potentialities is diffused through the community it tends to unify all types upon the goal of attainment subjectively regarded as realizable. The intensity of interest in the end minimizes the differences of objective rank and condition with which social order was hampered and which the impulsion aroused by the harmonizing ideal enables the typal tendencies to surmount. The focusing of the social feelings upon the ideal tends to make all alike—to minimize class differences before a superior or rather a supreme end. This alikeness consists in being potentially integrated under the same transcendent ideal type of personal ascendency over conditions.* If only one member of the community succeeds in doing what others may desire but know not how to achieve, that one becomes the new center of social integration with the ideal as thus incipiently realized. The *first* realized ideal is solidarity with leadership (prowess); this is the physical element of the social ideal—the might which is the basis of right to rule among one's fellows. The *next* aspect of the social ideal to emerge in the societary process is the solidarity of personality with invisible powers—the reverence that results in the obligation of religion and morality, resulting too in the expansion of the area of integration so as to admit of variety in unity toward the ideal. The *third* ideal element is the utilitarian, which utilizes the realized ideals of so-

---

* Nash, Genesis of the Social Conscience, p. 3.

cial discipline and duty to conquer present natural
and social conditions in the interest of the future
type of personality; as when society seeks to bend
conditions to meet the requirements of the national
ideal. Here the ideal social order tends to become
the instrument of the realization of the perfect type
of personality. *Finally*, the fourth element of the
ideal social order is that of the solidarity of personality with the race in whose welfare lies the ultimate
influence controlling his conduct. Here the ideal
relationships bring all social beings into a single
solidarity in which each personality is at perfect
equilibrium potentially with the entire human
kind.* This is the goal of the societary process;
but the realization of the cosmopolitan ideal to any
extent in any social state or situation by any part
of mankind must either serve as the point of diffusion for a wider basis of typal integration under the
control of the ideal unto which other portions of
mankind not yet so fully developed would find
themselves drawn; or, in default of such diffusive
energy in the ideal, there must result that which,
in the case of the city-state of the Greeks, Aristotle
called *stasis*—that deadly exclusion of other social
interests from fellowship with the ideal by those
into whose control the social order had fallen and
in whose interest it was primarily engineered. Thus
the developmental process goes on beginning with
the organic, as yet undifferentiated and unassimi-
lated, and through these stages ending with the

* Cf. Giddings, Theory of Socialization, LII., and LXIII.

ideal, only to make the actualized ideal the integrating center and the potential basis for a new social
situation, thence differentiating into new interests
and assimilating into a new social order the tendencies that harmonize in the solidarity of a still remoter ideal. And the guiding genius of this evolution is the selective impulse of social being.

The necessary conditions and the universal relations, by which the developmental process of selec-

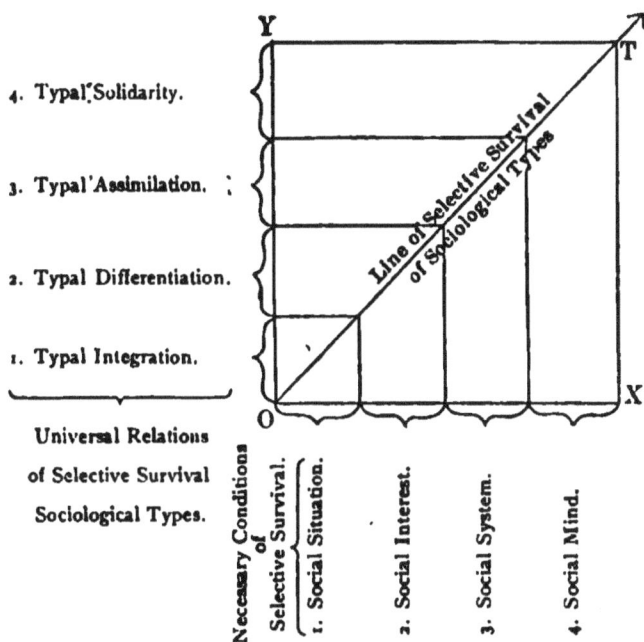

4. Typal Solidarity.

3. Typal Assimilation.

2. Typal Differentiation.

1. Typal Integration.

Universal Relations
of Selective Survival
Sociological Types.

Necessary Conditions of Selective Survival.

1. Social Situation.

2. Social Interest.

3. Social System.

4. Social Mind.

Line of Selective Survival of Sociological Types

FIG. 3.

tive survival can be conceived of and the life of
human association brought into theoretical consistency, have now been systematically outlined by the
analysis of the societary process.

The logical conceptions requisite for this presentation of the twofold aspects of this process—the
concrete aspect of natural association and the theoretical aspect of social organization—are logically grouped in Fig. 3.

BOOK III.

THE SOCIOLOGICAL AXIOMS.

CHAPTER IX.

TYPICALITY: SOCIALITY AND SYMBOLISM.

In the analysis of the societary process regarded from the standpoint of natural association we have shown on what necessary *conditions* and according to what universal principles human beings become social and develop typical qualities, how social types survive and are developed by functional tendencies of society, according to the law of selective survival of sociological types.

We now wish to show from the standpoint of social organization by what synthetic judgments personality, the social tendencies, and the community are guided in the selection of the *means* of social realization. These synthetic judgments are known as the Sociological Axioms. By them we see how it is and by what stages it is that the developmental process passes from the organic types to the ideal types. We see what part of the actual content of the community's resources is to be utilized. We have defined for us the *qualities*, the *conditions*, the *relations*, and the *possibilities* with which social evolution has to reckon. Society is organized

163

in accordance with a certain series of judgments which are the axioms of its development.

The sociological axioms are typicality, normality, institutionality and ideality. This is the normal and logically necessary order of their evolution and their validity. Each axiom has its subjective and its objective aspect by which the type in relation therewith adjusts itself to these two realms of reality.

The point of departure having been defined, from which we may proceed to take account of the sociological axioms, it is necessary to note that these axioms, while they are to serve as logical interconnections between the objective and the subjective aspects of the social process, are therefore the successive points of view to be followed in theoretical interpretation of social phenomena.

The first quality required for social survival is the logical quality of typicality, the subjective aspect of which is sociality and the objective aspect symbolism. To belong to no type is to be a member of no associative unit and therefore to lack the requisite of survival or of development. To be untypical is to be out of equilibrium with the natural forces and the spiritual motives which find their equilibrium in social types.

Nordau defines degeneration as " a morbid deviation from an original type," including in his classification, as the most notable examples, criminals, prostitutes, anarchists, lunatics. This negative definition implies the essential truth in our analysis of the social process, namely, that the normally typical is the essentially social, and that the abnormal types of personality are essentially wanting in the universally valid quality of sociality. Of course criminals cooperate, prostitutes are social, anarchists contrive together, lunatics are alike in setting at naught the assumed laws of reason; but nevertheless, an examination of any of these classes reveals the basis of our judgment respecting these abnormal types, namely, that the normally social or the typical quality is the test of fitness to survive as free members of society. Persons of kindred qualities congregate according to the degree of development of these integrating qualities.

Typicality is that social quality or that criterion of the organizing process which is least subject to change in the midst of changing conditions and relations. Changes in the social nature are changes of growth, changes of structure and changes of function. Childhood is full of changes of growth. The stamp which nature puts upon the individual organism insures that each portion of the animal world shall bring forth only of its own kind. Only the type that is reproduced after its own kind has anything like fair chances of survival. Sexual selection secures this result by the most persistent tyranny of the sexual impulses. But the direction of survival lies in the line of imitation of the typical, however the sense of the typical may impress itself upon the growing child. The waking consciousness of the child regards, we are told, the mother as part of itself. Certainly the psychic states of the mother are impressed upon the child in its pre-natal existence. . Growth differentiates the child into a separate personality; but wherever we begin to recognize its existence and wherever we may find its growth to end, the essential element that has made it social throughout its whole career consists primarily in its being typical. The changes of childhood serve only to reveal the more fully this consciousness of kinship with its own type of being.

Typicality as a sociological criterion involves more than a relation with a permanent object of a like kind. " A living being," says Clifford, " must always contain within itself the history not merely of its own existence but of all its ancestors." This guarantees unity of the physical or organic type. No amount of growth will outgrow the typical. But there is a step, a change in relationship between persons of like kinds which develops personality by separating it from other individuals and giving it the highest degree of typicality peculiar to organic descent. That change separates typicality into sociality and symbolism, and it consists in the " differentiation from surrounding minds which is the growth of individuality; and closer correspondence with them, wider sympathies, more perfect understanding of others. These, you will instantly admit," says Clifford, " are precisely the twin characteristics of a man of genius. He is clearly distinct from the people that surround him, that is how you recognize him; but then this very distinction must be such as to bind him still closer to them, extend and intensify his sympathies, make him want their wants, rejoice over their joys, be cast down by their sorrows." * As iron sharpeneth iron, so soul sharpeneth soul; and the sharper the wit of man becomes the more human, the more humane, the more social in spirit he is normally obliged to become. All the changes of growth, of structure and of function to which personality in society is subject only render him the more susceptible to the integrating unity with the type within the zone of whose influence he lives.

Typicality has thus these two normal aspects—sociality and symbolism. Nature's mode of perpetuating type is by the selective survival of the organic capacities required in association. But man bears within him those qualities in potential state with the advent into this life which must of necessity find modes of expression. These modes are what we call symbolism. If we were to write the one fundamental axiom over the portals of this human life of ours, for one just brought into it, it would be: Live the typical life of the community that harbors you by balancing membership and individuality. This sense of communion with one's kind, the sense of membership, is one of the first discoveries personality makes. To this fact of kindred coexistence we give the name of sociality. But the expression of the psychical results of this associative situation, that is, of this sense of member-ship, in such form as to make one's kind aware of this sense, requires all varieties of symbolic forms.

* W. K. Clifford, Lectures and Essays, Vol. I., p. 100. London, 1879.

The totem, the ornamental garb, the official insig-
nia, the religious symbols are of this kind. Sociality plus symbolism makes social organization realizable. No one is typically social in fact until his
sense of membership has developed and then found
appropriate forms of expression. Written or
spoken language is only one form of such utter-
ance. That form of expression may take any form
from the clinging embrace of the child and mother
to the systems of thought that science and religion
utilize to bring personality into touch through society with the true and the infinite with which normal society is livingly linked.

These two aspects of typicality must be kept distinct. Subjectively viewed, typicality is habitual
performance of the social functions of the type prevalent in the social situation. It is the subjective
standard which we see followed in the acts and
modes of life exhibited in the imitative movement
of offspring in association with their parents; of the
young in the imitation of their elders; of the members of a group in conformity to an efficient type
already realized. It is even more remotely apparent in those instinctive actions and reactions which
lie back of the strictly imitative expressions of self-
activity. Nature's first object-lesson in law is survival by instinctive and imitative conformity to
type. We may call this organic sociality, because
this relationship of survival by organic accordance
with type is the simplest and the most general requisite of the coexistence of animal organisms from
protozoon life up through the animal world ending

with the highest order of social beings in man. Our
acts, thoughts and feelings must be organized on
that basis. It is the vital principle of social existence.
In this aspect it is the fundamental physiological
relationship of sentient being having any regard
for coexistent relations with its kind. To be subjectively typical includes not only the consciousness of sentient beings of a like type requiring of it
certain functional activities, but also the capacity
of distinguishing a type like its own from one unlike its own whose functional activities it systematically avoids. The typical Jew could have no dealings with the typical Samaritan. In this sense typicality means that every creature shall live out the
creed of its own kind, by being socially susceptible
to the requirements of its type.

How far this susceptibility which we call sociality
goes back of the human life, the natural historian
of the social sense must be left to trace. Cuvier has
among his writings an interesting chapter on the
subject. Espinas and others have more fully described the extent of our knowledge of the sub-human sociality. Later still is Topinard's study of
organic man as a member of society.* We know
that man begins his life with the social sense as an
organic datum. For the sociologist's purpose it is
enough to point out that typicality, in these two
aspects of sociality and symbolism, is fundamental
as the criterion of social existence on the plane of
humanity. If proof were desired of man's natural

---

* The Monist, 1897.

sociality, and the necessity of its taking the form
of symbolism for expression as a means of development, we might quote some of this accumulating
evidence of the natural history of sympathy.   Of
this Professor Shaler says, " In the progress of social development we can, in a general way at least,
trace the stages of development from the more pri-
mal conditions of the altruistic motives, to the more
developed form in which they now find a place in
the mind of the more cultivated men."   And again,
" These   three   forms   of   the   altruistic   motive,
namely, the sympathy with the fellow-man, the
sympathy with nature, and the sympathy with the
infinite, have very different degrees of intensity,
and are otherwise divisible from each other, in
many ways.   Sympathy with the fellow-man is the
most intense of the three.   It is the simplest form of
the motive; it may exist with less admixture of
related motives than the other divisions of altruistic impulses.   It is the most universal among men,
and the most frequently active in any mind." * The
logic of sympathy is part of the mechanism of social
order.

  · It is this experiential content welling up in personality for expression in appreciable form that
makes symbolism an inevitable product of social
man within the pale of typicality.   The social being
is sympathetic in a normal state of fellowship, and
to be sympathetic is to be endowed with energies
needing direction.   The commonest forms of ex-

* The Interpretation of Nature, Ch. II.

pression give such direction as is necessary for living with one another in society. Hence symbolism is fundamentally linguistic. The community must, like every other embodiment of experience known to us, have its forms of speech, or what Tarde calls its ‘grammar.’ Into these forms nature and civilization pour their resources as fast as man in society makes it possible for his fellows to appropriate them. The typical quality may find expression in the building of a cathedral or temple, in the creation of an epic or in the ravages of conquest.

The social process therefore develops in personality a sense of membership with those that are typical—a consciousness of belonging to a recognized class, group or cult in which one has a substantial stake. The problem of giving understandable expression to these real and implied relationships is, however, a problem of the organization of social life itself. The study of social groups shows us the natural conditions of living together; social organization shows us the working conceptions. The symbolizing process is the process of making the concepts of social value available for communion with those with whom one has come into conscious appreciation of kinship. The two processes are distinct aspects of the societary process, in theory as well as in fact. When Sir Henry Sumner Maine asserts the fact that kinship is the basis of ancient society he takes emphatic account of the social process when the people are in close affinity with nature; that is, of a society whose sociality still retains the primitive limitations of expression. Social life hugged the shores of nature throughout antiquity. But wherever the greater facility of symbolic expression opened the way for the conceptual expression of social feeling there the bond of human association tends to become not so much that of organic kinship but rather one of subjective *communion* with one's kind by means of symbolism such as would satisfy the cravings of consciousness for expression. That satisfaction comes whenever sociality and symbolism find coordinate expression in the same social tendency. This requires of social man that he find his equilibrium of type by objective unity with nature as well as by subjective unity with civilization. Then must membership in society be organically safe and ideally free. Sociality and symbolism are the warp and woof of the societary process into whose texture is woven the typical pattern normal to the life of the times. The forces of sociality and the forms of symbolic expression weave all varieties of social experience into this unifying fabric. The triumphs and the disappointments, the sorrows and the joys, the exaltations and the humiliations of spirit of a people or any considerable portion thereof, become an inextricable part of the tone and temper of the type. The key to the social history or career of every people and every personality therein has to be found in terms of the type that normally tends to prevail.

It becomes evident from the foregoing analysis that the sociological axiom of typicality serves a twofold purpose in social evolution. These are:

First, that of coordinating the *community* to the structural conditions and the functional attainments requisite for normal conformity to type in the social process. Typicality gives in its functional quality of sociality and its structural forms of self-expression in symbolism, the two needed factors for the selective survival of the normal type of personality. In the school-life of the child, with a single social type in ascendant control, this process is most active. Fellowship and forms of expression for one's activity are basal axioms in development.

Secondly, the sociological axiom serves as a norm of gradation of members *within* the community. Development begins with gradation of attainment. Grades of typal attainment depend on the ratio of social to symbolic or individual efficiency in expression of natural capacity. One of high sociality and low symbolizing efficiency or vice versa tends to take a quite different rank in the community from that taken by a person in whom the two elements of efficiency are at equilibrium. But the question as to which of the three were the more valuable type depends on the question of what the requisites of survival are in the community taken as a whole, at a given time and place.

This twofold character of the sociological axiom as a means (1) of survival for the community and (2) for the development of personalities taken one by one in that community, may be illustrated by Fig. 4.

Let *YOX* represent the area of a social situation the objective basis of which is *OX* and the subjective aspect of which is OY. Then the normal line of typal development or survival will be Ot—Typicality, the two respective factors of which are YO, Sociality, and Yt (OX), Symbolism. From this it appears that the development of the type goes forward in the community as fast as sociality and symbolism can find their equilibrium in the integration of personality, t. This assumes that the subjective and the objective requisites of typal evolu-

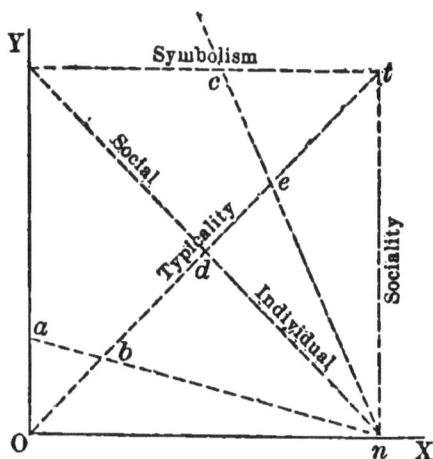

FIG. 4.

tion are equal. If their relation is not that of a unitary ratio then Ot takes a different direction to bring the community to equilibrium with its conditions. But there is a limit, to that change in typal direction, in the typal constitution of personality.

For each personality, if Ot be the line of typal survival normal to the community, the tendency is to *balance* its social and its individual units of personal efficiency on Ot. A slave introduced with low sociality *(aO)* and high efficiency of conform-

ity to objective conditions *(On)* would find his
typal equilibrium at *b*; a perfectly balanced member socially and individually, of an old family say,
not yet socially abnormal at *d*; and a member of
extraordinary potentialities *(ce)* plus the maximum
of symbolizing efficiency would tend to find his
equilibrium, by the aid of the typal axiom, at *c*, that
is, would be a leader of the typal tendency. The
conclusions may further be drawn as follows: (1)
That the social type normal to the community finds
its typal equilibrium by adjusting itself to the subjective forces and the objective conditions of the
social situation in the direction of maximum potential, *t.*

(2) That the members of the community, taken
one by one, find their respective equilibria by adjusting themselves to the line of typal survival of
the community on the basis of the ratio of the social to the individual units of personal efficiency
each member may have, *ab* to *bn.*

(3) That the valuation which the community
puts upon any member or class of members is determined by the position of personality on the scale
of typicality normal to the community *(bde).*

All this is true on the assumption of homogeneity of type in the same social situation; but, when
those conditions or forces which contribute to diversity of type once set in, then we have to show by
what sociological axiom the social process succeeds in diversifying the membership of the group,
typicality having been incarnated in the community member by member.

CHAPTER X.

THE second sociological axiom by which social development proceeds and under which we may logically group. the phenomena of social life is normality. Normality has two aspects—subjective and objective. The subjective aspect of normality is conventionality—a measurable element that resides in the community and which the social sense regards as its own common possession or criterion, to which one who is of any value to the community is expected to conform as a rule. It is a sort of subjective sovereignty within limits. These limits the objective claims of property put to it. Property* and conventionality† balance the forces of the community under normal conditions.

This second sociological criterion serves to *normalize* the social process when changes in conditions or causes require readaptation to type. Typicality serves its essential purpose by providing for the *vital* requisites of social existence. It puts personality in touch with the center of gravity of the

---

* Maine, Ancient Law, Ch. VIII. New York, 1888.

† Maine, Early History of Institutions, Ch. I. New York, 1888.

social group. But how is the growing content of personality in which individuality and sociality have to balance themselves with the conditions of existence, to find the *limits* of its scope of action ? How does social man define to his fellow-members the limits of the social experiment of the community of which typicality is the center of divergent degrees of typal efficiency ?

Normality defines these constitutional areas by showing the line of activity upon which personality may have a free field of adaptation. And just as the convergent efforts in association are defined in typicality, so too the lines that mark off the divergent movements of groups seeking equilibrium with social interests, are the paths of the normalizing tendencies, so to speak. These divergent lines are the radii of the community's activities, dividing the field on the basis of the grouping of differential features in the nature of personality and in the needs of the community. A fundamental differential entering into the development of the normalities of the social process is that of sex.* No society is normal which does not rightly relate its members to this fact. The typical in society is differentiated into male and female, each with its *proprium.* Normality is the basis and the test of morality so far as morality finds its basis in nature. The social process centers its movements upon the line of sexual morality. On the basis of this adjustment to nature it seeks to ascend. And here, in the determination

* Morgan, Ancient Society, Part II , Ch. I.

of the criterion of normality, just as in the case of
typicality, the sociological equilibrium of personality is to be found in equal loyalty to nature and
civilization.

From the side of nature sexual selection is the
patron principle of the social normalities. From
the side of civilization the selective authority tends
to be established under the control of the superior
rather than of the subordinate factors in human
development; what was in nature primarily sensual
becomes in civilization sensuous, that is, lit up with
the sense of beauty. The normalities that are beau-
tiful, the attractive manners and methods of association, are the ones that tend to prevail. They are
in keeping with the theoretically normal type. *The
normalities are the preferable practices among typical
people.*

The transition from typicality to normality is
readily definable. The child, passing from the parent's presence to the street for play with its fellows,
illustrates it. Under typicality symbolism serves
the necessary and universal purpose of personal expression by sign or symbol of language, image or
individual motion. Here parental imitation guides.
But soon the child seeks to be more than expressive or receptive and strives to become self-assertive
in influencing others to act with reference to him
and his desires. Then the creation of such codes
of social normalities as would preserve the type not
only in any condition but in a conceivably superior
condition of enjoyment than if left to the riotous
regulation of impulse, becomes the axiom of devel-

opment toward the potentially superior type. Social selection enters upon the second axiomatic
stage of development as soon as the social sense
singles out certain movements which it recognizes
as normally necessary for typal survival and development. To be socially normal requires conventionality; to be socially efficient, that is, to develop
with the community requires property in the sense
of personal appropriation. Conventionality and
property give man his social opportunity. Without
them in a right ratio he dies socially.

The *survival* of personality is *normally* secured
by the existence of those conventional practices
peculiar to the community. The common conduct
of the community we call conventionality. Conventionality is the first tax society lays upon personality. We chafe at these semi-mechanical vir-
tues now and then, when we feel that the individuality in us has to be kept in leading-strings by the
regard for the conventional and customary; it is
this state of things that makes men abnormally
social or abnormally conventional at times in the
social movement; yet the conventional is the only
way that the social world knows of setting limits
to associative action in such a way as to secure the
continuity of the typical. The absence of the conventional in a member of the community immediately disarranges our logic of social valuation; because conventionality gives a certain set to our associative behavior which we take for granted as one
of the postulates of our existence. Conventionality
secures survival therefore by settling as many as

possible, for the time being, of the questions that
arise in the intercourse of members of the community. The social habit being set by the selection
of those practices helpful to survival of type and
by the rejection of those hurtful to typal survival,
the body of tradition grows by personal contribution to the customary code of social intercourse.
This may go on to the point at which every incre-
ment of personal energy is socialized, until growth
has been swallowed up in convention and individualization has nothing left to which it would give expression in other than conventional modes. Like
the savage in his relation with the European, he
would do anything, even steal and cheat, to be
conventional.

Over against this static aspect of normalization,
which marks the social process, stands the other
aspect which might be properly called dynamic.
Conventionality compels personality to accept conditions as they are found; property-relations put
personality in the position to create changes within
or on the basis of the conventional limitations, by
setting more largely in motion primordial social
tendencies which gradually undermine or modify
the conventional cult. The history of property and
of custom, or conventional regulation of society,
shows that these two aspects of normality have
grown up reciprocally. Much conventionality, little property; less conventionality, more property;
little convention, much property is the record of
the evolution of the normalizing effort of human
communities. Here we have the real reason for

private property in social evolution. This represents three historic stages in the social process after
that of *conflict* in which property was the community's possession; the stage of *status* in which conventionality preponderated and property was a class
possession; the stage of *contract* in which property
has become 'sacred' and conventionality is barely
coequal with property interests of individuals; and
thirdly, the stage of '*conscience*' in which conventionality is subordinated to a sense of responsibility
or personal stewardship of property in the interest
of the type that is normally realizable. This puts
the control of property not on the basis of status,
nor of contractual right but on the ground of personal efficiency in the socially acceptable uses of
properties. And the acceptable uses are, in the sociological sense, those uses which secure the survival and the development of the normal types of

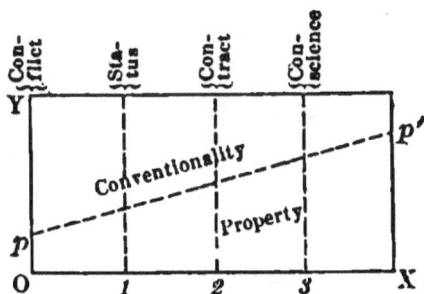

FIG. 5.

personality. From this principle we must deduce
the form of the social organization. This tendency
may be represented by the parallelogram, in which
property is taken to mean any quality, action, con-

dition or relation which the individual member of
society may appropriate. It includes all kinds of
goods capable of appropriation—utilities in which
individual man has sanctioned proprietorship. Individual proprietorship is the complement of social
conventionality, normally decreasing as the conventional factor in the social process increases and
increasing as the conventional factor decreases.

The *development* of personality in society and
thus of society in appropriative power is normally
secured by the growth of this very factor of property as an individual quality in social composition.
Professor Nash sets forth this truth when he ana-
lyzes the criteria of the social process of Christian
history by showing how the individualized qualities
of personality released from conventional bonds affected ancient society. He says: " The idea of personality dawns on the Western mind. There's a
good in each man, and for each man better than his
best, the good of self-knowledge and self-master-
hood. Personality means individuality creating
itself. This involves Freedom. Fate is that which
cannot be assimilated. To the reformer Fate is
the dead matter of society which he cannot hope to
vitalize. But to the Christian thought of Personality, that is, individuality creating itself through
covenant with God, there is no Fate save lack of
time." *

Why should not conventionality control the social process with its belief in the fatal maxim that
whatever is is right ? Simply because convention-

* Nash, Genesis of the Social Conscience, p. 4.

ality can only absorb and conserve the energies of personality in association. It can acquire but not create after the image of the sociological type—the logically superior reality which only persons free to project and to perform can get society to realize for its members. This again has been admirably put by the late Professor Clifford in stating the case against the conventional control of propriety over personality. The first condition of mental development, he declares, is that the attitude of the mind should be creative rather than acquisitive; for, as it has been well said, intellectual food should go to form mental muscle and not mental fat. The negative condition is plasticity; the avoidance of all such crystallization as is immediately suggested by the environment. A mind that would grow must let no ideas become permanent except such as lead to action. Towards all others it must maintain an attitude of absolute receptivity; admitting all, being modified by all, but permanently biased by none. To become crystallized, fixed in opinion and mode of thought, is to lose the great characteristic of life, by which it is distinguished from inanimate nature; the power of adapting itself to circumstances.

" This is true even more of the race. There are nations in the East so enslaved by custom that they seem to have lost all power of change except the capability of being destroyed. Propriety, in fact, is the crystallization of a race. And if we consider that a race, in proportion as it is plastic and capable of change, may be regarded as young and vigorous, while a race which is fixed, persistent in form, unable to change, is as surely effete, worn out, in peril of extinction; we shall see, I think, the immense importance to a nation of checking the growth of conventionalities. It is quite possible for conventional rules of action and conventional habits of thought to get such power that progress is impossible and the nation only fit to be improved away. In the face of such a danger *it is not right to be proper."* *

The problem then arises, as to the equilibrium between the conventional and the plastic, constructive forces in development. The solution lies in discovering the point at which the theoretically normal type, which any stage of the social process is capable of realizing, is being sacrificed or forestalled by the preponderance of the conventional proprieties over the individual impulse to creative activity. A community may readily be detected in the act of cramping the tendencies to change by throttling individual initiative. Likewise, it may be guilty of sacrificing the type to which it is normally destined by giving undue range to the sway of individual qualities. The truth lies in the balancing of these two elements of normality—the conventional or conservative and the creative or individual propria—in the direction of the potentially normal type. When the conventional suspends the development of the adaptive elements the existing types become impoverished and the capacity to

* W. K. Clifford, Lectures and Addresses: Conditions of Mental Development, pp. 115–6.

utilize for society what the individual has or may acquire is impaired. The socius subordinates the individual beyond recovery and reaction. The rise of a new kind of property, such as the rise of commercial wealth in the middle ages; or such as the growth of a new sense of personal capacity like the transition from slavery to serfdom or freedom brings into play—these exemplify the influence of the proprietary leaven of individual resources by which alone the conventional tendencies are counteracted. But conventionality must always to some degree serve as the point of departure of individual effort to appropriate the jural, the ethical, the economic or the æsthetic potentialities. The ruling ' style ' is more than a convenient admonisher. It requires courage to set it up or put it down before its time. As a matter of fact typal evolution comes normally by some one individual or group of interests discovering the direction in which these desirable elements of social advantage lie, and then, after their appropriation is made practicable, in making them available for the satisfaction of social wants. But these means of satisfaction must not be too remote from the level of conventional conditions to excite endeavor after their enjoyment. As Ruskin unfolded the elements of beauty in common interests of life, as the workman lives in the sense of satisfying world-wide variety of desires, as the servant of duty makes his life-interests nobler by letting the light of love in upon all relations with the community, as the advocate of justice strengthens the purpose of personality, the whole social process is swung into line with the conceivably superior type toward which the increasingly conscious community moves; so the proprieties of individual possession, as they are diffused throughout the community, tend to become conventional that they may not be lost to the greatest of all consuming demands—the developmental process of human association. Conventionality and property —the social and the individual factors in normality —are complemental factors in the evolution of personality toward the sociological type.

Normality is thus seen to be a necessary criterion by which the social process subjective and objective balances its course to secure the selective survival of the types of personality, under conditions requiring *adaptation to environment as a requisite of survival.*

Oxty in Fig. 6 is the area of typicality—the first axiomatic requisite of typal survival, and the first criterion of social valuation. But, where conditions require the community to pay primary regard to adaptivity to changes, this requisite of normality becomes a primary axiom of social valuation. This is prominently the case where a highly typicalized community is driven to adapt itself to a new territory, as when a mountainous people is forced to adjust itself to the conditions of the plain or vice versa. The type becomes more elastic, legal symbolisms are used to give formal sanction to changes in the typal group as in adoption into family or people. The individual element of personality for the time being receives more recognition and the com-

munity as a whole does not survive solely by adherence to a single standard of typal efficiency for
all its members. Freedom favors variety and circumstances require normality rather than typicality

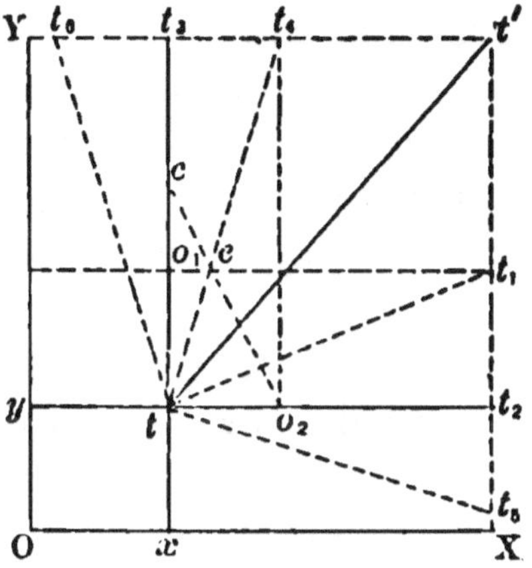

FIG. 6.

as a coordinate requisite of survival in this stage of
evolution of specific interests.

The community which has reached its limits of
homogeneous typicality at t can give no further
guarantee of development except on one condition
—that it allow each ratio of personal efficiency to
adapt itself to those conditions in which it can find
its equilibrium. Three typal tendencies thus arise:
tt_4, tt^1, tt_1 in the social situation t_3 tt_2. One set
of persons, on this condition, having high conventional efficiency (tt_3) but low proprietary efficiency
(to_2) will take the line tt_4; another set with low
conventional efficiency (to^1) but high proprietary
efficiency (tt_2) will normally take the line tt_1; and
that group of persons in whom both phases of effi-.

ciency are equal will tend to find its equilibrium along the line tt^1. This whole process is the normalization of the community into tendential groups or grades of adaptability on the basis of the traditional type of personality common to all groups. Groups on tt_2 and tt_3 are marginal groups barely efficient enough to be tolerated in social estimation. But groups on tt_5 and tt_6 are far too low in one or the other of the coordinating factors to be even tolerated. They must be excluded from society.

The relative value of conventional and proprietary factors determines the place of the group or of any member. The group with high conventionality and low proprietary qualification will find its potential equilibrium between tt_4 and tt_3. If it goes much below that it will be sub-typical and be eliminated, tt_6. The group in which the conventional and the proprietary potentialities are balanced will be at equilibrium somewhere on tt^1. The group of social interests within which proprietary potentialities are at the maximum but the conventional elements at a minimum will be at equilibrium somewhere between tt_1 and tt_2.

For each member of the several groups there is an equilibrium somewhere on the line of that normalizing tendency, the group being made up of kindred ratios of adaptability. The maximum of normalizing development in the typal tendency tt_4 is determined by conventionality (tt_3) and by property (t_3t_4) ; and there may be within these limits all grades of variety, among the members making up that tendential group, according to the ratio of conventional (social) and proprietary (individual) units of efficiency in each personality. We find any member's normal place in any typal tendency (tt_4, tt^1, tt_1) by a diagonal which connects the coordinating values of that type of personality. A member whose conventional value (social) is tc and whose proprietary capacity is to_2 finds his equilibrium at c. He would be at equilibrium nowhere else in the community in any other typal tendency. But one whose conventional value is to_1 and proprietary capacity to_2 would find its equilibrium only where o_1o_2 crosses tt^1, not tt^4. That is, he might not yet be differentiated into the organically normal group to which he potentially belongs.

We are led to the general conclusions, therefore, that normality requires of the *community* that as a whole its selective survival shall be effected through the capacity for groupal differentiation on the basis of kindred degrees of development in the qualities and capacities of its members.

Normality, as an axiomatic requisite of typal evolution, requires of each integrated *group*, into which the members of the community are divided, to socialize its members by means of conventional criteria common to the group, and to individualize its members by the influence of proprietary interests (property) upon personality through responsibility in possession, use and control, consistently with the typal welfare.

Normality, from the point of view of each member, requires each member of society to identify himself with that group within which he may find the equilibrium between the social and the individual factors of his personal constitution, that is, *within that typal group whose equilibrium of conventional and proprietary factors corresponds with the ratio of social and individual factors of personality.*

The value of each or any *typal group to the community* will depend upon the degree of efficiency with which it tends to perform its particular organic function, for the more normal survival of the type of life for which the whole community stands *(t)*. Hence this must be done without impairing or prejudicing other organic functions of the social process then and there requisite for normalization of the community to conditions.

The value of each and every *person to the community* depends first upon the degree of development, that is, the ratio of efficiency above the minimum level *(t)* of integration; and, secondly, on the personal capacity to normalize himself to that social interest to which his ratio of efficiency potentially assigns him.

The value of *the community to personality* depends on the degree to which conventional and proprietary interests are balanced in potentially normal equilibrium for survival of the generic type (typicality) *plus* the provision systematically made for personal adaptation to the grade or group of social interests in which his ratio of personal efficiency potentially finds its equilibrium.

For this axiom of organic *reciprocation* of groups

of social interests we shall have to ascend to the
next norm of selective development by assimilation
under the social system or *institutionality*, by which
the method of relating groupal tendencies and the
potentialities of typal attainment are alone made
capable of realization in order and progress.

CHAPTER XI.

Just as typicality was required to explain the coherence of kind in a simple social situation, and just as normality was required to be assumed to enable us to conceive of the phenomena of adaptation of variety of types or degrees of individual capacities, to conditions of existence; so, now, we have to find or suggest that axiom of social thought by which both the *typical* and the *normal* are reciprocally related in such a way as to provide for the realization of the *tendential* in the evolution of complex communities. How do the organic tendencies in society manage to develop ?

The situation is as follows: on the basis of established typical groups each of which is adjusted around a center of social interests in which its traditions, customs and possessions are comprised, another step in the unfolding of the socializing process appears. In this complex organization each group of interests is normally balanced on a center of gravity of its own. The prevailing degree of differentiation peculiar to each group locates it in the social system somewhere on the line of some one of the organic functions of the community.

Institutionality is the coordination of separate interests into a third form of social activity called a tendency. The interests of two persons are coordinated in a household by the institution of marriage, the interests of two or more *gentes* are coordinated to form a tribe, of two or more tribes to form a nation, a people or other political unit of organization (*ethnos, polis*). But all such coordinations have one feature in common; they institute such reciprocal relations as will require each and every social interest both to compete and to cooperate as a means of survival and development. The establishment of a sovereignty is the institution of liberty and of social leadership.

In this way society rises to higher types of character. It preserves the several interests which are capable of performing some organic function in the same social order by putting each interest between the alternatives of elimination and individuation of character. Actual decadence is therefore possible only by resistance to the sovereign social spirit, and potential advance is provided for as the normal outlet of human activity.

This yoking of reciprocal interests is effected through institutionality. All institutions might be classified as cooperative and competitive. When some essential social interest seems to be going to the wall, these reciprocal relations are so revised and cooperative institutions so coordinate the interest in jeopardy as to reclaim and restore this social function to its rightful place. This is the case with the family as the basal organization of the social system. Its function is axiomatic and its integrity is vital to social organization.

All institutions must be regarded as agencies to preserve the right ratio of competitive and cooperative functions. Social interests must be organized for survival of the actual and the development of the potential types of character. There must be a mutual recognition of complemental capacities to that end. By the cooperation of interests survival is secured. This institutional relation of interests we call order. By the competition of interests we guarantee the development of the potentialities which is the only practicable means of enabling the social system as a whole to enjoy the benefits of progress.

We saw that property was a necessary stimulant for individualizing the members of a conventionalized society. But by what means does the social process prevent proprietary interests of individual man from so dominating the developments of the community as to set at naught the conventional restraints which really serve the purpose of making men civil rather than savage in the type of social beings to which they belong ? Selective survival requires that these two, conventionality and property, normally constitute an equilibrium, each ministering to the evolution of the superior type. But as a matter of fact one of these two normalizing factors is always tending to overshadow the other. And at this juncture of civilized society, in the

Western world particularly, it is property interests which are believed by many to imperil the possibilities of the social process in evolving the normal type of attainment for the community as a whole.

Edward Carpenter forcibly portrays this tendency of property to forestall or to disturb the typal equilibrium through the effect of the growth of property upon personality in relation to the theoretically normal type. " It is evident," he says, " that the growth of property, through the increase of man's powers of production, reacts on man in three ways, to draw him away, namely: (1) from Nature. (2) from his true self, (3) from his fellows. . . . The true self of man consists in his organic relation with the whole body of his fellows; and when the man abandons his true self he abandons also his true relation to his fellows. The mass-man must rule in each unit-man, else the unit-man will drop off and die. But when the outer man tries to separate himself from the inner, the unit-man from the mass-man, then the reign of individuality begins—a false and impossible individuality, of course, but the only means of coming to the consciousness of the true individuality. With the advent of a Civilization, then, founded on property, the unity of the old tribal society is broken up. The ties of blood relationship which were the foundation of the Gentile system and the guarantees of the old fraternity and equality, became dissolved in favor of powers and authorities founded on mere possession. The growth of wealth disintegrates the ancient society; the temptations of power, of possessions, etc., which accompany it, wrench the individual from his moorings; personal greed rules; ' Each man for himself ' becomes the universal motto; the hand of every man is raised against his brother, and, at last, society itself becomes an organization by which the rich fatten upon the vitals of the poor, the strong upon the murder of the weak.

"And then arises the institution of government." *

In this analysis the central truth is the fact of the tendency of property to dislodge conventionality even to the extent of desocializing personality.   In the face of this tendency in the social process, how is the normal development of the potential type to be guaranteed ?   That is, at this critical stage of development by association, what sociological criterion or sociological axiom normally guides the social process in order to prevent any such a maladjustment as has actually overtaken countless communities ?   What enables the social aggregate to keep on the road of right reason ?

This third axiom for the guidance of the social process on the path of normal evolution of types of personality is effected through agencies of assimilation by social institutions, in which order and progress find their equilibrium.

Institutions are necessary to individualize the resources of the community and to socialize the capacities of the individual members.   The social

* Civilization—Its Cause and Cure, pp. 26-7.   Humboldt Library.

process has therefore much to do with institutions at every step. The common relations of men with one another and with properties call into existence social institutions. The community can never appropriate to the service of the normal type any of the gains or properties of individual acquisition or capacity without in some way institutionalizing that element of social value. Individual energies have thus to be socialized. To institutionalize any power or property is to set a value upon that power or property as an indispensable requisite in the selective survival or development of the types normally adaptable to that social order. We institutionalize the proprietary, the sexual, the governmental and the religious relationships as requisites. It is not that some value and others do not value these elements which enter into selective survival of types, that the institutional standard has to be maintained as a requisite of survival and development; but rather, that either too great a degree of equality or inequality may totally suspend the normal action of associative selection and thus of typal development. Now inequality is an indispensable condition of development. But there are physical and psychical limits to inequality beyond which not only progress but even sympathetic association ceases to hold in unity the members of the community. But there is no escape from the fact that the type that ceases to grow is in peril of dying, however useful it may have been to the social order.

Institutionality as an axiom of the selective sur-

vival of types defines these limits of the social movement in its two aspects of order and progress—
order requiring the likeness of typal quality and
progress requiring inequality in degree of adaptive
capacity in the complex community, both of which
find their equilibrium in institutionality by which
the course of the community is normally balanced,
within the limits of survival, in a third tendency
which we now designate progress.

In its normal character, institutionality is that
methodical aspect of human association which
makes the social process systematical or orderly
without destroying or depriving it of its progressive quality. It therefore is positive and preventive
in its normal function. It prevents the social energies from spreading out prematurely in the direction of maximum limits or from contracting within
the minimum limits of associative survival; it conversely focalizes the personal powers and proprietary means with respect to the main tendency of
typal progression.

Structurally regarded, institutionality is the
frame-work of social organization. It is that in the
social structure which gives a methodical setting to
the factors of socialization natural and historical,
and secures for the social process a sane direction
of effort after typal individuation. The function
of institutionality, as an organic agency, is to guarantee a certain quality which enters into the primary needs of the social order, to maintain that
equilibrium between individual tendencies to exploit society and social tendencies to exploit per-

sonality, so that typal attainment may find society the normal realm of realization.

Method and attainment, or order and progress, are the complemental aspects of institutional activity regarded as an axiomatic gauge of the selective process. In backward communities and undeveloped portions of society, where the institutional agencies are rare and simple, institutional method is less evident in regulating the life of men; there it takes the form of conventionality rather than that of institutions. But the social habit is institutional. Progress institutionalizes the conventional, if it accords with the ideal. Apart from the ideal trend of development conventionality becomes unduly dominant as institutional order, rendering change for the better more and more difficult. Where the institutional method of living is but slightly developed everybody is officially authorized to enforce the conventional upon all others. If not by legal still more fatally by other modes is social pressure exercised in the name of conformity to the conventional type. This method makes with certainty toward an equally intolerable monotony, if unbalanced by provision for the attainment of personality toward normal variety of social type.

From this bondage to the conventional method required for survival the escape has to be made by insisting on the complemental function of the institutional as an axiom of selective development in the formation of character. *Ennui* is the psychical outcome of the failure to do this. Suicide is to no small extent referable to this want of connection for reciprocal helpfulness between personality and the community. The remedy lies logically in the development of the individual in the institutional quality and the institutional capacity to help toward development.

This complementarity of order and progress, of method and attainment, in one axiom of typal individuation is a balancing factor in the midst of change. Method is the conservative system of socializing properties and powers deemed requisite for the type of personality entitled to survive. Progress is the individuating of those increments which order and invention have put at the service of attainment. It is the individualizing of resources by combining the actual and the potential in the personal achievement. Whatever one typal group attains to, that is socially useful for the survival or development of all groups, is methodically appropriable by these groups through institutional agencies. And this appropriation is done by individuating these new elements of attainment into the type of personality in other groups. Institutions are sociological clearing-houses, but primarily through the appropriation of new increments of social *qualities* from one group in which these qualities first arise to another among its members, thus heightening the *degree* of attainment in the community as a whole.

It is therefore evident that on the side of order institutionality is subjective. It is systemized habit. Social order is a thing of the common disposition. We do not associate peacefully by virtue of physical pressure but rather by reason of sympathetic habit. We are policed by the leadings of a sympathetic sense of social relationships. On the side of progress institutionality is objective. We see changes by reference to outward criteria. As these changes become established in our subjective life, they then for the first become part of the systematic order of our lives. The quality and the degree of attainment both enter into the formation of the types of personality; and all such types have upon them the developmental stamp in proportion to the degree of assimilation they enjoy. Order provides for unity of social type by institutional methods—it guarantees survival in association; progress provides for the assimilation of individual elements, or differential qualities, into the accredited course of typal development, thus securing relative equality and inequality in the same social system; but the equality is that of typal *quality*, the inequality that of typal *degree* of attainment, by which inequality among men progress is made possible.

There is in every community the institutional type of personality combining the orderly qualities with the progressive degree or capacity of social foresight. This type stands for those reciprocal relations without which the community would collapse. This type has a facility for combining the contingent with the conventional. It is the institutional type that alone can serve society in selecting the point of equilibrium between the past accumulations of the community and its progressive possibilities so as to incarnate into the sociological type the union of the two.

The multiplication of social institutions in modern life out of their primitive and ancient beginnings has opened a thousandfold the springs of power and property for the services of the higher type of personality. However far the institutional methods of the social process may have fallen short of realizing the normal level of well-being for any particular class or condition of persons, this defect is rather due to a lack of individualization of resources. Voluntary associations are rapidly remedying this defect. The potentialities of. attainment are great indeed which have seemed realizable from resources which civilization has taken unto herself. Through the efforts of individual man to utilize his powers over the properties of nature and the possessions of society these must be individuated by personality or prove a source of developmental weakness to the type that fails to do so.

Opportunity of attainment, however, in one social class or lot in a given social order, is not equally an opportunity in another. Station in life is a handicap or a hindrance. Status ever discounts opportunity. The latter situation may be such as to make typal attainment impossible. If governmental institutions fail to guide the social process so as to bring each organic tendency of the social population to the equilibrium between method and attainment, then some other institutional agency representing clearer conceptions of adjustment of personality to the potential type is normally called into being. Thus Rome called the family into a larger service in social organization, as compared with Greece. The Christian church first opened the fountains of spiritual attainment, as all great religions have done, where regulation by methodical forms of ceremonial authority suspended the exercise of the voice of a social conscience. When the ecclesiastical institutions lapsed into purely methodical functions to society, and ceased to assimilate and diffuse social resources by reason of institutional stagnation, the industrial institutions arose to give scope to personal capacity and character; for the institutions of industry and commerce afford no less effective inducements to order and attainment than other social institutions. Each in its time serves the potentially normal type. As the social process becomes capable of utilizing domestic, economic, governmental, and ethical and religious institutions they or their substitutes in social organization must appear as essential agencies in the formative realization of the best attainable type of personality for all portions of the community. In them we have united in equilibrium the institutional forms that give us social order and the institutional forces that are required for progress. This unity of structure and function must appear in the type in which all these institutions find their highest use. For the definition of the highest use we must look to the next sociological axiom— ideality.

These conditions lead us to infer that social evolution by selective survival of potentially normal types is not realizable apart from that coordination of interests and tendencies which we call institutionality. This takes up the typical which is qualitative and the normal which is quantitative, and assimilates these elements into a reciprocal tendency involving both the fact of order and the possibilities of progress.

Institutionality appears thus to be a derivative quality of social man. We have it in the quality we call law-abiding in any people. The invasion of a foreign foe finds people and their leaders appealing to the love of their institutions. Institutions are the product of this common quality in the social nature.

This quality is, however, unequally developed in the same people. Some classes of people, for various reasons, make little use of institutions on which other classes are very dependent for their survival and development. The breaking up of a household has cost society many a suicide. The severance of the family from cultural institutions tells fatally upon its quality and its capacity as a unit of social life. The classes among whom economic interests are uppermost are prone to undervalue the services of æsthetic and ethical institutions. The classes whom the necessities of survival tax to the uttermost are not able to develop beyond that. To share the life of a superior type of life is beyond their reach.

The test of institutions in the social process is their success in the organization of the population with reference to the solidarity found in the social ideal. Institutional development of the people as a whole cannot go beyond the common capacity of the population to participate in the attainment of a common end. Hence social ideals must react on institutions of popular service. The primary function of any institution—ceremonial, industrial, ecclesiastical, political and professional—is to organize the people upon the basis of their maximum appreciation of their position and their possibilities.

It is just this appreciation that gives rise to the second test of institutional capacity in a people, namely, its success in coordinating the main tendencies arising within the population. Governmental and industrial institutions organize the population on the basis of their *necessity*, as seen in the estimation put upon their lives and their labors. But for the progressive possibilities of a people civil and cultural institutions are required which emphasize the *potential* advantages of cooperation. These potential values have to be brought out, if real progress is to be made. There is no other way of making progress among a whole people except by stimulating men to participate in the type that normally tends to sum up in itself the best there is in that civilization.

The only normal process by which great populations develop, on the assumption of the selective survival of sociological types, is that which conventionalizes the social quality among the self-asserting tendencies, and potentializes the capacity or quantity of attainment among social interests. Conventionalized quality gives us those *relations* among interests which we call order. Potentialized *capacity* gives us progress. And order and progress are the subjective and the objective aspects of institutional efficiency.

On this basis of reciprocal influences among social interests social evolution sees wider scope of realization than ever, lying out before it. As fast as a superior social quality becomes an available object desirable for further selection, the conditions of a new degree of progress are present by which the actual type passes up into the potentially higher level of progress.

The coordination of the qualitative elements of tradition with the adaptive elements of action, by establishing orderly relations among natural tendencies, secures survival of the potentially more normal types and is a necessary and universal aspect of institutional evolution. Such was the case when monogamic households became institutionalized. The institution of private property involves both social order and progressive attainment. Likewise, when personal liberty became institutionalized, in established social relationships, a new type of personality or a variety of types is potentialized. Also, when a commercial custom becomes first conventionalized among a class and is institutionalized into a law imposing responsibility on all classes whose interests bring them under this relationship, we have the social process passing up into the higher level. The potential passes into a social norm of realization.

The institutionality of typal survival and development may be graphically represented by Fig.
7. Let $t_4 t^1 t_1$ be the points at which the three

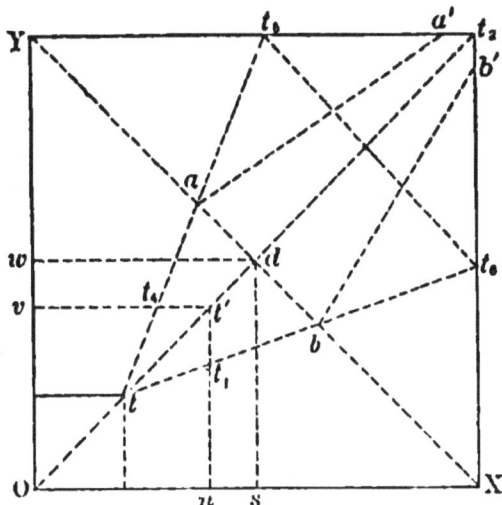

FIG. 7.

social interests emerge into typal tendencies of
$t_4 t_5$, $t^1 t_2$ and $t_1 t_6$, and designate these tendencies
as traditional, institutional and adaptive tendencies
respectively.

The area $wdsnt^1v$ will represent the potentially
normal gain from the institution of a common
social order as the basis of typal attainment.

By measuring social order on OY and progress
or attainment on OX we may state the relative
value of any typal tendency to the community,
within the social situation YOX, if $t^1 t^2$ be taken as
the norm of maximum possibilities of typal evolution.

The value of any organic typal tendency to that

complex whole which is the life of the community depends

(1) On the degree of potential participation with the selective trend of the institutional order by means of which typal attainment is normally realizable.

(2) The value of any community (social system) to any typal tendency depends on the relative need that typal tendency has for the institutional qualities at any given degree of typal development in such tendency.

If, for example, the traditional tendency in the community, after reaching a, has before it the alternative of at_5 or at_2, it will take one or the other according as conservatism or progress of its peculiar type is a requisite of survival. If it selects at_5 it becomes the prime exponent of social order but reaches its limit of development at t_5—long before its possibilities would be exhausted on aa^1. Hence the latter is the line on which it will normally proceed, for maximum typal survival and development, short of absorption into t^1t_2.

If, again, the adaptive tendency at b, takes bt_6, it realizes its high potential capacity for progressive adjustment to conditions, but reduces relatively its scope or extent of typal continuity in a complex social order. Only the line bb^1 seems to offer this tendency the equilibrium of both order and progress, short of absorption into t^1t_2.

Hence the traditional type, having need of progressive attainment, normally selects aa^1; and the adaptive type, having need of methodical order, selects bb^1, as in both cases the lines of maximum typal evolution.

The axiom of institutionality brings both the traditional and the adaptive type into equilibrium with the institutional type and thereby each co-operates in the survival and the development of all. Together they tend toward a still more perfect type in the ideal.

CHAPTER XII.

NATURE decides the question of the relative usefulness of any typal tendency, or of its products, by the elimination of the untypical, the inadaptable, and the unorganizable. The facts of warfare between families, tribes, classes, peoples, nations, parties and policies sufficiently illustrate this.

But the tendency of history, that is, of the sympathetic social population whose criteria of social value have become axiomatic, is to appeal all her deeply marked differences, which arise in the social process, to the standard of ideality. These standards are always evolving by different degrees among different interests. On the scale of ideality all social choices find their ultimate valuation. In ideality all social systems tend to find their judgment-seat. It is true equally of personality and of the social population taken as an aggregate, and the ideal element, in which the fellowship of man comes to its fairest fruition, thrusts it root, actually or potentially, far down into every stratum of the social nature.

Of course the ideal elements have their origin in the conceptual capacity of personality, from which, like fledglings trying their wings, they escape only to find that others have had kindred experiences. And thus, by the process of logical association, conceptual currents arise from congenial groups of ideal elements. Schäffle has pointed out the impossibility of keeping the ideal element in one's inner life to one's self; its nature and process are such as to seek expression.

We have seen how the subjective forces of human nature in association crave for expression in some kind of symbolic representation, the most universal forms of which are linguistic and artistic. We have seen that the symbols serve the purpose of intensifying a natural sociality into a sovereign sense of membership, uniting the community by specific modes of self-expression until it comes to act as a unit upon being subjected to certain stimuli or changes in its conditions of existence. This conception of the typical as a goal of development provides the social sense in us with the objective *form* of the ideal as an object of imitation or attainment.

Certain typical persons are constantly serving as the ideals of certain as yet undeveloped social beings. The relations of parent and child, of teacher and pupil, of pastor and parishioner, of ruler and subject, of official and citizen, of hero and his worshipper, all illustrate the fact that the ideal element as it appears in imitation of actual social types runs back into the simplest relationships of the social process ; and they show that wherever typicality is a dominant quality there the ideal element is present in some degree at least. But wherever the typical, apprehended as the standard of imitation and attainment, has once served as an idealizing and formative force, the growing consciousness of man sooner or later differentiates the actual from the conceivably more perfect type. The idea of the perfect grows with the mind's acquaintance with qualities, conditions and relations which the imitated person does not contain. The sovereignty of the typical is ultimately broken as a social ideal. Such a crisis comes in the minds of all of us. ·Likewise is the integrated community discomfited at the inadequacy of the old and the sense of the need of a renewed ideality.

The typical gives us an ideal element which we may call social quality—an indispensable property of the social species. But when this quality of typicality—the conformative quality in social man —fails to guarantee survival, then normality or adaptivity to conditions calls for the property of action as the criterion by which the typical becomes differentiated toward the ideal. The social situation in which typal integration has full play enforces upon all therein the property or the quality of being socially typical. But when the simple social situation breaks up into groups of social interests the element of action enters as the differential separating one interest from another. The element of action under the two aspects of conventionality or propriety and possessions or property physical and psychical, material or immaterial, may be conveniently called the criterion of ca-

pacity. It is quantitative, as a criterion of social
value. It asks what a man has *done* in society,
which was Napoleon's test of social efficiency; not
what a man *is* in society, which is the test of tra-
ditionality.

If the typical gives us social quality and normality gives us social capacity or the property of
action, what does the criterion of institutionality
contribute to the constructive creation of the social
ideal ? We have shown that within the social
order the condition of institutionality arose from
the necessity of coordinating the several tendencies
of typal activity into an assimilative process. Thus
the several social interests were organized into established and systematic conditions. Among them
there was a necessary interdependence of parts
each in some way conditioning the idealizing tendencies of the other. Hence out of the criterion
of institutionality as a characteristic of the social
process we get the ideal element of reciprocality,
that is, that the social ideal is conditioned by
responsible relations among those interests involved in its synthesis.

It is apparent then that each of the three axioms
of developmental selection—typicality, normality,
institutionality—leaves over some residual requisite of progressive survival which must find expression in the succeeding axiom. The goal of
development is not yet sufficiently defined.
Furthermore, each successive axiom exhibits an
increasing degree of potential ideality. In ideality
—the next higher and final sociological axiom—

these elements find their supreme synthesis and the developmental process comes to its most complete equilibrium in human character. Personality attains this balance between conditions and community to the extent to which it realizes through society the two necessary aspects of ideality—religion and science.*

Social ideality, as an ultimate axiom of development, is the conscious anticipation of the typal qualities, normal conditions and institutional relations requisite for the solidarity of all organic social tendencies in the progressive individuation of a potentially perfect type of personality.

We must not confuse social ideals with social illusions † as is often done in the estimation of the axiomatic function of religion in development. Illusions are incidental, however common they may be, to the societary process. But religious ideality is creative of social solidarity by being true to fact under social conditions. The ideal is the object upon which convictions converge often for survival only, but more frequently as a goal of development. An illusion is a state of conviction based on the want of accurate information. Illusions arise from ignorance of fact, of the actually real; ideals arise from a belief in the conceivably perfect end to be attained. The one has to do with the present and the other with the future; the one with the actual, the other with the potential. The societary process is such that though it is conceivable that there may

* Guyau, The Non-Religion of the Future, Part III., Ch. II.
† Sully, Illusions, p. 326.

be as many social ideals as there are social beings, still the subjective factors in the societary process, by constant communication of man with his fellow-man in any social order, works out a convergence of belief which favors the most forceful because the truest ideals. "Amid all this apparent deviation of belief from a common standard of truth," says Sully, "there is a clear tendency to a rational consensus. Thought, by disengaging what is really matter of permanent and common cognition both in the individual and still more in the class and fixing the quantum of common cognition in the shape of accurate definitions and universal propositions, is ever fighting against and restraining the impulses of the individual imagination toward dissociation and isolation of belief."

If the societary process really presents us with the axiom of ideality that corresponds to the needs of the social order in its highest equilibrium with natural conditions and spiritual intuitions, then we can see clearly that ideals are subjects of development quite as much as social traditions, social activities and social institutions. No one will pretend to say that, if society is part of the cosmic process, ideals are wholly independent of the world that lies outside of the societary process. The process which constructs its own sociological types to which attainment normally tends, has but to present to the social consciousness an end or goal of achievement remote enough to combine the minimum demands of natural conditions with the maximum potentialities of social character to present society with an ideal of typal achievement. Thus the thought of man projects for himself and his fellows in association a type of personality in which are found all the characteristics of perfection. This is the essential quality of the social ideal—that it be a type of personality or of social organization distant enough to shade out of relief the hard *conditions* of the actual existence and definite enough to satisfy our sense of completeness and of harmony of typal *qualities*. It is therefore true that the social ideal is the *ultima thule* of the socially typical: it is the typical advancing to perfect relations by the ascendency of qualities over conditions. Religion and science as idealizing efforts have together made this axiom practically available in development.

These three norms of social development—typicality, normality and institutionality—contribute toward the formation of the social ideal. The element of ideality aids us, only so far as the ideal anticipations after which the social process is working is true to fact in its combination of the socializing elements. This is the scientific requisite of attainment to the ideal; and as long as human socialization has its procedure conditioned upon nature the contemplative or reflective in social life must take its point of departure toward the perfect type from the practical conditions in our natural existence. But starting with respect for knowledge of the natural requisites of survival, which is science, and projecting the ideal in which these three axioms enter harmoniously into the

selective process, which is spiritual communion
with the universal, personality, in whatever social
situation, must normally tend to lift itself toward
the level of its harmonized potentialties. Typicality serves to furnish the qualitative elements
which we may continue to call traditional; normality provides the adaptive element of action; institutionality serves the process with the utilizing,
the organizing or the reciprocating element which
gives every essential element its interdependent
place in the social order. All these elements ideality individuates into the potentially perfect type.
These four axioms are therefore the sociological
axioms, the universal marks of the social process
and the necessary modes of the typal evolution of
personality. So that the kingdom of ideality lies
next to any social existence in which the traditional, the adaptive and the reciprocating factors in
the social process are truthfully controlled by a
harmonizing faith in the attainability of the progressively perfect type—the ideal.

Religion and science are the essential aspects of
social ideality. Midway between lies the realm of
art—the creature of both. They find their equilibrium only in the sociological ideal, that is in some
ideal which results in typal solidarity of social tendencies at equilibrium with natural conditions and
with the moral history of man. If science serves
only one typal tendency in society and is shut off
from another, or if religion inspires only one typal
tendency to the exclusion of others, the sociological
ideal must either lack respect for universal law or

reverence for the rule of righteousness. But where these two are equated in the truly logical conception of their sociological relation, as undoubtedly they were in the mind of Kant, the moral order of the inner life of man in society and the natural order of the world find their equilibrium in the conception of the ideal type of personality. On this condition personality is reverent alike toward the truth in the science of nature and the truth in the fellowship of man with the Infinite, because they are but two different paths of human progress toward equilibrium of both in the ideal of solidarity. The end of both is truth not for truth's sake but for the sake of a more perfect type of personality.

Our analysis of the typal tendencies in the social system would therefore lead us to look for a traditional ideal, an adaptive ideal and an institutional ideal. As a matter of fact social history confirms this analysis. The traditional ideal is found in the ideal of equality—not equality of social efficiency of personality but *kinship of typal quality*, or equality of the ratio of typal efficiency, or likeness of type. If the traditional type of personality were given free scope to direct the social process toward its ideal it would arrive, as it always has, at none other than this one of likeness of type as the main characteristic of the ideal social order.

In view of the tendency of modern democracy to take this trail, it is worth while to follow out this tendency to traditional ideals of social realizations to some of its remoter implications.

First, the traditional ideal involves a relatively
static order of social existence. By assuming this
one element of the social process to be relatively
permanent and dominant, and other elements as
transient and insignificant or abnormal, the order
of our social progress would be reversed by substituting the actual or some past social order as the
standard of attainment. The easiest conceivable
ideal to attain to is that which finds and keeps the
equilibrium at any given point at which the mass
of men are themselves in command of their conditions of existence. But that implies or requires
that the social order or the force of natural selection shall eliminate any disturbing factor tending
to convert static into dynamic capacity. But no
static order of society can escape deterioration of
type which so violates the sympathetic quality in
human nature. So that the traditional type of
equality as a social ideal if left to sway social policy
not only lowers the level of moral attainment but
takes the leaven out of the social process.

Secondly, the traditional ideal constantly conceives of the social order as having power to cause
the desired social forces to develop and grow and
the undesired factors to diminish by dying out.
Remove this relation to an infinite distance or infinitely increase the rate of the transformation and
the process presents us with the social ideal of the
golden age of equality. The social process is an
experimental process, it is alleged.* If we can ex-

* Jevons, The State in Relation to Labor, Ch. I. *.

tract the abnormal or disturbing tendencies or hold them in check long enough to cause their extinction, and give full scope or greater impetus to the development of the normal factors in the process, then the attainment of the ideal seems to be only a question of applying the results of past experience to the new circumstances according to the law of the selective survival of potentially normal types of personality.   We have only to magnify the chances of the normal tendencies of past experience under present circumstances and minimize the abnormal to zero and our ratio will be one expressive of the ideal equilibrium.   But the answer to this line of reasoning is conclusive in this fact—that *the competing tendencies* into which free peoples are organized—tendencies, each seeking to socialize personality after its own preferred ideal yet increasingly conscious of the possibilities of cooperation toward the common ideal—*are the source of the energy inherent in the developmental process*, and the elimination of these tendencies which now compete and now cooperate on well-defined institutional conditions would be equivalent to the attempt to convey mechanical power from wheel to wheel without physical contact.

The logical fallacy of the traditional ideal consists in the attempted application of a generic concept to a specific social situation, and therefore overlooks the differential characteristics which distinguish any specific social type from the genus to which it belongs.   We have, that is, not to construct social ideals for generic social man but for typical men of like passions with us. Logically, this social ideal of equality is dim-sighted as to differentials.

The scientific fallacy of traditional ideality lies in failing to respect the fact that development is essentially a process of typal individuation. To suspend individuation in the interest of homogeneity alone, or to disregard differentiation by cutting the bond between personality and those social interests which act as spurs to personal endeavor after power and property, is wholly out of line with the developmental possibilities ; the typal consciousness that we belong to a class or a people is the very ground of developmental possibilities as well as the essence of social survival. So far then as this ideal emphasizes a solidarity of feeling or a common plane of social condition and fails to recognize development by differentiation and individuation, to that extent the ideal is logically impossible and scientifically inconsistent with fact and law as we know them now.

But apart from this tendency to regard social ideality as static rather than progressive, the traditional ideal of equality or likeness of type is fundamentally consistent with typal evolution in the following two respects :

(1) It insists that each member of the community be integrated to the type of personality normal to that social station, below which if any one should fall he thereby ceases to be a typical member of his species—social man—and that the higher types of potential capacity must forthwith seek to rein-

tegrate this sub-typical member to the recognized level of sociality, lest he become the center or nucleus of a sub-social class—that is, a dependent member of society. The traditional ideal stands for the organic solidarity of personality with the community in any social situation. This integration of personality with the normally organic type which enters into the composition of the community is the principle governing the attitude of the communities within Christendom toward the dependent and defective, but only tendentially so toward the delinquent classes. The traditional ideal wants guarantees from the community against typal reversion.

(2) The traditional ideal furthermore insists upon the integration of all communities under the universal category of humanity. This theoretical or sentimental canon of kinship of all peoples is exhibited in such noble practices as that of hospitality to strangers, in society's respect for the claims of personality to the very verge of his claims upon life, and in the natural growth of the affective sentiments, which is apparently the common characteristic out of which this constructive ideal could be developed. To this theoretical ideal of racial unity must be referred the tendency to make a common law of humanity the object of religious or moral aspiration, also the conception of natural law as an ultimate ideal to which to appeal from social policies or processes that tend to impair the typal integrity of a people's life.

The adaptive tendency of social life calls for a

corresponding ideal as the goal of the social process. This is *the naturalistic ideal or the ideal of liberty*. Its essential relation is seen in the satisfaction of personality with some group or other of social interests; this ideal sifts society, and therefore to that extent also tends to intensify inequality of capacity. It thus guarantees variety of types in the social process. Its danger lies in developing such a heterogeneity of degrees in the consciousness of the social ideal as to prevent the social tendencies from concentrating upon any commanding social ideal, provoking reaction of the lower against the higher types of efficiency. This incongruity results in the effort to soothe the social mind with an ideal in which the weakness and the strength of the social situation, the right and the wrong impulses pervading it, the usefulness and the useless tendencies therein, are formed into a whole in which the defects are not only rendered harmless by being restrained but are really required to bring out in compensatory relief the truly inspiring elements of the ideal. The effect of this is to substitute a variety of different social ideals between the organic and the potential ideal to meet the needs of diversity of type arising from the different degrees of typal potentiality in different social interests. But this series of successive ideals serves as a series of steps " to higher things " in typal progression. There is thus developed a sense of superior and subordinate ideals in the service of selective survival. Nevertheless this compromise is an evasion of solidarity as an axiom of development.

This brings the development of social ideals to the point at which the social process begins to institutionalize the order of ideal values; for the social process is fundamentally selective. In the conflict of interests, ideals are assorted and among these ideals the institutional ideal alone has in it the capacity to coordinate the ideal elements or values. This is the ideal of superiority. Its function is to assert the ascendency of the superior ideal against any social interest or set of social interests that may lack the sanction of the typal consciousness of the normal needs of society as a whole. To assist this ideal we must appeal to the social mind. The coordinating function of the institutional ideal is constructive; it brings together the component elements of both of the other idealizing tendencies, the traditional and the adaptive, each of which contributes an essential element to the ultimate or potentially perfect type. The traditional process or tendency guarantees the selective survival of the *generic* social type by keeping it in vital touch with the traditional ideal of typal *quality*. Hence the ultimate ideal must be *typically* social. The adaptive process or tendency guarantees the selective survival of *specific* social types by keeping these types in vital connection with some ideal of normal *activity*. The ultimate ideal must be ideally *normal*.

The institutional tendency guarantees the development of newly individuated social ideals by selective assimilation of the dynamic elements of the adaptive ideal with the static elements of the traditional or generic ideal.

The ideal of solidarity arises whenever the institutional process succeeds in awakening in the consciousness of the community an idealizing appreciation of the characters in history with which the social experience of the people is most fully in sympathy.

The axiom of ideality, as Royce has said, calls for the organization of life. But there are always two banners under which human life in society may be organized in response to the consciousness of the ideal as the controlling norm of action. We may follow the spirit of history and seek the ideal in organization of life and its tendencies in worship and in what social effort offers for realization. Or we may take the ideal of the scientific search for the truth in its impersonal form as that under which humanity should organize itself for the perfect typal realization.

The first of these ideals is thus formulated from the ethical and religious standpoint: " Find work for the life of the coming moral humanity which shall be so comprehensive and definite that each moment of every man's life in that perfect state, however rich and manifold men's lives may then be, can be and will be spent in the accomplishment of that one highest impersonal work. If such a work is found and accepted, the goal of human progress will be in so far reached." * This is in

* Royce, Religious Aspect of Philosophy, p. 211.

reality simply the reformulation of Comte's practical program of Employment and Education—an ideal which schemes of social reorganization are constantly endeavoring to realize in the name of religion whether of humanity* or of divinity.†

The supreme goal of science on the other hand is the synthetic development of knowledge to find the truth—the law of the progressive equilibrium of the human type of being with the cosmic process. It seeks to arrive at a statement of man's normal place in nature and of personality's place in society. It is interested in his adaptation to conditions objective and subjective, as the primary requisites of survival. By associating with his own kind, that is, by being typical, he has selected the social organization as the sphere of survival subject to conditions past and present in his objective environment which he cannot eliminate but may master. These conditions must therefore be understood; they must if possible be made calculable; at least they must be rendered helpful to man's development. Not only the fact of man's connection with nature is required by the scientific ideal of society, but the law of that connection, progressively unfolding to him the principle of his typal evolution in association. The ideal of science is selective and the instrument of selection is the reasoning process of personality in association—the reasoning of social man into right relation with nature and his fellow man by natural pressure or

* A. J. Booth, St. Simon and St. Simonism, pp. 35–47.
† Booth's " Darkest England, Preface."

spiritual promise at every step of his development.

From these two aspects, the scientific and the religious, the social process works at the realization of the ideal type of personality. We may contrast these aspects, to bring out their complemental character by reverting to the axiom of institutionality, by which the traditional and the adaptive tendencies in the same social organization were reciprocally coordinated but not reconciled into ideal solidarity. Of these tendencies the traditional is the logical exponent of the religious ideal as the goal of typal perfection. This tendency sets before us the infinite personal spirit, a subjective fellowship with which is the ideal *relation* of religion. By virtue of humanity's solidarity with the infinitely perfect type of personality all tendencies normal to society are made one in this intuitive conviction called faith. Hence the precise contribution of the religious consciousness to the sociological ideal is the conception of a perfect type of personality subjectively apprehensible as the goal of the institutional order of society, through the systematic guidance of which the community progresses toward a potentially more perfect equilibrium in the solidarity of the spiritual ideal—the kingdom of God.

On the other hand, the adaptive typal tendency is the logical exponent of the sociological ideal which science presents. This requires ideal normality by adaptation to the objective conditions of development, just as the traditional type required ideal typicality by affiliation with subjective type of ideal personality. The method of the scientific ideal is essentially rational, not intuitive. The ideal of science is attainable only as we rationalize the cosmic order environing us and find where man normally belongs therein and what is the law of his survival and development as a part thereof. With the law of his typal evolution given, we must deduce the social organization requisite for the attainment of the ideal. According to this ideal of science, personality is of value to the degree to which he tends to identify himself with the potentially normal type of personality, that is, with the perfect type of his kind—the universally human. And this tendency to equilibrium of personality with the perfect type of humanity depends upon his adjustment to the condition of his existence by association with the actual social type under institutional organization as a means of attainment toward the ideal possibilities of his nature.

It must be evident from this contrast that the religious ideal excels in its *conception* of an ideal social organization, but that the scientific ideal gives us a superior insight into the *law* of that order conceived of as realizable under the conditions of natural association. Religion insists on the subjective content of an ideal that its *quality* shall be *personal;* science insists that any progressive realization thereof must be *normal.*

The history of sociological theory reveals these two elements of personal quality and degree of normality with nature as the sociological ideas that

have led the race in its meanderings after the goal
of its half-revealed destiny. Everywhere we recognize one of these complemental axioms of social
evolution—a personal Divinity or a normal Humanity. All that we can do is to individuate both as
fast as each brings into our treasury of knowledge
its growing revelations from out of the vast realm
of the unknown. From one source the developmental process gathers spiritual content for its
ever-renewing ideals, from the other it learns the
conditions of its progressive realization. In the
equilibrium of the typal content with the typal conditions lies the promise of ideal development. But
*the logical goal of that development is the spiritual
solidarity of both Divinity and Humanity in the
same society.*

We may now graphically represent the developmental process in the four stages of its axiomatic
succession within the limits of a social order which
begins with a homogeneous type, expands into a
variety of interests or type-developing centers, is
coordinated into a system of reciprocal tendencies
and finally consolidated in a social ideal. The ver-
tical lines measure the socializing or subjective
aspects and the horizontal the individualizing or
objective aspects in the process. The diagonal line
represents the line on which personality, any tendency or any community finds equilibrium under
these successive conditions. For example, in the
simple social situation *Onta*, Fig. 8, the requisite
axiom of selective survival is typicality *Ot*, the subjective and the objective factors in the location of

which are respectively sociality *nt* and symbolism *at*.

When typal integration has reached these limits at *t* the reaction in favor of divergent interests results in the differentiation of typal tendencies,

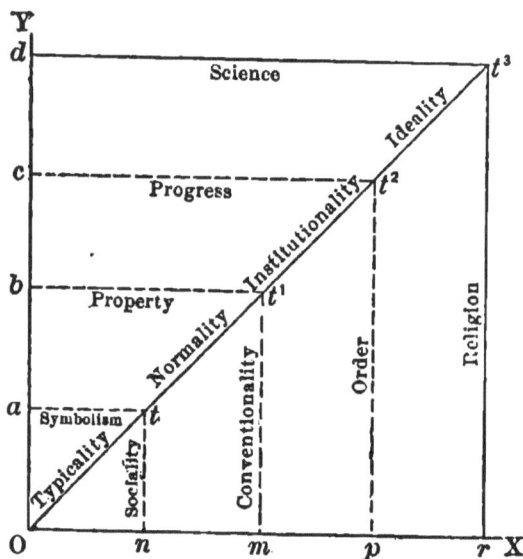

FIG. 8.

throughout *bt¹m nta,* but reaches its limits at *t¹* where the subjective interests of conventionality *mt¹*, and the objective interests of property *bt¹*, coming to an equilibrium locate the line of normality *tt¹* as the line of selective survival among rival interests. Anywhere from *t* to *t¹* any set of social interests may find this equilibrium, but it will always be located by the joint influence of considerations of conventionality (manners, morals, customs) and property, involving social and individual values tending to an equilibrium in a type normal to the situation of each set of dominant interests.

At t^1 order emerges and the conditions of progress appear under the system of typal relationships called institutionality t^1t^2, until typal assimilation under this order reaches its limit of progress at pt^2 and ct^2. Thence the ideal factors of science (object-ive) and religion (subjective) compete for control of the typal process and the axiomatic requisite of survival becomes ideality.

Nothing has been noted about the occasions or causes that produce or break the equilibria of these several factors. But normally the equilibrium at t would be broken by the growth of symbolism over sociality bending the homogeneous typal tendency of Ot in the direction of mt^1 only to recover its course and find its equilibrium at t^1. So throughout the typological process the individual or objective factors property bt^1, progress ct^2 and science dt^3 are the occasion of change and disturbance of the equilibrium. The breaking up of or the failure to form an equilibrium causes the rhythmic movement of social development.

The factors that tend to resist the disturbance of the equilibrium are conversely sociality in the simple social situation, conventionality among variety of social interests, order in the reciprocally related tendencies, and religion except in the time of ideal enthusiasms which impose considerations of change; and yet the quiet effect of conversion upon social character far outweighs the occasional enthusiasm. Consequently religion is essentially a conservative factor in society.

From these conditions and causes typicality becomes the requisite of survival in a simple social situation; normality, based on typicality, becomes the requisite of survival among divergent social interests; institutionality, in a complex social situation whose typical groups of interests are to be organically coordinated; and ideality, where a community has passed from the sole guidance of institutions to the capacity to apprehend the normal course of evolution of types by the light of subjective standards of development.

BOOK IV.

THE SOCIOLOGICAL PRINCIPLES.

CHAPTER XIII.

AXIOMATIC ASPECTS OF SELECTIVE SURVIVAL.

OUR presentation of the logical conceptions characteristic of the social process has thus far led us to recognize the general nature of this process as that of an individuating series. Social man finds expression in passing from the actual type to the potentially normal type to find equilibrium with the conditions of survival. This is the part of typical personality in association. This tendency in the groups of population is designated The Developmental Process.

In the second place we were led to inquire into the conditions and the relations in human association that must be postulated to make this process of the evolution of the typical in the aggregate naturally conceivable. These requirements we call The Sociological Postulates. They are the logical forms by which the social aggregate reasons, or rather which it takes for granted and uses in the course of its existence.

In the third stage of our inquiry we ventured to indicate those axiomatic judgments or norms by which the life of society is kept in the path of typal evolution. The normal social criteria were defined by which the course of human development is balanced between the particular and the universal, the individual will and the social sense of the race. These were called The Sociological Axioms, or those synthetic social judgments by the aid of which social man finds his equilibrium both with the actual order of nature and the conceptual process of human history. They are the logical judgments of social development arranged in the order of their historical evolution.

To those who may take the trouble to compare the several stages of this inquiry it should appear that we have here the conceptions necessary for a science of the conformity of human character to types.* Beginning with what appears to be the fundamental feature in the logical character of the social process—the type of personality—we proceeded to define those necessary forms and those universal functions by which, in the social process as known to us, these typal products tend to appear, to persist and to make progress from actual to potential life. Secondly, we sought to show by what axiomatic means man in his twofold capacity as individual and as social, manages to be obedient to the subjective dictates of the community and to the objective demands of its dependence upon nature. Our answer was: By following the axioms of social organization. Thus the logical connection of personality with the community in the common process of socialization is elaborated in the logical mechanism of social selection.

* Holland, Jurisprudence, p. 25.

There now remains for us to formulate the principles which belong to the process as thus presented. Having by analysis and synthesis revealed the logical categories required for society's survival and defined the axioms of development in their order in the history of social organization, we have now to show how social aggregates make use of these formal conceptions and axiomatic judgments in social selection.

The primary relation of each personality, interest and tendency to the community and of the community to its natural conditions, is *a selective relation.* This selective sense pervades society. The survival not only of personality but of society itself depends upon this selective capacity in the quality of the personal unit or the aggregate. The whole social process is pervaded by the causal relation which we call selective survival of potential capacity. There is no society that would not inevitably go to pieces but for this all-pervading principle to which every specific result and every relationship in any way considered as social can be referred for explanation.

The axiomatic qualities of the social nature or rather of the individual, as we know him in contrast with the community of which he is part, are defined by Carey—a too much neglected authority—as (1) the impulse to association up to a definite degree, (2) the estimate placed on individuality, (3) the sense of responsibility, and (4) the capacity for progress. All of these qualities of social man are normal and necessary phases of the more generic principle of selection of the conditions and the connections according to which survival becomes a matter of realization.

Social selection by the community of the typical quality in personality, of the normal conditions in nature, of the institutional relations in civilization and of the ideal ends among developmental possibilities, gives us the essential aspects of this process of development. We may consider it (1) from the standpoint of personality, or (2) from the standpoint of the axiomatic tendencies, or (3) from that of the community as an aggregate.

The selective principle is well brought out by conceiving of personality as occupying a point of view between the two great factors of the human development—nature and organized society—with respect to which typical groups of men make selective adjustment. The effect of this relationship is to develop a selective capacity in every such group and a corresponding selective foresight in the community. Natural conditions and organized society hold up before such a group the alternative of struggle with nature or of striving after solidarity with other groups in responsible activity.

Immanuel Kant has formulated this principle of the selective development of personality, individual and social, to show the process by which the principle of selection rises from a mere animal impulse to the rank of a controlling ideal. " The means by which nature has availed herself, in order to bring about the development of all the capacities of man, is the antagonism of those capacities to social organization, so far as the latter does necessitate their definite correlation. By antagonism, I here mean the unsociable sociability of mankind— that is, a combination in them of an impulse to enter into society, with a thorough spirit of opposition which constantly threatens to break up this society. The ground of this lies in human nature. Man has an inclination to enter into society, because in that state he feels that he becomes more a man, or, in other words, that his natural faculties develop. But he has also a great tendency to isolate himself, because he is, at the same time, aware of the unsocial peculiarity of desiring to have everything his own way; and thus, being conscious of an inclination to oppose others, he is naturally led to expect opposition from them.

" Now it is this opposition which awakens all the dormant powers of men, stimulates them to overcome their inclination to be idle, and, spurred by the love of honor, or power, or wealth, to make themselves a place among their fellows, whom they can neither do with, nor do without.

" Thus they make the first step from brutishness to culture, of which the social value of man is the measure. Thus all talents become gradually developed, taste is formed, and by continual enlightenment the foundations of a way of thinking are laid, which gradually changes the mere rude capacity of moral perception into determinate practical principles; and thus society, which is originated by a sort of pathological compulsion, becomes meta-morphosed into a moral unity." *

The grouping of persons in moral unity of type inevitably results in the development of axiomatic judgments which become the selective norms of social choice of the united body of persons. These norms of experience are then taken as the standards of the social mind in selective survival. It is by these standards that communities are guided, under the necessary conditions peculiar to associative life. In the simple social situation typicality is the di-rective principle; in the differentiation of social in-terests it is normality; in the assimilation of active social interests or tendencies under social order it is institutionality; and, in the solidarity of these tendencies, ideality becomes the prevailing prin-ciple of social procedure.

The sociological axioms therefore have to be reckoned among those selective principles by which the four organic tendencies of the community under the given conditions perform their respective functions. Tradition, adaptation, assimilation, sol-idarity are the standards by which personality ap-prehends the equilibrium between the social and the individual factors in personal efficiency. The social tendencies such as the amatory, the eco-nomic, the political and the ethical and religious, perform the organic functions in the evolution of the community by the guidance of axiomatic judg-ments.

* Quoted from Huxley's "Administrative Nihilism," pp. 75–76.

The relation of personality to the selective process of the community is not direct but through these tendencies. Here he finds the axioms of social choice for his class and condition in life. The selective problem of personality is to equate his degree of personal efficiency with the tendency that connects him most directly with the convictions of the community. Then his typical group or tendency becomes the organ of his choice. For each of us is affiliated with some typal tendency which in turn must be congruent with the sanctioned aims of the social consciousness that controls the system in which we live.

We are here concerned with defining the function of the sociological axioms as successive centers of choice by which typal tendencies are kept within organic limits. Hitherto, we have spoken mostly of these tendencies in their logical quality; but when the axioms have become conscious data to guide the choices of men in survival and in development, each tendency or group—traditional, adaptive, institutional and ideal or creative—exercises an authority over conduct within its limits. Every such tendency has its distinct psychological quality. The diffusion of that quality organizes the choices of its members for social action.

Social selection may be defined as the preference of the social process for the type that normally tends to prevail. This requires that every man adjust himself so as to be at equilibrium with that tendency which corresponds to his degree of efficiency, that each tendency be purposefully adjusted to the trend in the social mind which controls the social organization, and that the social organization be adaptable enough to meet the demands of its environment.

Typicality is survival by the selection of such associative relations as are required to bring one into equilibrium with the organic *type* sanctioned by the community. The traditional tendency in society is the special guardian of typicality. It is survival by selection of the comradeship of kindred.

Normality is survival by the selection of those conditions of existence to which one's *degree* of attainment corresponds, that is, the selection of that social interest, or such tendency as that in which one's degree of typal attainment finds its equilibrium and which is coordinated with the conviction of the community. Normality is survival by selection of the comradeship of capacity.

Institutionality is survival by the selection of those reciprocal relationships by which typal qualities and different degrees of development are assimilated to the social system tending toward individuation into a potentially more normal type. It is survival by the selection of responsibilities of social organization.

Ideality is survival by selection of that goal of achievement in which the individuation of the potentially more normal type tends progressively to find its equilibrium in the perfect type of personality. It is survival by selection of social possibilities as ends of life.

From these distinctions of the selective tendencies in association we may formulate the axiomatic principles of selective survival as follows:

1. The *selective survival* of personality in a simple social situation is *by typal imitation*—by conforming to the traditional tendency of organic imitation.

The effort of any man of given social and individual ratio of efficiency to find equilibrium with the community requires that the relation of the community with its conditions of existence be known. The relation of the community with the conditions of existence is expressed in the state of conviction in the social consciousness. This typal consciousness is a conviction as to what personal relations (sociality) and what modes of expression (symbolism) are consistent or inconsistent with the survival of the community.

This typal consciousness wrought into conviction is typicality. It affirms the average type of man it is capable of tolerating. Its enforcement is the function of the traditional tendency in the social mind. It represents the sum of increments of conviction as to what is consistent with the associative existence of beings of the given kind. It therefore becomes the first synthetic judgment with which the personal impulse to choose must reckon in the effort to find its equilibrium with the community or with any integral portion of it. We know a community best through the imitative tendencies by which it executes its categorical judgments in favor of its own traditions.

This selective impulse of man to arrive at or maintain an equilibrium with the community by that tendency whose type of personality is nearest kin to himself, is essentially an act or series of acts of typal imitation. Here the social impulse finds sway in sociality. Sociality is, as Tarde says,* imitativity. Not only of the feelings and the thoughts expressed, but also of the symbolic modes of expression, the same may be said. Selective survival under such circumstances consists of the imitation of type which has become the axiomatic key to that social tendency. It is the method and thus the causal principle at work to bring personality into equilibrium with the controlling quality of the community through the mechanism of that tendency to imitate the traditional type.

2. The *selective survival* of personality in a complex of social interests in any given community *is by normal adaptation*—adaptation to the conditions of survival in the community by affiliation with the adaptive tendency in social activity. Survival by normal adaptation requires that adjustment to circumstances or to that tendency with which one is most apt to find his degree of efficiency, provided that that tendency is congruent with the prevailing conviction of the community.

In the case of typal imitation as the mode of survival, personality was primarily social, and secondarily individual. In the case of normal adaptation personality's functions are relatively reversed —the individual in relation to nature is ascendant, the social is relatively subordinated and taken for

* Les lois de l'imitation, p. 78.

granted. Selective adaptation to conditions with which one's degree and ratio of personal efficiency correspond is normality. Normality requires the negation of what is other than normal in the relation of the personal member to his environment subjective and objective. The selection of the normal as the right relation and the rejection of the abnormal as incompatible with survival are both acts of selective foresight. By selecting the right social tendency a man is made by his society. Apart from the admonitory service of normal social tendencies no one could unaided find his equilibrium with environment. But he must choose with normal man lest the tide leave him ashore. Given any personality whose individual and social elements of efficiency are known, he must measure his actions to meet new conditions or circumstances for survival's sake. But there is only one possible way by which that survival can be continuously effected, namely, by being loyal to that tendency whose function among all others is that of adapting its members to conditions. The selective process not only requires man to be typical but to be normal. The development of personal capacity by adaptation brings out this inevitable differential.

In imitation the selection of a *qualitative object* as the standard of imitation was the object of choice. In the adaptation to conditions the selection of a *quantitative degree* involves the choice of differentials. Typal selection was by personal imitation of a common standard or type; normal adaptation is by individual discrimination between the actual and the potentially more normal typal conditions, that is, by the discovery and choice of that differential in adaptation by the selection of which and its incorporation into the conditions of existence, that type increases its chances of survival.

3. The *selective survival* of personality in any system of competing typal tendencies *is by institutional assimilation.*

The third axiomatic aspect of selective survival is the choice of institutional agencies. This is conditioned upon the prior development of imitative quality and of adaptability in us, through the agency of the traditional and the adaptive tendencies. Through imitation of a homogeneous type a typal self or likeness is consciously realized by which the community becomes possessed of social convictions to which its members conform. Through normal adaptation to environing conditions differences in individual capacity, that is, degrees of personal efficiency are developed. These two tendencies—one to conformity to the actual or traditional type and the other urging adaptation to potential type—compete for the control of the social process. The past and the present meet in rivalry for the control of the future.

Under these conditions those convictions upon which men think and feel alike, become organized into *the institutions of social order.* They set the seal of social sanction upon the relations regarded as normally necessary for association. The sexual relation becomes the established institution of wedlock, *because* it is normally necessary for selective survival of the type regarded as congruent with the community's convictions respecting its kind. So too the other institutions of the social system act as assimilative agencies of typal tendencies, resulting in the individuation of both imitative and adaptive tendencies into an institutional tendency.

On the other hand those convictions upon which the social consciousness is at variance in the community become the *institutions of individual progress.* Progress comes to the community by a diffusion of *individual* conviction of the potential type of attainment throughout the community until it becomes part of the conviction of social mind. All progress is first individual, then social; first potential then actual in the choices of men. All order is first social and then individual. Order is the result of social selection; progress is the result of individual selection. Institutions serve as transformers of the individual into the social and of the social into the individual. Institutional assimilation makes selection of the typal qualities common to the community *plus* the differentiated capacities peculiar to its more normal individuals; the outcome of which is not only a reciprocally established relation between the traditional and the adaptive tendencies, and the individual and the social impulses, but a still more normal type of personality as the selective result of assimilation of the actual and potential toward the ideal. Personal survival under these circumstances is by selection of the institutional method of equilibrium between the two typal tendencies to socializing order and to the individualizing effects of progress upon personality, by which there tends to arise a new individuation in the direction of the ideal.

4. The *selective survival* of personality in a progressive social system of complemental typal tendencies is *by ideal individuation.*

The final axiom of selective survival is ideality, under which the perfectly coordinated nexus of typal tendencies, each with its contribution to the progressive social system, tends to find its equilibrium. We pass from the competing to the complemental system of tendencies in passing from the institutional to the ideal standard of selection.

The enrichment of the social consciousness through the tendency to wider or more varied . adaptation to individual effort together with the facility with which the actual passes on into the potential type of achievement, not only proves the inadequacy of any social order of institutions as a finality in human evolution, but makes it inevitable that ideal systems of association should be conceived of as attainable. It is said of Thomas Jefferson that he spent his life reducing his idealities to realities. This faith in the perfect type as achievable is precisely the axiomatic relation of personality to these authoritative norms of our social life. But such achievements if ever personally realized, cannot rest there. They must be socialized. In the socialization of the ideal we really reconstruct society. In the words of Martensen, " It is an illusion constantly recurring that the aim of history lies first and foremost in outward conditions, circumstances and institutions, instead of lying within man himself. . . . Human orders of society—the Family, the State, nay even the Church in its earthly constitution,—are only temporary forms which must be broken down when perfection arrives." *

Ideality as an axiom of selection appears only when the community of a potentially perfect social organization is prefigured to the social mind, into which on given conditions the actual community is deemed capable of passing. These conditions have to be sought in the progressive proposals of the apparently rival but really complemental revelations of science and religion. Each of these in its own way inspires the social consciousness to the conviction of the possibility of passing from the actual through the potential into the ideal in typal realization. The nearer science and religion bring the social consciousness to reverence the same ideal type the more will these great revelations become complemental.

Enough has been said to show that the sociological axioms, each in its own sphere, are centers of selective relationships governing the survival of personality in association with its kind. But these selective centers of association indicate to us the principles also which govern the progressive development of the community.

Enough has been said also to indicate the part that the social tendencies play in the evolution of man. Selective survival is by affiliation of person-

* Martensen, Christian Ethics (General), p. 139. Clark Translation.

ality with the type in which the community finds its normal equilibrium. The normal equilibrium is to be found by identifying one's self with the social tendencies which are consistent with the judgments of the community. The consistent convictions of the community are given us in the sociological axioms.

Personality is therefore coordinated with the convictions of the community through the intermediation of the axiomatic tendencies, each of which is the exponent of some organic function of the community, and all of which potentially converge in the ideal type of development toward which the social process moves.

The selective principles of personal survival by axiomatic association are therefore

1. Typal Imitation.
2. Normal Adaptation.
3. Institutional Assimilation.
4. Ideal Individuation.

Inasmuch as all principles or laws are expressions of hypothetical tendencies among phenomena, each of these principles can be given a tentative form of statement which is tendentially true as a statement of the relations peculiar to the social process.

1. The principle of typal imitation may be tentatively formulated for the simple social situation: In any simple social situation the tendency to survival by typal imitation varies directly with the degree of typal integration regarded as requisite for survival, and inversely with the ratio of the indi-

vidual to the social units of efficiency. Or, the process of typal imitation varies directly with the difference between any organic type and the social type normal to the situation and inversely as the ratio of these two types.*

2. The principle of normal adaptation may be tentatively formulated for the social interests as follows: The general process of normal adaptation to environment varies directly with the capacity of any tendency to differentiate itself from the common interests of the community and inversely with the capacity to integrate the membership of the community to that tendency in which each member tends to find his normal equilibrium with his kind and through this tendency with the community as a whole. More briefly, the process of normal adaptation in any particular tendency varies directly with the difference between its social and its sociological type and inversely with the ratio of these two types.

3. The principle of institutional assimilation is tentatively formulated for the social system as follows: The general tendency to institutional assimilation among the social tendencies in any social

---

* A fractional ratio is used to indicate the individual and social elements of value in any type of personality, the numerator serving as the individual and the denominator as the social elements of value. If $\frac{6}{10}$ equals the value of a type normally at equilibrium in a social situation, $\frac{5}{10}$ and $\frac{4}{10}$ may represent two organic types one of which is only $\frac{2}{3}$ and the other only $\frac{1}{3}$ developed as compared with the normal standard. The ratios of these two typal values correspond to the degrees of development in the respective types.

system varies directly with the degree of efficiency of any organic typal tendency to assimilate itself with the potentially normal type of personality toward which the social system tends, and inversely with the ratio of integrating to differentiating efficiency. Briefly stated, the assimilation of any social tendency with the social system varies directly with the difference between the social type of that tendency and the sociological type of the social system and inversely as the ratio between these two types.

4. The principle of ideal individuation may be tentatively formulated as the law of the social mind within a given social system, as follows: The tendencies to ideal individuation of type vary directly with the difference between the sociological and the ideal type and inversely as the ratio of these two typal values.

CHAPTER XIV.

THE SELECTIVE SURVIVAL OF SOCIOLOGICAL TYPES.

EVERY science presents two kinds of problems; the first, to determine the particular causal relations; the second, to coordinate all such relations into a self-consistent system which will unify all separate and individual instances.* In the previous chapter we pointed out those causal relations which prevail within a series of postulated conditions necessary for survival. Now we proceed to coordinate this series of logical relations under a single sociological hypothesis—the selective survival of sociological types, as the fundamental law of the developmental process.

The term law in its logical sense always has one unvarying meaning—a universally valid hypothesis by means of which the phenomena under consideration find rational explanation. In its scientific sense its fundamental meaning is that of an observed order of events in which are coordinated a set of particular causal relations or principles into a self-consistent system. Lotze presents these two aspects of the same idea when he says, " In theo-

* Hibben, Inductive Logic, Chap. XVIII., pp. 281-7.

retical investigation of reality we mean by a law the expression of the particular inward relation which exists between two facts and constitutes the ground at once of their conjunction and of the manner of their conjunction." This is the logical aspect of the meaning of law. The other aspect— the scientific—is much nearer to the thought of every-day life. " In practical life," says the same authority, " a law determines a state which is to be brought about."

By putting these two statements together we may include both the logical and the scientific conception of law in the same fundamental definition. Thus our definition should stand as follows: A law is a statement of an intelligible connection pervading things by which on given conditions a different state of things comes to pass.

There are two distinguishable parts in this conception of law. *First,* there is the fact of a uniform connection usually called the hypothesis by the assumption of which to be true we explain why and how it is that under the same circumstances things remain as they are. *Secondly,* there is the change of conditions on the occurrence of which one state of things takes the place of another state of things. All laws of a fundamental character are hypothetical and must be expressed in conditional terms. In order to reduce any set of phenomena to rational explanation we have not only to account for a pervading uniformity by assuming a prevailing relation—the *coexistence* of two facts or states; but we have also to account for the occurrence of change—the *sequence* of one fact, state or event upon another. The first of these—the uniform coexistence of men under types of character in successive conditions of human association—was given in the sociological postulates. The second —the explanation of the sequence of one type upon another—was given in the sociological axioms.

We may conveniently express this coexistence in the formulæ,

$C = E$, that is, if C occurs E is sure to occur; or $C^1 = E^1$, that is, if C^1 occurs E^1 is sure to occur.

We may express this sequence by asking what it is that, if added to or taken from C will bring E^1 to pass and thus give us the state of things expressed in $C^1 = E^1$. What is $C - C^1$ equal to, apart from E^1, as the incremental or differential factor in the situation ? The discovery and formulation of law requires us therefore (1) to find an *hypothesis* which will explain an actual coexistence of facts comprising a given situation, and (2) to define or measure this *differential* which will explain why one existing nexus gives place to another succeeding one.

This strictly logical conception of law is applicable to theoretical investigation in sociology. If $C =$ the conditions of existence under which any social type E exists, then $C = E$ expresses exactly the equilibrium between the given social type and its normal conditions of existence for the time being. That is, $C = E$ is an expression for the typical group—the nexus within which the coexistence of C and E occurs and for which there must be some cause. $C^1 = E^1$ is a second step in a series of social situations of which the same can be said. $C^2 = E^2$ is a third, $C^3 = E^3$ a fourth, and so on to $C^n = E^n$ in each of which the same problem occurs—of suggesting an hypothesis by the assumption of which each coexistence will have received a satisfactory explanation. This is the first part of the problem in the formulation of sociological law. But as yet the hypothesis is assumed to be valid only for each typal nexus: we want an hypothesis valid for the series of typical groups of persons to which they all owe a common allegiance.

That requisite will appear in the search for the differential element. Here we have a series of differentials representing a consecutive series of changes in the social process; C changes to C^1, and E to survive is disengaged from C and projects a potentially normal life for itself, $C^1 = E^1$, into which it passes to find a new equilibrium. Thus we have a series of *actual* situations corresponding to a series of *potential* situations; the differential in each case represents the change which must occur in the conditions of existence of the type in one social state in order to impel it to project a potential social state into which it must pass to arrive at the new equilibrium which awaits it. The social type E^1, seeing that its environing conditions C^1 have changed to C^2, is required to project a potential social type E^2 to which E^1 will succeed when it has passed over to C^2 and actualized the potential type by ceasing to be E^1 and becoming E^2. The same or similar transition occurs in each member of the series until C^n has finally impelled E^{n-1} to pass over into the potential type which will bring E^n at equilibrium with C^n.

Now this differential between the actual social type and the potential type is the pivotal point to be grasped in this conception of the social process and the formulation of the process into the sociological law of the development of types.

The statement of sociological law requires us therefore to include not only this bond of connection between the actual condition and the social type in any situation $(C = E)$ and the sociological type, but also this tendency of the social type, on condition of change in the actual surroundings, to give the preference to the potential social situation over the actual social situation which has been discounted by a dislodging process of change.

It would seem that the first of these requirements is to be met in the assumption that under the conditions of natural association where the type is realized the social type E *selects* that social situation or condition C within which, on penalty of becoming abnormal and being eliminated for failure to select, it may find its equilibrium, and that this is sufficient to account for the coexistence of C and E. And it would seem equally adequate, if we were to account for the transition of the social type E over into the potential type E^1 by assuming the capacity in E to rationally *project a potential state* E^1

into which E, in the event of impending change in its once normal conditions of existence, might pass over, as a requisite of survival into a theoretically more normal social state, thus selecting the *differential* element which makes the potential equilibrium a realizable one.

The capacity of personality in common with his fellows of kindred type to select this potential differential requisite for equilibrium as a normal mode of development out of one type, condition, situation, into another is the fundamental induction under which all other typal relations find their rightful unity. The formal ratio of the social to the sociological type is the fundamental relation in the process of social development.

But the *selection*, by the actual type, of the normal differential as the potential requisite of equilibrium is not enough. The social type must *individuate* the relation; that is, it must make itself master of that changed relation by assimilation of the differential element into the social type of personality which tends to prevail. The direction of the assimilative process must be from the organic toward the *ideal* type. Development of social types is by the constant selection of the differential between the social type and the sociological type in order to normalize the type to new circumstances. The typical group that continuously individuates the results of that experience is sure of social development.* In a word, the law of social

* Fouillée, Education from the National Standpoint, Ch. IV. International Education Series.

development is survival by selective striving to realize the potentially normal type. Individuals survive by selection of the typical ; social tendencies survive by selection of the normal ; communities or other groups that make up social aggregates survive by the selection of the organic or institutional. The selection of the potentially more normal type by the social mind leads the social process from the level of mere animality toward the ideal. Logically, therefore, the *selective connection* between the social and the sociological type and the appropriation of the *right differentials* are the essentials of the law of social development.

From the side of logical analysis and inductive synthesis this law of selective development would seem to follow from what has hitherto been said. But do the ordinary facts of our experience justify us in accepting any such an hypothesis ? By a series of postulates we have defined the several conditions under which the given facts of social development—the survival of social types by the selection of the potential—are alone conceivable as subject to this law. The sociological postulates of the simple social situation, the social interests, the social order and the social mind, together with the conditional principles of integration, differentiation, assimilation and solidarity, did not, however, go so far as to suggest on what *one comprehensive condition* all of these conditions of development could be satisfactorily accounted for. According to the postulates, if we have given us the organic type of the human species, with a capacity to dis-

criminate between more and less normal conditions
of survival, to organize institutional relations and to
work by an ideal norm, between the generic and
the perfect example, then we can by the aid of our
logical powers lay down the conditions under
which the reality of a developmental process is
conceivable as pervading the whole world of human
association.   But it is quite another thing to suggest that comprehensive supposition which will put
the reasoning mind in such a position that the
separate areas of conditions and relations which
have been postulated will no longer be regarded as
simply conceivable conditions, but which, from
that hypothetical point of view, must thenceforth
be regarded as belonging to the phenomena that
are *hypothetically explainable* under all conditions.
And this is exactly what the law of the selective
survival of sociological types seems to do—it em-
braces all the facts of social reality in one self-consistent suggestion.   And, besides furnishing us
with this first requisite of a logical hypothesis—by
adequately accounting for the phenomena of human development—it fully meets the other requisites by coordinating into a consistent whole the
postulated conditions.   The residual contradiction
in each typical group—family, class, community,
nation—drove us on to the next, toward the ideal,
and forced us thus to seek for some underlying explanation.   The absence of any such contradictions
in the theory of the selective survival of sociological types compels us to consent to it as a form in

which we may think rationally of the entire social life.

A universal law must, therefore, square itself (1) with the series of working postulates or conditions without which we cannot think of phenomena in the form in which they are presented to us, and (2) with the differential content of these axiomatic experiences in association. The first of these requirements we deem ourselves as having met in defining the conditions of social development. By the definition of these conditions we have shown how under natural association the social process evolves types of personality. The typical group passes from the actual to the potential and thus ascends to the ideal from the organic type, by successive selection of developmental axioms. And this is without in any wise being inconsistent with the real processes of thought and things as we must conceive of them in all our thinking and doing. Logically regarded, then, this hypothesis seems to have left no impediment in the way of our entertaining it as a universal law for the explanation of social phenomena in terms of types.

But is it equally free from suspicion on the side of the facts of our social existence ? Do we find a selective sense at work there ? Does the social type select the potential type as the compass of its guidance ? Do our social institutions regard such a selective relation ? Are our social feelings attuned to typal standards ? Are our emotional impulses governed by such criteria ? Do the reflective conclusions of the social mind find expres-

sion in typal tendencies that survive by virtue of
selecting the potentially normal equilibrium within
which the community is aware of its conscious
strength, and restless in the sense of its weakness
until it tends to attain thereto ?   Or is this whole
theory of social reality a fiction of fictions which
belies the facts as they are to be seen from observation of our social system ?   We have shown how it
is conditionally conceivable.   We have explained
by what means the results are possible.   Is it compatible with the axiomatic judgments which sustain our social life ?   It agrees with our logical
conceptions of the objective aspect of the social
process: does it accord with the content of these
conceptions as it is given to us in social experience ?   This, really, is the whole question.   The
content of our social experience is given in the
sociological axioms.   The typical, the normal, the
assimilable and the ideal are the objects of ceaseless selection in history.   They are the resources
of our development.   Do we in our every-day associations live by selecting the typical, by adjusting
the typical to the normal, by assimilating the increments of the experience of change into established
types of character, and do these rejuvenated types
tend to select the ideal ?   If so, then we have the
law of social development in the selective capacity
of social man to keep alive before himself the potentially normal choice anywhere between the
organic and the ideal level of social living.

    If our living together really depends upon the
trustworthiness of typical qualities and axiomatic

relations, an analysis of our social experience ought to help us far on toward a reasonable answer. We know, for instance, that the moment we step into a community, or come to some understanding with another of our own species, there arises a result which we call a social relation. If we advance into the community our relations thicken, or multiply. We are soon beset with ruling connections, upon which, regardless of our own disposition, there is a common way of thinking and feeling and acting. That is, we discover that in this community there is a prevailing way and also a will of its own, the fact of which is a reality to their mode of existence. This may take the form of an intuitive or habitual manner, a conventional propriety, an institutional system or an ideal authority. But it is part of the logical equipment of the community in any or all phases of development.*

If we extend our acquaintance with its members one by one, or class by class, we soon discover that the acts of some are governed largely by what others do and say; in other words, we see that certain ideas are current and prevail. If we trace these ideas to their source and ask who vouches for them particularly we shall not fail to find that certain persons or classes are the recognized representatives of these phases of thought, feeling and will among their fellows. Upon further inquiry into the grounds of this fact we ultimately reach the

* Durkheim, La Methode Sociologique, Chs. I., II. Paris, 1895.

conclusion that these ruling ideas in the custody of the community are regarded as an indispensable condition of men's living together in society. In proof of this it is enough, in the first place, to observe that whoever attempted to depart materially from the accepted modes of life and thought would be quite likely to discover that there really existed apart from himself or from any single individual a social force or forces positive and effective enough to be properly regarded in theory or practice as the general will. This is the fact of normality to·the existing conditions reappearing in a preventive form. For, the too open and radical departure from its typical standard, accepted as a normal requisite of survival, must result in the suspension of the social activities of the individual transgressor by reason of this disturbance of the normal relationships. Persecution, expulsion, involuntary migration and ostracism are but ordinary illustrations of this species of social reaction in favor of that logical reality—the type of personality which is normally at equilibrium with the mind of the community and with the objective condition of its existence.

In the second place, we should find that this condition of association which insists on normality of type, both in relation to the conviction of the community and to the conditions of objective life, then and there prevalent, has fortified and economized its resources by the institution of accredited agencies of administration. These give force, efficiency and directness to the general convictions logically wrought out of the experience of the community. Designated individuals or classes are selected to serve as exponents of the same general consensus of experience. Under such conditions of living it is inevitable that there should be developed types of personality in more or less complete harmony with the conditions in the midst of which they live.

A social type always represents an equilibrium either in fact or tendency. This equilibrium is the point at which personality in associative relations with the community balances itself between the conviction of the community on the one hand and the objective conditions of survival on the other. This equilibrium once found other persons are integrated thereto and the type arises. How does the social type, or any particular typal tendency, with which personality is thus integrated, keep the highway of normality and thus succeed in surviving progressively between the upper millstone of the social conviction and the nether millstone of objective conditions in nature? The limits of sociological law are between the organic and the ideal types.

We have to look in two directions for our solutions. From the side of natural history organic types appear and prosper. What is the way by which biology, for example, accounts for typal survival and development? The evolutionary process usually accounts for continuity of type by the theory of heredity—the theory that the same or similar marks tend to be reproduced from parent to offspring. The same process explains variety of type by the effects of environment requiring adaptation to its changes and consequent departure from the unity of type. But the organic type of biology is the generic datum of sociology. And our problem is not biological but historical and logical. Given a member of the human species in association, as the organic type of physical structure; let him be so situated as to have simultaneously to adjust himself, in order to live, both to the conviction of the community as his psychical milieu, and also to the demands of his physical environment; what other outcome could there be either in tendency or in fact than a typal equilibrium which is the result of progressive or rather successive selection of the potentially more normal type as the logically necessary result short of elimination? That is to say, that, if under these circumstances there be survival of the organic type now taken up into the social situation, and if there be a social tendency which has both to reckon with the categorical convictions of the community and with the sturdy conditions of external existence, then, personality being what it is, and knowing as we do what it tends to be, there can be no other outcome. This outcome is logically and historically inevitable—that personality constructs in ceaseless succession hypothetical types of personality as the logical answer to the demand on the part of social conviction and natural conditions for a potentially more normal social organization of life. The sociological type is not a composite picture of the requisites of survival. It is the potential *ensemble* of all that goes to make up a more normal society. A proposed line of development is alone calculable by personality on the basis of past experience registered in the typical character, supplemented by the assumption of the reality of the potentially normal type. A category of development which man can hypothecate out of the content of his experience with his kind and with his natural conditions is a logical necessity.

The sociological type, which social man selects in accord with the suggestion of the sum of his experience, is the deepest function of this experience. It appears as a categorical nexus thrown out in advance of attainment by the typal consciousness, speculatively as it were. In it are focused all the elements of man's conscious capacity to arrive at a potential order of association upon which to set his seal of conviction. In the intenser moments and the trying stages of the race, of the people, of the classes, of the personality that lives with and leads the multitude, it is " a cloud by day and a pillar of fire by night." It is the companion of every one, vague and even fictitious to the dull of heart it is true, but still the object of effort to most men; the hope of society in times of unrest, but the social counterpart of every being who has any part in the winning of his fellow-beings on to the solidarity of our social life in the potentially normal type of man.

We can only appeal to the selective genius of the species in association to verify the reality of this connection between the actual and the potential as a universal relation to which we give the name of law because under it all the principles of social choice find their unity. Typal integration, variation, assimilation and solidarity are conditional aspects of the selection of the potential by the actual types.

The other part of our answer takes us back to the discussion of the sociological axioms. Does the law of the selective relation of the actual and potential types agree with these settled judgments of social experience ? Social types, that is, men of a like kind in associative quality—organic likeness being granted—keep the track of development by being axiomatic, by respecting the series of judgments with which man in association is instinct. Whether instinctively, intuitively, emotionally or reflectively, the type that survives at all tends to prevail by progressive assimilation of men to the *potentially normal.* How shall we distinguish this from the actual type ?

The distinction between any social type and the type that normally tends to prevail is the *axiomatic differential* between the social and the sociological types. He who conforms to the axiom of typicality survives by the imitation of the objective or subjective (logical) standard of equilibrium. But the social or typal conviction may so change its tendencies or the change in conditions may require a readjustment such as to leave a wide gap between the type imitated and the type normally tending to prevail. Here is a task of selective calculation or discriminative selection that is vital to the member of society, to a social tendency or the community at all times. The nation, for example, that does not see its meaning and adapt itself accordingly goes on imitating what tends to become a sub-normal type and is in danger of extinction. Adaptation to the tendency of the potentially normal type is the only way of regarding this change rightly. And this can only be done by determining the value of the axiomatic differentials. The typal consciousness normally is always active in the determination of this key to the ever-changing life of the type—the typal differential. This axiomatic differential is the difference, for example, between an outgrown domestic code and the demands of new conditions of existence upon family life. Or, if, after normal adaptation by one class, new or changed relations between the class and the community arise, the axiomatic differential indicates the elements of order that should be institutionalized. The axiomatic differential is the difference that is worth assimilating and diffusing throughout the popular life. It is that which makes a people richer in wisdom and clearer in its power of prevision. The burden of development always falls first upon sensitive souls, because they are taught by the spirit that tends to be.

The law of social choices must aid us in giving right values to these intimations. If this can be done, then the elements of strength can be socially assimilated and the factors of weakness be eliminated. Otherwise revolutions must supplant evo-

lutions. The axiomatic differential is the pilot of
the social process.

If the social type be located at x—in Fig. 9—the
limit of survival at equilibrium by typal imitation—
the potentially normal tendency of the community
takes the direction of x^1 then the axiomatic differential would be represented by xx^1, and we determine its value by defining to ourselves $1x^1$ which

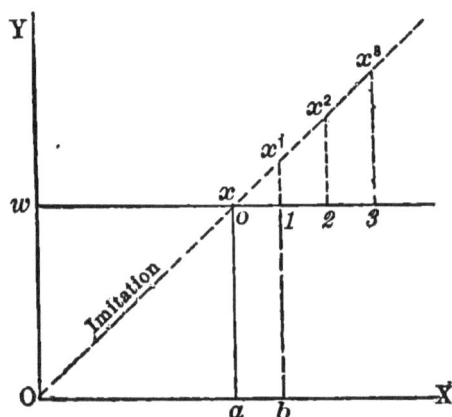

FIG. 9.

represents the changes in subjective qualities (sociality), and $o1$ which represents the changes in the
objective conditions (symbolism). So likewise,
with each of the other differentials, we measure the
changes in circumstances by defining the qualitative and the conditioning factors that are demand-
ing a transition in the life of the type as it has become known to us. Thus we determine the differential which dislodges the typically normal by finding out the changes in subjective qualities which we
call custom (conventionality) and the changes in
the objective conditions which we call property.

These enable us to locate the typical group with respect to the institutional tendency by which that state of society is controlled. This tendency may be military, industrial or religious. The subjective elements of order and the objective elements of progress enable us to calculate the differential in the tendency of institutions as they affect the type of character with respect to the ideal, by detecting the changes as they record themselves in the behavior of the type. So the changes in religion and scientific knowledge enable us to anticipate the trend of ideality in the spirit of a people, a class, an institution or an age.

By conceiving of the social process as one governed by the selective anticipations of the potentially normal course of associative effort, and then expressing that policy in the form of the type that tends to prevail, we put the whole social process in terms of a scientific experiment and make social evolution a calculable tendency.

The selection and use of the axiomatic differential is a perfectly scientific procedure both in theory and in practice. Here we can pass from the known (the social type) to discover the scientifically probable event (potentially normal type) in case of changes. For scientific thought is the recognition of an observed order of events by the aid of which we apply past experience to new circumstances. The new circumstances are the axiomatic differentials as shown by comparison of the actual with the potentially normal type. The past experience is given in the disturbed equilibrium of the actual type. The observed order of events is the selective connection between the type and the requisites of survival for the type that normally tends to prevail. It is an observed order of selective development by idealizing the potential.

We may state this in another way: The evolution of personality in association under all circumstances consists in the individuation by the actual type of the differential which brings man into equilibrium with the type that normally tends to prevail.

The essential character of the law of selective survival of types has now been sufficiently defined. We have yet to define the *limits* within which the law is operative, because like all universal laws it is conditioned upon the presence of the qualities, conditions and relations from which the law itself is an inductive generalization.

Moreover, it must be shown why, according to this law, typal *devolution* and *extinction* are destined to occur in the social process; that is, under what conditions does the selective survival of the potentially normal types cease, and the selective function divert its choices toward ends that lead away from the straight and narrow path of typal normality ? Or, does the selective function ever cease to select at all, contenting itself with the situation it holds, until the capacity to advance toward the ideal is lost through the malady of disuse, and the impotence of the community leaves its memory to decay because neither history nor nature has any possible fellowship with it ?

The selective survival of sociological types is the logically formulated law of the societary process. Taking this law as the theoretical aspect of the subject,* the process finds in this hypothesis the law of social progress in relation to nature and civilization. Nature gives us the organic limits and civilization the ideal limits of typal selection. Social progress consists in the capacity of human association to assimilate the differential increments of social value in the direction of the ideal. Progress is a typal tendency by differential increments graduated from the organic to the ideal type.

From the side of nature we have progress secured by pressure for selection of the more normal conditions of survival on penalty of elimination of the type that ceases to select; or, after selecting, is impotent to enter into its projected conditions of life. Nature provides no nurse for impotence apart from a brief infancy. Civilization is fundamentally sympathetic.

From the side of civilization we have progress impelled by a conscious sense of the promise of perfection. Between this pressure to select which nature puts on social man and this promise to become perfect which man offers to himself, the whole scope of progress lies with all its actualities and its possibilities.

Natural selection in the long run simply selects the *materials* with which social selection has to work, if it works at all on its own account. If it does not work at all, natural selection simply sees

* Supra, Ch. I., p. 25, B.

to it that the abnormal does not control the social process. But where social selection involves social self-consciousness and with that the cognizance of potentialities of typal attainment, we have a species of selection the distinctive feature of which is the choice of *methods* by which nature's supply of materials is to be utilized for the attainment of self-selected ends. This is the aspect with which the social process is concerned, in the main, among civilized nations; so that for them natural selection may or may not be involved in social progress, except in the sense that society being conditioned upon the cosmic process social selection is conditioned upon natural selection, as two terms in a selective ratio.

Now what does natural selection supply as materials for the social process to utilize through its conscious methods to attain its ends ? Nature at least supplies society with organic types in which there is a more or less definite ratio of structure to function. It also supplies in some form or other the means by which the given organic types may survive by adaptation to their conditions of existence. The appetite for food and the sexual impulse, by the birth of enormous numbers in the absence of parental care, and in case of parental solicitude by the birth of a comparatively few of the species *—these together with the growth of the familial instinct, which exists among the greater

---

* Letourneau, The Evolution of Marriage, Ch. II., pp. 20, 34. Darwin, Origin of Species, Ch. IV., pp. 127–30; Ch. VI., pp. 205–6.

number of vertebrates and among many inverte-
brates, are aspects of natural selection whose end
is the preservation or perpetuation of the organic
type.*

It will appear that, in answer to these questions,
the limits of selective survival of potentially normal
types are at any time to be found between (1) the
ideal that tends to prevail in the form of the religious and scientific tendencies of the existing civilization at any place in the pale of association, and
(2) the organic type of personality which the conviction of the community is willing to tolerate as
the personal unit of its organization. All others it
lets go to the wall by the least painful way possible.
The maximum limit of selective survival of the
sociological type is reached when the typal tendency is ultra-ideal in any stage of development;
beyond that the community ceases to hear or read
the message of a higher life for its members. The
ideal then offered is neither imitable, adaptable, nor
appropriable by that type of personality. The minimum limit of selective survival is reached when the
organic type loses its capacity to be typical, that is,
ceases to be socially organic and is incapable therefore of becoming the basis of any individuation of
ideal qualities. That is, it cannot develop with its
kind.

Those familiar with the social tendencies of modern life will not fail to recognize the entire agreement of this theory of selective survival by faith in

* Romanes, Darwin and After Darwin, Vol. I., pp. 264-70.

typal normality as an attainable aim of the social
process in general and of its most active social tendencies in particular. " The reality of this selective
capacity," says Caird, " this guiding organon effecting the synthesis of social life—is the essential
truth in all social reactions and reorganizations.
Men believe in their capacity to enter into a realization to which they are entitled by being men. This
. . . capacity may be overestimated or be an illusion, but it is none the less real, as a causative force
in social history." Referring to Rousseau—as one
of the prophets of the sociological type of potential attainment of personality in normal association
—the same writer observes, " By such writers the
mere *capacity* of man for a higher life is treated as
if it were the higher life itself; and it is forgotten
the capacity is nothing unless it be realized, and
that its realization requires the surrender of individual liberty and private judgment to the guidance
and teaching of those in whom realization has already taken place. But it is none the less true that
the consciousness of the capacity, and consequently
of the duty, of becoming not merely a slave or an
instrument, but an organ of the intellectual and
moral life of mankind, is the essential basis of modern life." *

The selective survival of potential types then
goes on within definite limits set by the nature of
the factors involved. Just what, then, within the
limits of natural pressure and spiritual perfection,

* Edw. Caird, Social Philosophy and Religion of Comte,
p. 199.

does the social process do with the materials at its
disposal ? We have said that the selective individuation of a normally required differential is the
mark of human progression. This would seem to
imply that with the organic type given by natural
selection to the social life of man there is something
to be done which is different from what the natural
process has done. That something is individuation
of the differential in the direction of the ideal, or
the potential in the direction of the ideal, at any
given time and place in the social order.

If this orderly selection, and individuation of the
organic type, with the potentially more normal in-
crement in the direction of the ideal, be the fundamental law of the social process regarded as progressively selective, then the method by which potentially normal survival is realized is that of functional selection, on the part of the social types of
personality, of that axiomatic differential which—
among all possible differentials capable of contrib-
uting to the sociological equilibrium—lies next in
the direction of the ideal. The hypothetical law
thus formulated may be finally stated as follows:
*The social type normally tends to prevail by func-
tional selection of the next axiomatic differential
that is potentially assimilable in the direction of the
typal ideal.*

From this way of conceiving of the law of selective survival of sociological types it must be easily
inferable why communities die, why classes disappear, why families become extinct, why nations and
peoples disintegrate and cease to function in the

creative movements of human history. To the law of survival and development by the selection of the potentially normal or sociological type of realization there is no exception. To cease to select the potentially attainable is to cease to develop; and to cease to develop is to prepare to die. The selective capacity may be impaired in many ways, but principally either by severing the typal consciousness of any social tendency or function from connection with or *interest in the ideal* or by defects in the organic character of personality as a social being. This is the case particularly with the adaptive types of the population. If the institutional machinery of selection be beyond their reach or operated in the interest of other types, and the ideals of the times be too remote for participation by the adaptive types, then these types, whose proximity to nature is closest, instead of becoming more selective in their social capacity, tend to survival by the law of natural selection. The law of survival by selecting typal normality is in force as long as choice of personality is possible. It is possible so long as the construction of the sociological type is not a mockery or a meaningless thing to consciousness. It is not a mockery so long as the typal consciousness is capable of conceiving it and using it for the control of action in the direction of the ideal.

The other way by which the selective capacity of the community, or any tendency organically part thereof is impaired, is by gradual *deterioration of the organic types* of personality which served as the materials of the social process. The physical type is primarily a matter within natural selection. Sexual selection is an aspect of social selection as well as of natural selection; but the idealizing social consciousness can only reach it to elevate and enlighten its choices by means of the infusion of the ideal into the animal selection. Without such infusion of the ideal the process of typal imitation, in its simplest and most elementary form of integration by the child copying the character and conduct of the adult parent, is short-lived and totally inadequate as a basis for building the nobler types of a highly-conscious civilization. As soon as the household ceases to be the unitary mechanism of selection, by reason of the organic defects in its physical or psychical character, society at that point begins to die at its roots. Normal adaptation becomes inadequate, typal assimilation is impotent in the individuation of new types, and the heavens of social ideals hang low, like the heavy mists of Bœotia, upon the social mind.

Normally, social selection by types requires that organically sound types shall serve as the starting-point and the imitative standards of the social process. Hence we admire athletes rather than scholars in educational life. The organic types of personality are the materials of selection which nature furnishes. Hence the development is conditioned upon nature for the organic materials of the evolution, however ideal its end. The organic quality of personality as a social being determines the height toward which our ideal types of life can attain.

On the other hand history in its broadest, or

civilization in the subjective sense, is the source of the ideas by which the social process in its selective character is influenced. The union of both in the selective process is necessary for normal evolution of types. We must regard this process as preeminently a process of the present tense, organizing its factors—its conditions and its forces—from nature beneath and from history around or within us. Selection coordinates with precision all the elements of past and present that we give it upon the sociological type of the future.

Survival by selection of historical forces unnurtured by the close connection with the conditioning factors in nature strengthens the type ideally but weakens it organically and tends to produce an ultra-social product. The tendency of history apart from nature is to eliminate these ultra or extremely social types. The tendency of history apart from nature is to produce a sub-social product and thus to eliminate this sub-social or extremely individual type. The selective process takes its course toward the potential by the individuation of both the conditions of nature and the forces of history in the type that normally tends to prevail. Selection is a social capacity of the community equally dependent upon history and nature.

If at a, in Fig. 10, in the social situation YOX. the selection of historical forces and natural conditions forms an equilibrium, the persons thus actually situated will be socially typical; but if the historical forces are selected for survival and the natural conditions relatively ignored, then an *ultra-*

typal tendency *(ab)* sets in. If natural conditions
preponderate at *a*, a sub-typal tendency sets in *(ac)*.
O^1 is the potentially normal type to be attained by
development.

If the preponderance of historical considerations

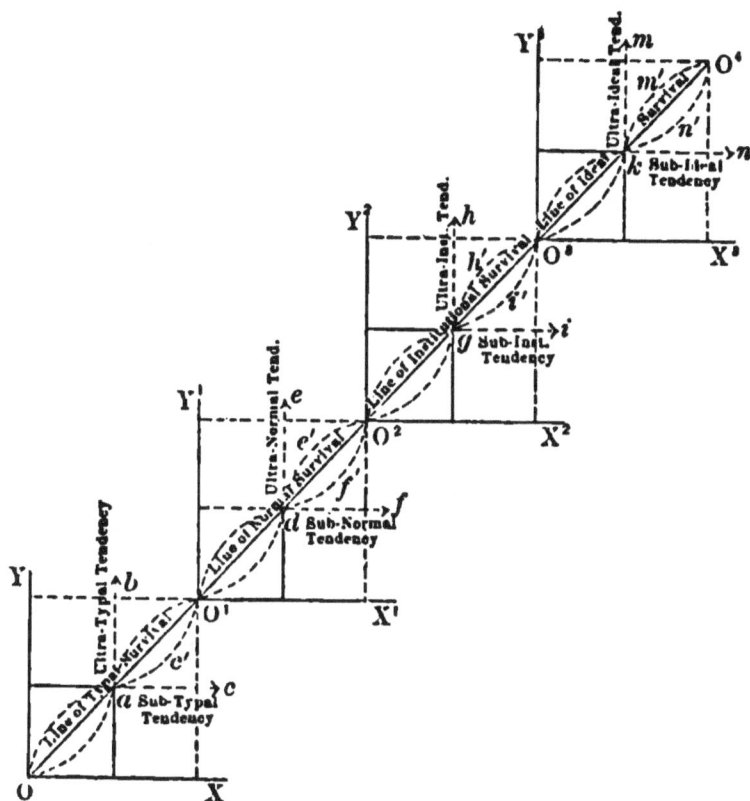

FIG. 10.

occurs at *d* we have the ultra-normal tendency *de*;
if natural influences preponderate we have the sub-
normal tendency *df*. O^2 is the sociological type.
If at *g* we have the historical forces alone ascendent, we have *gh*, the ultra-institutional tendency;

if natural conditions dominate, we have *gi*, the sub-institutional tendency.

If at *k*, the historical forces control selection, we have the ultra-ideal tendency *km*; if the natural conditions control we have the sub-ideal tendency, *kn*.

The *rhythmic course* of the selective process is produced by the reciprocal effects of the natural and historical factors on either side of the line of equilibrium OO^1, O^2, O^3, O^4, by diverging from the actual type *(a, d, g, k)* and converging within the limits of association toward the potentially normal *(O^1, etc.)*.

The process of the selective survival of sociological types varies with the degree of unity in any social population. But we may put the law of this evolution of the actual toward the potential as follows: The development of types of personality, in any social population sufficiently integrated to consciously formulate a social policy under which its great functional groups of social activities are organized, varies directly with the difference between the social type normal to any functional tendency and the sociological type of the community, and inversely as the ratio of these two types.

CHAPTER XV.

PROGRESS: ITS NATURE, METHODS AND AIMS.

" PROGRESS in effect is not," says Guyau, " simply a sensible amelioration of life, it is also the achievement of a better intellectual formulation of life, *it is a triumph of logic.*"

What are the necessary logical conceptions involved in the easy-going word progress, as applied to society ? The following analysis is an attempt to answer this question.

It would seem to be true beyond cavil that the tendency of human development, as we follow its course from the standpoints of nature and history, is to transfer the seat of authoritative control over the evolution of society more and more from the outward forces to the inner motives.

If this be the case, then we shall generally find the law of human evolution less among the objective conditions and more among the elements of the social consciousness. We shall have to traverse the area lying between the borderland of the brute-world, where organic man in his lowest natural estate still lingers in many lands, and the achievements of human emancipation. The nature of progress, therefore, never changes: it is always, as

283

Spencer affirms, from the generic to the specific—towards the perfect in its methods and aims.

But the same cannot be said of the methods and the aims of progress. In these we must look for the variable features. Races, nations, classes and families have all grown in scope and penetration of social vision. With conscious enlargement of the social mind comes widening of horizon. The effect, for example, of the discoveries of the larger world with which the middle ages came to a close, told with marvellous force upon the methods and aims of the peoples of western Europe. The contact of the Christian nations with the races of the outlying world brought to our knowledge a new revelation of the methods and the aims of peoples among whom progress was at first supposed to be wholly wanting. But a nearer view has left no doubt as to the fact; only the methods were so different and the aims so remote as to require a truly sociological orientation before the points of view could be reached from which to understand their evolution in the light of sociological laws.

Progress must first of all be axiomatic—that is its unfailing nature. When it ceases to integrate social types, to normalize society to changing tendencies, to systematically individuate or assimilate the increments of personal worth out of variety of typal tendencies, or when its heart waxes gross for want of inspiring ideals, then the social process has ceased to be progressive.

1. Progress must be *typical.* Of every social order whether it be the family, the class, the com-

munity or the nation, we have to ask whether, at
one and the same time in its history, it is typical in
the social quality or organization which it pos-
sesses, and whether that quality tends to be multiplied by imitation to such an extent as to be ever
renewing by integration the unity of life at its
foundations. There must be this equilibrium of
personality, at the bottom of every social structure,
with the conditions of existence; and there is no
bond by which man can be cemented into an im-
pregnable association completely enough to conquer nature, except in the loyalty of personality to
type at equilibrium with its conditions of survival.

The first step in social progress is the discovery
of that type to which the persons in association
can conceive themselves to be normally capable
of conforming. The mental terms on which they
live together constitute a sociological protocol,
however they may express it or take it for
granted, by which they are guided in their relations. This typal self is a logical reality and it is
the sociological organon by which in the last analysis all association of personalities proceeds. There
is a typal self—a conscious criterion of sociality.
This sociological self constitutes the first equilibrium for the members of the social aggregate. It
is tentatively projected before the ever-changing
social process as a norm of tendential reckoning.
The successful selection of the sociological type is
the secret of social evolution. It involves both the
discovery of the connection and also the differential

between the actual and the potential types. *Carpe diem* is the world's confession of decadence.

This overlapping conception of community in personal propinquity, as we may call it, is the logical norm or organon of progress. We have given this quality the name of typicality. In its subjective content it is an ever-persistent social sense with a method of its own. It is to sociology what association of ideas is to psychology. The persistence of this sense of membership in, and common loyalty to the sociological conception is as natural to us as it was to the persons comprising early communities. This deep-seated tendency to be typical is an organic function established as the seat and center of authoritative progression throughout the race. From the typical standpoint, by which we apprehend the generic quality of progress, we thus get a view of the methods by which the selective survival of types is realized both from the side of nature and of civilization.

(1) *The historical method of social progress is by subordination.** The early human communities exhibit the relation of subordination of the individual will to the social mind to an extent that the modern can scarcely conceive of, to say nothing of appreciating its full meaning as a method of social evolution. This tender thing which we designate the early community was greatly in need of guardianship. It consisted of the mother with the infant at her breast. " The first social unit," says Pro-

---

* Spencer, Principles of Sociology, Part III., Chs. I., II.

fessor Thomas, " is not the family but the mother and her group of children, and the tribe is primarily an aggregation of those related by blood to a group of females. Both social feeling and social organization are thus primarily feminine in origin—functions of the anabolism of woman. But natural selection operates still further in favoring both the offspring and the community where the male is associated in a supplementary way with the female in the expression of social feeling and the extension of social activities." *

(2) The whole history of primitive progress shows that the subjective and the objective phases of survival by typal integrity present methods peculiar to themselves. In what we may designate the first or integrating stage of human evolution in society, the objective or *natural method of social progress is by Conflict.*† There was no other method known to primitive man by which his sociality could find expression against danger than that of persistent reaction against those who strove to intrude upon the inner circle of his typal sanctum. Sociality was bought at a great price when it was once known to be the subjective requisite of survival. And the quotation of that price in the ' open market ' of the early world was given in terms of conflict for the first fruits of social conviction. Here we have the genesis of the social mind, around which from that date to this the battle-line of man-

* W. I. Thomas, Am. Journal of Sociology, July, 1897, p. 61.

† Bagehot, Physics and Politics: " Age of Conflict." Giddings, Principles of Sociology, pp. 14, 19.

kind has always been drawn up, though the
methods of preserving the convictions of typal integrity have greatly changed with each stage of
progress.

The method of conflict takes two forms in the
performance of its function of typal preservation.
It has to preserve the simple social unit by repelling
persons not of its own kind.   The preservation
from the capture by another tribe of different descent or blood-relationship—a different type—is
what the heart of archaic man prayed for above all
things else.   Besides this it had to keep in control
the constant tendency of the members of the community as individuals to assert the individual and
exalt it above the social, thereby exposing the community to the foe from without by the tolerance
of freedom from within.

The natural method of social progress consisted
therefore in antagonism to all that was non-typical
from the standpoint of the homogeneous community.   It stood guard over a sacred experiment of
the selective survival of the potentially normal
type to which every member of the community
was a sworn friend.   Toward every other type in
conflict therewith he was equally a sworn foe.

The historical method of social progress consisted in the subordination of the individual to the
potentially normal type as the sheet-anchor of an
associative existence that was at all worth having.

Both the historical and the natural methods of
progress had, however, a common function in this
stage of social evolution in which they worked as

one: they both cooperated in the *subjugation of nature.**

The nature of progress, therefore, is characterized by the method of conflict with all that is nontypical in nature in general and by the method of subjugation of every impulse that is not primarily social in human nature in particular. The typical in human progress is thus selectively developed by the elimination of the non-typical and the non-social from the process. This is not only true of the primitive social unit, but equally true of the modern social unit—the monogamic family, which is the selectively evolved organization for the development of normal types of personality each after his own kind. Whatsoever in the constitution of the family is foreign to its own type and wanting in sociality is a peril to its normal function of type-development.

(3) The *aims* of the community in its first stage of progress are (*a*) sociality—a common sense of each other's need, or the preservation of kinship of blood; and (*b*) symbolism—modes of self-expression in harmony with the common conviction. The union of these two determines the development of typical qualities needed in the community and therefore its entire social progress is dependent upon them. Progress being guided by the potentially normal type, which the social consciousness constructs as the logical aim of cooperative effort, progression must be realizable only to the extent

---

* Mackenzie, Introduction to Social Philosophy, p. 341, seq.

to which sociality and symbolism are equated in this normal type. Where the axis of sociality, which represents the social motives, and the axis of symbolism, which represents the communicable forms of expression meet, we have the locus of the realizable type of attainment.

2. Progress must, in the second place, be *normal.* This requisite of normalization is defined as the degree or capacity of adaptation to conditions in the community. Normality is equilibrium with nature on the part of society, but it involves the idea of change with the changes in environment or from one natural environment to another with a gain arising from the transition—a tendency to a more perfect degree of adaptation. It requires that the typal consciousness of the community picture for itself a potentially more normal type which it is theoretically capable of substituting, for the one actually realized, by readaptation.

Thus for the community as a whole. Within the community in which various classes and conditions of interests are integrated and organized, each having a distinct tendency and a distinct degree of adaptive efficiency to assert, normality as a progressive characteristic requires that every interest shall tend to find a potentially more normal equilibrium with the conditions of existence. The differentiating process of social interests by which these varieties of types have been evolved has been described under the Sociological Postulates. Here the important problem is to put each tendency or each social interest in a position to bear the brunt

of changes in environment by bringing each tendency to that degree of self-consciousness which will
enable it to calculate the potentially normal type of
attainment for itself. Instead of each community
having therefore a single sociological type to which
it must address itself in progression, we now' have
each tendency comprising the community—organic
group of interests—exhibiting the selective capacity for progressive survival which in the earlier
stage of progress characterized the community as a
whole. The degree of adaptation to equilibrium
has been developed throughout the population,
class by class and interest by interest, until each
becomes conscious of its own capacity at normal
adaptation.

(1) The historical method of progressive normalization of the community and of its classes, conditions and interests is by the *substitution* * of the potentially more normal for the actually less normal
equilibrium, for each separate interest or class
within the given conditions of existence. Here the
method of conflict already developed comes into
play to displace the abnormal or subordinate it to
the normal.

It is thus only that personality within any class
can ever find its equilibrium, wherein it reaches the
maximum of social valuation. Within the separate
social classes the proprieties are developed by which
personality is kept from becoming abnormal or
sub-normal. As each modern occupation which

* Spencer, Principles of Sociology, Vol. I., Part III., Chs.
I.-II.

has been long established and has developed a self-consciousness of the sociological type to which it is taken for granted that men will measure up to, so all pursuits which the normalizing process requires in the community create a cult by the aid of which each generation is habitually integrated into the conventionalities of the class. Notable examples of this kind of progression are the ethics of the medical, the legal and the clerical professions, as well as that of the military class.

(2) The natural method of normalization is by *Status*.* This method marks the second objective stage in human progress by typal selection, just as conflict was the first mode of typal development. After a series of conflicts, subordinations and substitutions a class or a community's equilibrium tends to become an established fact or an established order of events with which that group of the population learns almost instinctively to reckon; the result is a social status maintained by the performance of distinct social functions for the community and by the relative absence of changes in the conditions of survival. But in normal conditions the typal tendency within each social status is not suspended. Where, however, the typal tendency to more normal adaptation to conditions is arrested permanently on the part of all constituent classes and interests of the community we have status crystallized into Caste. A dynamic tendency is caught between nature and authority and pinioned

* Maine, Ancient Law, pp. 163-165.   New York, 1888.

there as a static type. A status, therefore, is a necessary aspect of normal progress; a caste is a proof
that progress has been arrested and a typal equilibrium becomes stationary.

These being the methods by which population
secures adaptation to conditions through the reactions of class-interests, what are the *aims* which ani-
mate the normalizing of man in progress toward
the completer equilibrium ?

(3) The aims of normal progression are (*a*) conventionality—the selection of relatively fixed
modes of intercourse within each cultural group,
in which the kinship of morals, manners and customs is binding upon the conduct of each member.
That is, next to sociality, the most important elements of progress are class-codes of conduct. The
proof of progress is the facility with which a class
acts together and with the community. Within
each class the obligation to progression by more
normal adaptation to class-conviction is laid upon
all of its members. The conventional is the creed
of the class. To reach and to respect its requirements is to be integrated; to violate it is to ' lose
caste '; to be indifferent to it is to be eliminated.
To conceive of and seek successfully to realize a
type which carries one beyond the conventional
type of the class is to be differentiated into another
class.

(*b*) The second aim of normal progression is
property—the selection of the means most useful
in normalization of type to conditions. In the subjugation of nature so as to utilize its resources we

have the most comprehensive aim of the progressive impulse. Conventionality is, in a real sense, the
limit of the claim that the community has upon
the behavior and the attitude of personality. Property is personality's claim to a quality, a degree, a
relation, a means to an end—the equilibrium of the
individual with the tendency or social function to
which he normally belongs. Property in the sense
of a personal requisite of progression is not only
the necessary means of maintaining one's status
in society but equally necessary for adaptation to
the type that tends to prevail within that status.
Hence it is the objective requisite of progress.

The relation of conventionality to property is
complemental. The direction which the conviction
of the community takes will depend on the ratio of
these two factors in normalization of life. If the
customs of a community transcend their normal
function as the conservator of the manners and
morals in the popular life, then the static and form-
giving forces cause it to grow rigid in its relations
to changes, thus preventing adaptation to the type
that normally tends to prevail. If, on the other
hand, property transcends the normal function as
the dynamic agent of adaptation and becomes the
end to which the type that normally tends to prevail is subordinated, then the abnormal is sure to
arise in that community.

If, in YOx, Fig. 11, a class or profession be normally at equilibrium at t, the typal tendency Ot will
be at equilibrium by the complementarity of the
conventional (at) and the proprietary (wt). But

if *at* transcends the line of normality by ascending
to *d*, without any change in the proprietary factor,
in the aims of the community, the social tendency
will be potentially abnormal by the distance *db*. If
at *d* property aims begin to have the ascendency,
the normal tendency will be restored in the equilibrium of both aims in *b*. If property aims become

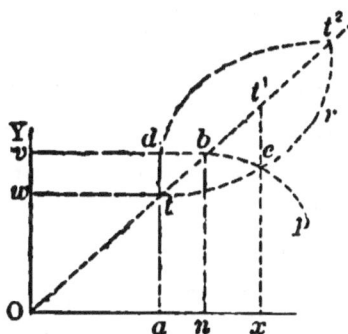

FIG. 11.

ascendant in social progression when conventional
aims are at their normal *(t)* the course of progression will be in the direction of *tcr*, not *tbt¹*. If property aims become ascendant at the maximum of
conventional aims, then the line of progression will
be *dbp*. The equilibrium will be found at *c*, rather
than at *t¹*, as would be the case if the two aims were
balanced.

If each ascendant tendency in social aims is well
enough organized to have a conventional standard
and a proprietary influence sufficient to sustain itself more or less independently, as the Guilds of
industry were in the middle ages and the landed
aristocracy of the same period and later, then each
would take its own course of evolution; *tdt²* the

course of the latter, and trt^2 the course of the former, both tending to meet in equilibrium in the mercantile or industrial nexus of the later social reorganization. This illustrates the rhythmic tendency in social development.

3. Progress must, in the third place, be *institutional*. We have seen that normal adaptation by tendencies requires substitution of types within the limitation of status. In the aims that dominate progress by normalization the conventional and the proprietary required equation in order to get to a newer and truer equilibrium. In the experience of some peoples, India and China for example, the limitations of status were such as to leave personality practically no room for development into a superior type. The more perfect contentment with the actual was the law and the prophets of progress. Property—natural gifts, attainments or material goods—enables personality to substitute the potential for the actual type of attainment. To that extent the individual, and thus the class to which he belongs, becomes more capable of differentiating himself from the limitations of status to the liberty of contract.

The institutional stage or aspect of progress does not become conspicuous until the social process has sufficiently differentiated both property and personality and then assimilated them under some more perfectly fitted type regarded as vital to social progress. Institutional relationships among classes are the necessary means of assimilation. Only by such

assimilation of the traditional and the adaptive elements can better types arise.

(1) The historical method of progress by institutional assimilation of social qualities of character
takes the form of an individuation of a more normal
type of personality. Property is the school of personal responsibility. The possession of property
under social guarantee is one of the most powerful
springs of attainment known to our species. The
attitude of personality is thereby changed with respect to the potential type of life toward which
property is the instrument of progressive individuation. Property and responsibility between man and
man grow apace. Property may be commercial
or cultural. The right proportion is a question
of public or social policy. Cultural possessions of
a community or a class, incorporated into the life
of its members and institutionalized as the basis of
a new social order, come to have an immense sig-
nificance in the individuation of the community
toward the potentially normal type of life. This
individuation is largely accomplished through increased social organization.

This coordination of property and personality in
the individuation of the more efficient man is not
a matter of accident, nor of conspiracy of proper-
tied classes against a proletariate. The uses of
property determine its relations to personality and
the community. The same is true of social power
as a possession of the community. It is a power
available for individuation or degeneration of social
type. Extinction of the actual social type rather

than individuation of the more efficient type became the inevitable outcome of the tendencies rife
among the tribes of the Germanic migrations.*
The once normal became the typically abnormal,
until the turmoil of the migration gave way to the
two great institutions of the Roman church and
the Germanic state. The one individuated personality with the spiritual possessions of the church
and the other individuated personality with the
possession of territory. Each aspect of this institutional individuation gave orderly direction and
control to these vital relationships in the same social system. Out of them arose the type of national
character. Progress is not possible without this
individuating capacity in the community. It is the
potential type of personality, which guides the subjective aspirations of the community, that determines whether or not the possessions can be differentiated into separate classes and then through
them into the life of the individual. But if it is
done, and done normally, it must be by institutional assimilation.

The institutional test of progress is to be found
in the effect of any institution upon the capacity of
any class to individuate the resources of life for attainment. How does it affect the several classes
of the community to utilize the social order ? Does
it vitalize the ideal, utilize the potential, assimilate
the elements of strength ?

(2) The natural method of institutional progress

* Francke, Social Forces in German Literature, Introduction
and Ch. I.

is that of *Contract*.* When in the intervening stage
of progress only a single kind of attainment was
the *sine qua non* of survival, conflict was the method
of evolution toward the potential. When this tendency had become differentiated into several similar
tendencies centering in social interests about which
these groups or classes normalized themselves,
status becomes the method of social growth. Value
of personality under status was a class-category.
But now that personality has become differentiated
from status, and property is differentiated from the
community, progress takes the form of contractual
relations. It establishes reciprocal relationships in
the form of rights and obligations, defining the
conditions upon which those obligations may be
assumed which have their roots deep down in the
rock-bed of our social consciousness. This method
of development of the type of character by responsibilities that can be enforced by property
damages is of the utmost sociological importance.
Every contract takes for granted a typical quality
of character. A lends to B on specified terms,
property of specified value, payable six months
hence. Back of it all lies the assumption that the
type of personality which each assumes in the other
will persist, and that under these institutional conditions each will be true to the type toward which
the community tends. Economically we call this
by the name of the risks of speculative loans. Sociologically it is a method of prediction of tenden-

* Stimson, Labor in its Relation to Law, Lecture II.

cies. The actual type taken for granted is beneath
and beyond the contract; it is not 'nominated in
the bond,' but is the basis of the bond itself. The
two circles of personality intersect and the type is
that within the intersecting arcs. It is by that type
that we find the basis of institutional progress. It
is that upon which reliance is placed for future pay-
ment and future claim. But for the logical capacity to construct such a series of conceptions on
institutional conditions there could be no more
progress by means of subjective individuation and
objective contract than there is among a school of
fish or a flock of sheep.

Both contract and individuation, as methods of
progress, require a typical understanding by which,
in all kinds of personal agreement expressed or
implied, a basis of reciprocality is reached.

(3) Progress as an aspect of social policy has two
normal aims. They are (*a*) order, and (*b*) progress
(improvement), both of which are the characteristic
ends of the process of assimilation. Progressive
assimilation requires authority (sovereignty) and
liberty. The former is social, the latter individual.
Order is individual opportunity which is a condition of improvement.

Order as an end of organized progress involves a
conscious effort at giving consistency to certain
social convictions which have become assimilated
into the subjective life of the people. " Life, liberty and the pursuit of happiness," is a trio of convictions as to what ought to be institutionalized in
the social order of national life. Government guar-

antees this result within constitutional limits. These limits express the permanent will of a people as a whole. But new possibilities realized by a class disturb the constituted relationships of order. Individual or class progress requires the whole people to appropriate new increments of power or be eliminated from the progressive process.

To say that the second aim of progress is progress is simply to affirm that the progressive policy seeks to establish the progressive purpose in the mind of the individuals to be reached thereby. A progressive social order whose aim is the assimilation of all tendencies of social life toward a unified type of national character provides the conditions on which individual effort daily seeks its own betterment. The progress of institutional order is the progress of personal attainment.* Indeed, the progress of individual welfare, toward the ends which society approves as admissible, is the function of institutional order on which rests the possibility of social progress.

4. Finally, progress must be *ideal* in its aspirations. This simply implies the presence in the life of the community of two methods of ideal attainment.

(1) In its subjective aspirations society must seek the solidarity of the potential with the perfect type. This method of subjective realization then becomes the practice of the community which regards the ideal as an imperative to which its members are

---

* Aristotle, Politics, Bk. IV., Chs. XII.-XVII.

bound to aspire. This is the highest standard of subjective activity in the community. We find it written out in the moral codes of nations, that all men should equally seek certain realizations. Progress of the type of personality in social development requires some such equalizing authority to make the end of effort equitable.

(2) From the standpoint of the individual what form does the ideal in progress take ? Evidently that of *Conscience*.*

(3) The *aims* of progress, in its ideal aspect, are to be found in (*a*) science and (*b*) religion. This equilibrium which the community seeks with nature can only be realized by the knowledge of science through which to guide it in the development toward the ideal type. This type is the highest available expression for that equilibrium into which the knowledge of nature must enable the community to pass.

The embodiment of the scientific aim in personality does not, however, stop there. The knowledge and insight into nature's uniformities, its equipoise of tendencies and its harmonious beauty of movement—these only impel the spirit in personality to a deeper yearning for fellowship with the mystery of the cosmos, the sense that comes in toward us from the vast untravelled sea to whose shores science has simply led and left us in wonder and awe.

Religion is the expression of this aspiration, and

* **Nash, Genesis of the Social Conscience, VII.**

as such is a social factor. Among factors in social progress none have quite played the part that this tendency has. The soul of social man transcends the potential and aspires to communion and conformity with the ideal type of infinite personality. This is the essence of religious aims at all times. In the words with which Herbert Spencer concludes his chapter on Religious Retrospect and Prospect, " But one truth must grow ever clearer—the truth that there is an Inscrutable Existence everywhere manifested, to which he can neither find nor conceive either beginning or end. Amid the mysteries which become the more mysterious the more they are thought about, there will remain the one absolute certainty that he is ever in presence of an Infinite and Eternal Energy, from which all things proceed." *

This survey of the nature, methods and aims of progress may be summarized as follows:

1. The *typical* nature of social progress is characterized outwardly by *Conflict* with all that is non-typical in nature; and inwardly by the method of *subordination* of every personal force that is not social in human nature.

The result is the elimination of the unsocial and the integration of the social under the category of the progressively typical.

2. The *normal* nature of social progress is characterized objectively by the method of *status*, by which the different degrees of social capacity tend

* Principles of Sociology, Vol. III., p 175.

to be localized into differentiated groups of homogeneous members each at equilibrium with its type and each type with its corresponding conditions; and subjectively by the method of *substitution* of the potentially more normal for the actually less normal degree of adaptation to conditions.

The result is the elimination of the abnormal and the integration of the normal by the differentiation of the social population into groups based on kindred degrees of efficiency and by the tendency to the substitution within these groups of the potential for the actual type as changes require.

This elimination of the abnormal constitutes a sub-typical class which is institutionalized in charitable organizations as soon as the social feelings and the surplus of property permit of their survival in connection with the social system.

3. The *institutional* or *assimilative* nature of progress is objectively characterized by the method of *Contract,* by which the tendency to attainment through reciprocal obligations between man and man and between the individual and society is realized under a system of rights and duties; and subjectively by the method of individuation of the newly developed elements of attainment by some, into the actual type common to the community, thus realizing the potential type of personality normal to the community through institutional organization.

The result is that contract eliminates the irresponsible and individuates the responsible into a superior service of the social system. The newest type normal to any social system is the truest type to past experience and present circumstances. Of course contract here includes all reciprocal obligations of which the social consciousness is aware.

4. The ideal nature of progress is objectively characterized by the method of *Conscience,* by which organized society tends to incarnate its ideal in personality as the law of social life; and subjectively by the method of harmonious *solidarity* of all degrees of attainment each in allegiance to the perfect type —the ideal normal to its degree of development.

The result is the elimination of the immoral, that is, the faithless or the disloyal to the progressive ideal. The ideal judges by man's degree of development; but the ideal also requires the equalization of *all* degrees of development into a social solidarity based on loyalty to and fellowship in the progressive ideal potentially normal to the people as a whole.

On this conception of progress, viewed both from the logical and the historical standpoints, we may say

1. That subordination to type is the logical principle and conflict with conditions the historical process, by which such an organization as the family could alone have been evolved.

2. That substitution of the more normal type of attainment, within each level of social efficiency, for the less normal type is the logical principle, and status or static adjustment with conditions on the basis of degrees of social efficiency, is the historical

process by which such a social result as the social classes could have been evolved.

3. That individuation of the main tendencies in the social population by assimilative institutions of social order as the internal principle and contract between man and man as the external method of developing personal responsibility in social relations, are the only processes by which the progressively social system, such as the modern state, could be realized.

4. The solidarity of all degrees of personal attainment by loyalty to the perfect type of social realization, is the logical principle; and the method of conscience as a tendency to derive social authority from the inner life of typically normal persons, is the historical principle by which it is alone possible to account for the appearance of social ideals, such as are in philosophy regarded as the goal of humanity, and in religion as the solidarity of humanity and divinity in the kingdom of righteousness.

The tendency of social thought has been to rest its criticism at this point, on the ground of practical difficulties in the natural character of man or historical tendencies in the social organization. But the case is not yet finally adjudicated, if one may profess to read the social spirit aright. In the estimation of the faith that moves mountains, there is a higher court than the social system, a higher law than that of social order—a diviner event toward which the social process moves.

There is a stage in the evolution of the typal consciousness in which the scepter of social authority passes from the structural system of order to the functional capacity of personality. The goal of all government is self-government. Man aspires to guide his feet and find his path by the light of the social ideal communicable to his kindred. Then the potentially normal type, toward which the social system moves, becomes authoritative, and the system as such becomes only a scaffolding. The modern State may be too repressive to endure as the end of association. We must rely on the reflective social mind, rather than on the invention of political machinery for the selection of materials, methods and ends. Only by this subjective growth can any social or governmental system control the tendencies of social service to find their unity and solidarity in the *perfect* sociological type—the social ideal.

Our conclusions may now be summarized as follows: The successive degrees of social development of types of personality arise by selection of the potentially normal tendencies of the community. In the sociological axioms personal development begins with the quality of typicality as the first requisite of social worth. Normality is the next criterion of value. By uniting both kind and degree of personal worth in the relation of institutionality we thus unify these three developmental tendencies in the ideal.

The next portion of our conclusion shows that these axioms fit into the subjective and the objective aspects of the social process as presented in the sociological postulates.

Thirdly, we saw that the facts, events and tendencies of the social process are reconcilable in every essential aspect with the universal hypothesis of social development by the selective survival of sociological types.

It then remained to define the exact nature of the selective function itself that runs through the social process as the law of social life. What part do the great organs of the social process—the family, the social class, the national community and the race, regarded as an organic part of the cosmic process, play in the evolution of types ?

As the family or tribe develops to the point of self-consciousness it becomes the organ of selection. It makes for itself a place in which only such developing activities are admitted as keep its members in the integrating process. The family determines, by the type of attainment it enforces, the extent to which a kind of character shall be insisted upon, when it shall give place to normalizing influences, when institutional relations shall be entered into and what ideals shall control its policy as an organ of selection. Through these respective axioms it connects itself with all aspects of the social process. By the connection of the family with some dominant social interest we preserve the best traditions of the past for present use in social service. By institutionality the family selects those elements in the social system which individuate its type toward the type of the community and is thus assimilated with the life of the people; by ideality it consolidates its highest aims with the aims of the race. In this the family consciously completes its selective function as the primary organ of the evolution of social man. The family selects the *qualitative* type that shall prevail.

Similarly, the next great organic agency of typal evolution is the social class. The essential function of the social class is to normalize mankind by linking personality to conditioning social interests the scope of whose claim is limited and yet is necessary as a function of the community. Within the class the family determines the organic type that shall survive, but the class determines the degree of social development that is potentially normal within its limits. By its own sociological standard a type peculiar to itself is evolved in accordance with the principle of differentiation by which its selective function is controlled. Through the use of social institutions it assimilates elements of worth within the community, thus tending to become individuated with the type that tends to prevail therein; and through ideal individuation the class becomes consolidated with the ideals of the race; more and more, as it becomes self-conscious of its actual and its potential worth, does it tend to impose, by its ideals and its institutions, its own type upon the community, as the modern commercial and industrial classes do and as the class-tendencies have ever done in almost all progressive communities at some stage or another. Hence the social classes become the organs of development for personality as well as for the whole people. The class selects the *de-*

gree of development required within its range of interests.

Likewise any social system, in the form of the established community, acts as a selective instrument in the elimination of the abnormal, and the assimilation of the normal tendencies of social organization. Here, in the make-up of municipal or national organization of society, the family constitution has already determined the qualitative types and the classes have determined the degree of development. Out of these the social system must be constructed. That social class which most completely approaches to the sociological type in which these tendencies converge contains the combination of selective capacities which secures it the leadership. The enlargement of the life of the people for which the energies have been gathering in each social class comes only by following this prophetic instinct—this loyalty to a larger life. By this sentiment of solidarity, of social feeling of loyalty to the national type of character that tends to prevail, the pressure toward typal realization calls for an efficient organ of social selection. The establishment of the State is the result.* The industrial relations are laid down as the conditions and limits within which assimilation is operative. Every agency of whatever kind from the constitution to the constable becomes the institutional organ of selection in the interest of the type of personality which tends to prevail in the direction of the

---

* Willoughby, The Nature of the State, pp. 120–1.

national ideal.* Thus the type upon which the self-conscious and reflective contingent in a community of people sets its heart and to which its classes tend to be assimilated seems to determine the nature and extent of political agency necessary to focus the social functions upon that potential end. Some of these functions are self-conscious enough of that end and of their own relation to it to need no political direction and control. Others are not. To differentiate the essential ends of social realization from the non-essential and to select for social man the instruments and the institutions of his own evolution are the social reasons for the modern State. As an organ of selection both of means, methods and arms, the State is the instrument of the national consciousness.

The race-ideals transcend the national type. The ideal types of personality toward which they are impelled who loyally assert them are among the most potent selective factors in human association. " The chief impulses of nations and peoples are abstract ideas and ideals, unreal and unrealizable; it is in the pursuit of these that the great as well as the small movement on the arena of national life and on the stage of history have taken place. The conscious deliberate pursuit of ideal aims is the highest causality in human history." †

* Burgess, Polit. Sci. Quar., Vol. X., No. 3, 404-8.
† Britton, An Anthropologist's View of History, Am. Journal of Psychology, Vol. VIII., No. 1, 132.

CHAPTER XVI.

THE THEORETICAL METHOD OF TYPES.

AFTER the statement and definition of the principles which are characteristic of the social process we proceed from principles to method. Method has first of all to respect the abiding relations which have been established by the analytic and the synthetic exposition of social life. The phenomena peculiar to associative existence having thus been resolved into recognizable outlines, the question arises, How should the mind equipped with a definite idea of the social process and its leading principles proceed to make for itself that investigation and that exposition which will enable it to gain an intelligible insight into social phenomena as a whole ?

Method as here viewed involves the logical process of observing social phenomena. It is therefore both subjective and objective, both logical and scientific in its requirements. Its ultimate object is to teach our reasoning powers how to interpret the facts of social reality so as to give them their due value in the formulation of social policy. From the logical side of its meaning method is concerned with discovery and proof of laws; from its scientific side, method is concerned with the selection of the facts and conditions under which such logical inferences are true to objective life.

To the sociologist these are complemental attitudes of thought in the method peculiar to his subject. We have therefore to keep this constantly before us in the formulation of a theory of the method of sociological interpretation. For if the end of method is social policy, we have equally to avoid a method which undervalues the concrete facts or ignores the conceptual forms according to which social aggregates behave. The service of theoretical inquiry into the nature of methods in their relation to facts and forms is consequently of the utmost importance to social procedure. This distinction is not a new one, however, between the theoretical method and the concrete procedure in social inquiry. In the opening analysis of his *Social Physics* Comte clearly indicated the relation between the two tasks in pointing out the necessity for the separation of theory from practice in sociology. " As the abstract history of humanity must be separated from the concrete, so must the abstract inquiry into the laws of society be separated from questions of concrete sociology. Science is not yet advanced far enough. . . . It is not that the material is scanty or imperfect. The deficiency is of a sociological theory which may reveal the scope and bearing of every view and direct all reasoning to which it may give rise: and in the absence of such a theory we can never know that we have assembled all the requisites essential to a rational decision."

This postponement of the concrete inquiry into social phenomena, until stock has been taken—to use a commercial phrase—of our own forms of thought under whose categories all our observations and conclusions must ultimately fall before they may be safely put to practice, Comte regarded as a necessary condition of successful investigation; and he also saw in the failure to observe this order the reason for the failure of sociology to achieve its triumph as the guiding principle of rational interpretation.. If the theory of the selective survival of sociological types be the true interpretation of the social process, then not only must the problems which concrete sociology proposes for solution and the solutions which it suggests, take this theory for the guiding of efforts in social policy, but sociological methods must, whether they be logical or scientific in their character, find their synthesis in the method of types. And with this relation of dependence of policy upon theory it is eminently true that sociology alone can serve as the guide to genuine speculation when its uses are once fully ascertained.

The sociological method of types requires us to be conversant with four features of the subject:

1. The *facts* of the natural conditions of the social aggregate. These are found in the postulates or integrating conditions of natural association.

2. The *events* in the historical sequences or social forces by which society is historically differentiated. These are found in the axioms of social organization.

3. The determination, from the integrating conditions and the differentiating sequences, of the social *types* normal to any integrated aggregates of a given time and place. We must know the *typical groups* by which selective survival is realized.

4. The determination of the typal *tendencies* which actually or potentially prevail. We must know the *organic tendencies* in which the typical groups are reciprocally coordinated in the effort to supersede the actual by the potential as the mode of development toward the ideal.

The logical conditions of natural association and the logical axioms of social organization have their content respectively in typical groups and in organic movements or tendencies of the social population.

The historical and the natural aspects are the universal and necessary coordinates from which a social process, whose nature or inner law is the evolution of types must be viewed, in all that is done in the way of investigation and exposition. For, any method intended for use in a field of phenomena so extremely complex as those of the social world are, cannot but take into account with full adequacy whatsoever is distinctly social in causal and conditional character. Any method of interpretation—and this is the business of sociological theory—that fails to find room in its process of reasoning for all essential factors of socialization, must logically be not only partial, preliminary, and piecemeal, but must be harmful in its effects upon the total results of social procedure. But on the other hand, that comprehensive method which balances every essential element in social reality upon the focus toward which the whole social process moves must be most helpful to thought and practice.

In the method of typal interpretation we have such a synthetic method of treating social phenomena. All other methods of which sociology has made use are specific methods of subsidiary service in the elaboration of the materials and conceptions without which the method of types could not have become possible. The sociological method of types is, therefore, the inductive basis of the other partial methods. And this result is consistent, moreover, with the way in which all successful efforts at scientific investigation have achieved their results. According to Mill—who, more so than any other of modern logicians, has crystallized the principles and practices of modern research*—in all scientific investigation " the way of attaining the end is seen as it were instinctively by superior minds in some comparatively simple case, and is then by judicious generalization, adapted to the variety of complex cases. We learn to do a thing in difficult circumstances, by attending to the manner in which we have done the same thing in easy ones. This truth is exemplified by the history of the various branches of knowledge which have successively, in the ascending order of their complication, assumed the character of sciences." †

Without pausing here to show more fully that

---

* Hibben, Inductive Logic, p. 312.
† Mill, Logic, Bk. VI., Ch. I., § 1.

the method of social experience is the method of
social types, and to reiterate the fact that the type
of character is ultimately the determining element
of social policy, it would be an oversight not to
refer to the contribution of Mill to sociological
method made over half a century ago, before the
data from which the axiomatic bases could be de-
duced were available for the typal interpretation of
social life. Mill's view of the subject of sociology as
a science of national types of character appeared fif-
teen years before Darwin and Wallace announced
simultaneously the theory of natural selection as
the method of survival in the animal kingdom.
There is therefore something almost prophetic in
the following statement of the sociological method
by which he conceived that the subject might be
brought from its then imperfect state to the level
of a science for the guidance of human communities. "The progress of this important but now
imperfect science," he says, "depends upon a
double process: first, that of deducing theoretically
the ethological [typological] consequences of particular circumstances of position, and comparing
them with the recognized results of common experience; and secondly, the reverse operation; increased study of the various types of human nature
that are to be found in the world, conducted by
persons not only capable of analyzing and recording the circumstances in which these types severally
prevail, but also sufficiently acquainted with psychological laws, to be able to explain and account
for the characteristics of the type by the peculiar-

ities of the circumstances; the residuum, if any, being set down to the account of congenital predispositions." *

The two coordinate features in Mill's logical conception of the method of the social sciences were (1) the circumstances of position or conditional situation which comprises those structural features of social organization to which we have given the name of the Sociological Postulates; and (2) Mill included in the complemental aspect of his suggestion as to method, those ethological consequences which arise from circumstances of position, and which we have elaborated into the Sociological Axioms. These two coordinating features are data of determination of the types of personality.

This method admits of schematic representation. We take the postulates as a series of social conditions or structural circumstances of environment necessary in any method of study of society as a natural process and thus in any inquiry into social factors. And we also regard the sociological axioms as furnishing the other coordinate series of social results, consequences, or functional qualities necessary to any historical process of association. Then we have the two coordinate series of sociological criteria by which to guide us in the "increased study of the various types of human nature that are to be found in the world."

We may determine roughly any particular *type* by finding out

    1. The social situation to which any person is

* Logic, Book VI., Ch. V.

integrated and the social quality it gives expression to in its relation with other types.

2. The social interests with which anyone is identified and the degree of adaptation to conditions which differentiate his manners and his capacities from other interests.

3. The social system under whose assimilating control his life is individuated by the prevailing relations of order and progress.

4. The social mind by which his convictions are coordinated to the solidarity of the social ideal by the normative influences of exact knowledge and religion.

More technically expressed the method of determining social types is by noting one's relation to

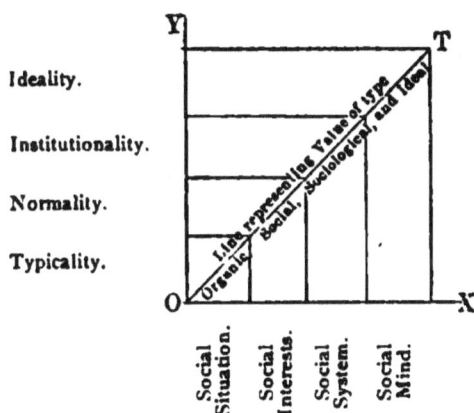

Ideality.

Institutionality.

Normality.

Typicality.

Social Situation. Social Interests. Social System. Social Mind.

FIG. 12.

each of the postulated conditions of natural association and the corresponding axiomatic qualities of historical organization of human life.

In the comprehensive social situation, Fig. 12, *YOX*, take *YO* as the line on which the axiomatic qualities are measured, and OX as the line on which the series of postulated typal conditions is to be represented. These are the coordinate series of data for the determination of types. Every type must have four sets of coordinating data to determine its value in the social process.

(1) Typicality coordinated with a particular simple social situation; that is, an organic typical quality coordinate with a corresponding set of circumstances environing it, and revealing a resulting *type of personality* at equilibrium therein.

(2) Normality coordinated with social interests; that is, a measurable degree of adaptive activity coordinate with a definite set of social interests, the type in its effort to find its own social class of capacity revealing a resulting *typal tendency* to which it normally belongs.

(3) Institutionality coordinated with a social system; that is, a set of institutional relations of that particular typal tendency to the other typal tendencies within the same social system, resulting in the *suggestion of the potentially normal type* toward which the assimilating system tends.

(4) Ideality coordinated with the comprehensive social mind; that is, a continuous series of ideal social aims, corresponding to the degrees of development of the social mind of each main tendency in the social system; by this there results a dissolving of the contradictory elements in the organized social system and the individuation of the potential types of the several tendencies into the solidarity of an ideal common to organized society.

In Fig. 13 the line *OT* is the normal line of development of any type of personality, the *organic* typal quality *(t1)* is relatively low compared with the influence of the environment *(at)* corresponding with it. Both together constitute the data by which we determine the *organic* value of the social type *(t)*—a value that falls below the normal by as

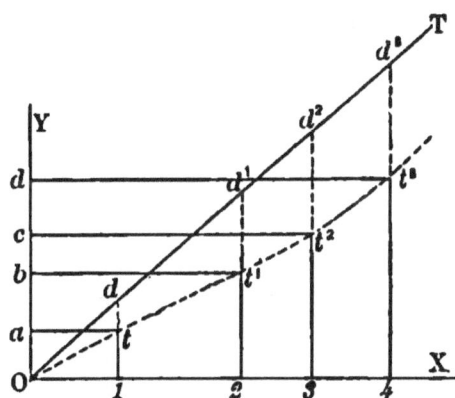

FIG. 13.

much as *td* in typal quality, showing that organically the type is below the possibilities of the conditions which it occupies.

The *social* value of the type *(t¹)* in any tendency is determined by its social interest *(2t¹)* and its adaptive capacity *(bt¹)*. It falls below normality to actual conditions by *d¹t¹*.

The *sociological* value of the type in any social system, that is, its capacity to serve not only a single tendency but to conform to the type toward which the community normally tends *(d²)* is given as *t²*, *d²t²* below the normal.

The *ideal* type is located at t^3 and is determined by the conformity of this particular tendency to its *own* ideal $(4t^3)$ and by the end (dt^3) which the social mind tends to impress upon this particular group in the social system. But this ideal falls below the normal ideal by as much as d^3t^3.

In Fig. 14 the typal qualities are relatively high and the type-determining conditions relatively low as factors in the process of development.

In Fig. 15 the type-determining factors in the

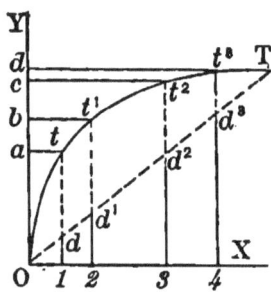

FIG. 14.

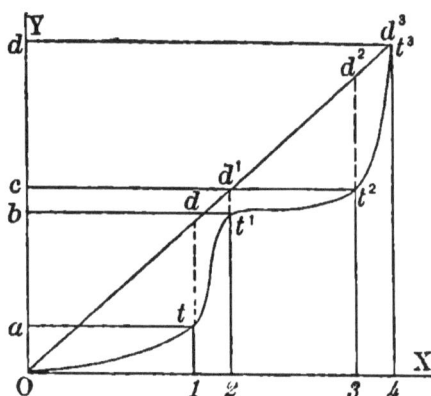

FIG. 15.

social process are irregular, with a strong tendency to relapse from and return to the normal in alternating succession.

In all of these cases the value of a type in a social process is consequently determined by its fourfold efficiency: (1) its organic capacity to integrate its members in a given social situation; (2) its social capacity to differentiate its members into a typal tendency based on social interests; (3) its individuating capacity to assimilate with other types in a working social system; and (4) its idealizing capac-

ity to consolidate with other types to realize a subjective solidarity. This is true of a family-type, a
class-type, a community-type or a national type of
character.

This is the logical method of types, concretely
defined in terms not unfamiliar to one accustomed
to social reasoning. Theoretical research cannot
evade these requirements and any method must
reckon these data among the requisites of the study
of types.

The hypothesis of survival of types by the selection of the potentially normal type serves as a guiding law and at the same time as a scale of normal
valuation. For, if the sociological method pays too
exclusive attention to the exposition of the conditions (postulates of situation, interests, social system and social mind) under which the types appear,
it explains the connection between conditions of
existence and the type in any given typal nexus,
that is, it explains *coexistences* simply; but it fails
to show why according to universal law the type
whose connection is thus explained passes out of
any given conditional nexus or coexistent relation
into another higher up or lower down in the scale
of social values; why, for example, a persistent type
finally becomes a resistent type, and then rises to
the level of reciprocal relations with other types in
the social order and finally finds its equalization in
the realization of its ideal. It fails to explain *sequences.*

This law of values Mill did not have at his command, because the law of natural selection had not

yet been formulated, to say nothing about its application to social interpretation, excepting of course the form in which Malthus had sought solution for the problem by competitive elimination. The selective survival of types gives us the positive principle of survival by development by means of association, which is the essential part of sociological method. In order therefore to apply this law so as both to explain the survival of types on given conditions and to account for the *sequential development* of actual types into the types that tend to prevail, we must not only know what are the *actual conditions* under which any type occurs, but equally important is it to find out what the *tendential* value of the type is; that is, we must know what motives universal to typal consciousness move typical groups to development. We must take into account both kinds of typal efficiency: (1) the organic efficiency to conform to the normal type in any given conditions, and (2) the capacity to recognize the *difference* between the actual and the potential type and the use of institutional and ideal means to attain thereto. The whole question of sociological method is summed up in the problem of determining the line of functional selection along which any social type in any given conditions of place and any historical period of time tends to find its equilibrium in the developmental process of selective survival. It is not solely a problem of logic ; for if it were, the actual line of selective development would coincide with the potential. Nor is it simply a question of actual fact; for then the type would be normally valued by its relation to actual conditions and remain static. But the problem of method is that of determining the *tendency* of the given type in terms of a particular series of conditions, and of a series of axiomatic qualities which are the axes of its loci in the line of selective survival. We can thus compare the actual line of selective survival with the potentially normal line, and detect the sequential or axiomatic differential which discounts or puts at a premium the given type of personality. We may thus plot the curve of a family, of a class, a community or a nation, or of any social tendency or aggregate which is sufficiently integrated and differentiated to have the typal consciousness which exercises selective control over the assimilative and individuating conduct of the group. We can plot the whole social population by classes, by communities or we can compare the tendencies of national life period after period.

To determine a *social tendency* we must compare the actual social type at one time and place or state of society with the corresponding type in another social situation, that is under the changed conditions of a succeeding period or date. By a series of determinations we should then be able to represent to our minds the rise or fall of the typal values of any social class, any people, any city, or any nation in the full course of its history.

The method of determining any typal tendency requires the coordination of the series of conditions with the series of axiomatic qualities in successive social situations. Given any social aggregate sufficiently integrated to have a typal consciousness of its own, in order to determine its tendency we must know,

1. The series of *particular conditions*, including (1) the physical situation of this aggregate, (2) the social interests of its membership, (3) the social system by which the sentiments of this aggregate are coordinated, and (4) the social mind by which this aggregate's course of conduct is reflectively conditioned and cantrolled. See Chapter II., p. 24.

2. We must also know the series of *axiomatic sequences* or causal motives peculiar to the associative life of the race as expressed in that aggregate, including (1) the *organic* consciousness of type, or the keenness of sense of superiority of man over the brute creation as a quality of this group (typicality); (2) the *tribal* consciousness of type, or the sensitiveness to social environment. The extent to which the aggregate is conscious of comfort at being with and of discomfort at being away from its equals in the degree of *development* in typal capacity (normality). We must know (3) the *civic* consciousness of type or the capacity of the aggregate to assimilate itself with the activities of the social organization in the more or less conscious effort at typal individuation toward which the social system tends. This is the sense of civic responsibilities (institutionality). We must know (4) the *creative* consciousness of type, that is, the effectiveness of this aggregate to provoke by example or precept a reaction on the part of the community or any

portion thereof in favor of the ideal types of personality under which all tendencies may find progressive harmonization of effort.

From these coordinate series of data we may determine any typal tendency at any given time and place in social history. Any inquiry made after this method into any typical aggregate, sufficiently differentiated to have a typal consciousness of its own, will readily find the social tendency or tendencies which exactly correspond to this synthesis of conditional and sequential factors. This method coordinates the *integrating conditions* (postulates) with the *differentiating sequences* (axioms of the social process) and deduces therefrom the *individuated type* peculiar to the tendency in question. By the integrating conditions the typical aggregate adjusts itself to nature. By the differentiating sequences it addresses itself to the content of history in its striving toward the ideal. By the union of both in the same social tendency we get the actual social type simultaneously undergoing an integrating and a differentiating process whose joint tendency is typal individuation. In the study of any social tendency we should have to approach the subject from the natural and the historical aspects by way of a series of sciences to get the general trend of its development as given in the following outline, always keeping in mind that the process centers in individuation.

By means of this outline of method we may represent graphically the social organization of any society during its successive stages of historical development. First, on a horizontal line represent the integrating conditions of such a society as Germanic society, in its four periods of social development—tribal, military, civil, and national. Secondly, for each of these periods determine (1) the social æsthetic or the primary tastes, likes and dislikes in the primary relations between man and man; (2) the economic elements in the organization of that stage of development, including property

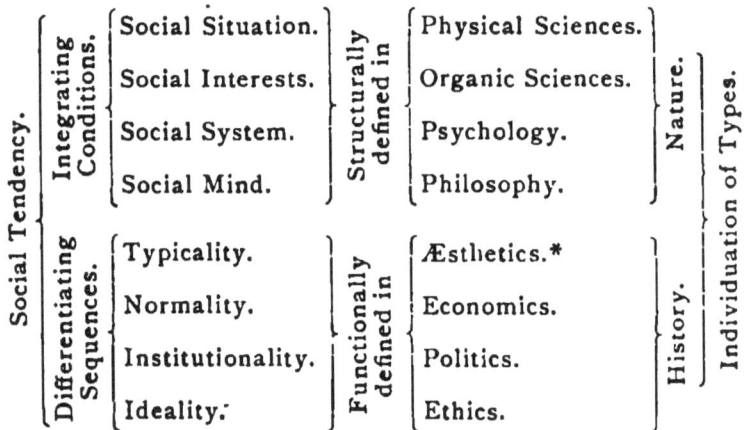

Social Tendency.	Integrating Conditions.		Structurally defined in		Nature.	Individuation of Types.
		Social Situation.		Physical Sciences.		
		Social Interests.		Organic Sciences.		
		Social System.		Psychology.		
		Social Mind.		Philosophy.		
	Differentiating Sequences.	Typicality.	Functionally defined in	Æsthetics.*	History.	
		Normality.		Economics.		
		Institutionality.		Politics.		
		Ideality.		Ethics.		

and its uses as affected by custom and conventionality; (3) the polity as given in the relations of superiority and subordination; (4) the ethical organization of conduct with respect to the ideal of character.

This being the logical outline of the method of types, what lines of inquiry must be followed to give scientific character and historical content to

* Æsthetics is not by any means a satisfactory term to use in designating the 'science of our likes and our dislikes' which really determine our primary social relations.

this mode of determining the nature of the process of social development ?

In the first place we must look in the direction of the relation of the social aggregate to nature to find the integrating conditions which fashion the developmental movement. What is the nature of the methods by which the coexistent conditions are best revealed to one seeking for a solution of the relation of nature to human socialization ?

Secondly, we must look in the direction of the historical forces—of the axiomatic relation of the aggregate—to history in its organized aspects to find the differentiating sequences by which the developmental movement is influenced. What is the nature of the methods by which the differentials in typal evolution are given concrete content ?

The methods of defining the natural conditions of development of types are those of the physical, the organic, the psychological, and the philosophical sciences.

These specific methods, on which the method of types relies, correspond with the points of view from which the part of personality in the social process must be investigated; the descriptive method being peculiarly fitted to present the phenomena of the social situation within which typal integration is the characteristic process and persistency of type the condition of survival; the naturalistic method being best adapted to make exposition of the phenomena of competing social interests during the rise of which resistance to uniformity of type and the normalizing conquest of nature is the primary requisite of survival; the psychological method being indispensable to define for us the governing relations which control the social aggregate when it enters into and develops within the social order by the assimilation of its tendencies under the conditions of institutional life; and the philosophical method being finally necessary to formulate for us the phenomena of ideality among which the characteristic process is social consolidation. Each method, therefore, makes a specific contribution to the truly comprehensive method, but none of them is capable either of interpreting the social process as a whole or of completely interpreting its own social meaning apart from its synthesis in the process of development.

The practical value of any theoretical method of inquiry into social phenomena depends on the extent to which it contributes to a wise social policy. The ultimate test of any social policy is the type of personality which it tends to produce. The social process is known by its typical fruits actual and potential. The sociological method, therefore, is preeminently concerned with the determination of the type—actual or potential—and the conditioning and the causal factors which enter into the process by which these types are or tend to be evolved.

If this relation of these four classes of methods to the sociological method of types be conceded as logically and scientifically compatible, then it must be admitted that the way has been pointed out here by which one more portion of the whole field of knowledge can be intelligently used in the service of the social life. By so doing, the social situation of any type of persons, the social interests of all distinct groups or classes, the social order in which all interests and types are reciprocally established in a social system, and the social ideal by which the consolidation of the whole objective life is developed into equilibrium with the social mind in mastery of the social situation—all these appear each in its own place and doing its own part in the evolution of a progressive policy of typal attainment. In their practical results, as well as in their logical relations, these methods give scientific content to the formal conditions of development. This will be evident from the following account of actual methods.

The descriptive method in sociology finds its best exponent in the writings of Spencer, in which the data, the inductions, the relations and the institutions of the social order are presented. The method is that of the physical sciences in the analysis of processes. The principle governing that method in this case is not historical but comparative, but yet not comparative in the sense in which writers on jurisprudence use the method. In juristic literature we have the comparative study of *kindred* institutions and jural relations in different communities of the *same* kind; in Spencer's exposition of social phenomena we have a comparative study of *analogous* relations existing among communities of *different* kinds, in the effort to illustrate the universality of the principle of evolution from the simple to the complex in social orders. Social types in Spencer's system of classification are types of social organization—not types of personality.* But no one can study his most direct contribution to method, without realizing that the underlying idea in *The Study of Sociology* is consistent with that of the type of personality which normally tends to prevail.†

The naturalistic method is a method of systematic description from the naturalist's point of view; from this method of organic interpretation has been derived the following aids: (1) The organic conception of society, (2) the idea of the equilibrium, between personality and its environment and of the social aggregate with its environment, (3) the solidarity of nature and civilization in the cosmic process of evolution, and (4) the recognition of the typical as the criterion of evolutional value (Romanes). This method defines social interests most successfully.

The psychological method marks a reaction from the naturalistic or analogical methods. Its material contributions to sociological method have been equally illustrious. They comprise, (1) the prominence of the subjective factors in social life (Ward), (2) the insistence that personality in conscious association with its kind is the core of sociological interest (Giddings), (3) the formulation of psychological laws in social life (Tarde, Baldwin), (4) the

* Principles of Sociology, Vol. I., Part II., Ch. X.
† Chap. iii., pp. 52-3.

service of sociology in the educational development of types of national character (Guyau, Fouillée).

The philosophical method often identifies sociology with the philosophy of history (Barth),* though the two are distinct—the quest of sociology being that of the typical groups in fact and tendency and that of the philosophy of history the ideal, as part of the content which enters into the social process. From the philosophical method applied to the interpretation of social phenomena we have (1) the determination of the social ideals which characterize the social process (Mackenzie), and (2) the definition of the function of intellect (Draper), and of religion (Kidd, Nash) in human progress.

The method of types presumes and underlies the other methods and can only be applied after the other methods have been sufficiently employed to bring the sociological data to light from which selection is to be made in the study of any particular problem. Without the descriptive method the quality of typicality could not be adequately grasped; without the naturalistic method the adaptive or normalizing efficiency of the social type as an organic tendency must lack the requisite degree of exactness; without the psychological method the social motives can never be given their right value in the analysis of the social process; and without the philosophical method the potency of ideal convictions as conditioning factors in social evolution must remain to be determined by the personal

* Die Philosophie der Geschichte als Sociologie, A, § 3. Leipzig, 1897.

equation of the investigator himself. But with the typical procedure we insist (1) upon the selection of only the typical as the subject of investigation, (2) upon the determination of the conditions of its existence or environment as a controlling factor in typal tendency, (3) upon the reciprocal relations which any typal tendency holds in institutional life, and (4) upon the goal of life toward which the type in question tends. By this procedure the essentials are made the subject of analysis and synthesis and the problem is cleared, from the start, of unessentials.

Whether a science of sociology can be developed as a science depends very much upon one's conception of terms. But, whatever meaning may be given, it is at least certain that we can think scientifically in social interpretation by the aid of this method. "By scientific thought," it is properly said, "we mean the application of past experience to new circumstances by means of an observed order of events." Here there are three conceptions requisite for scientific procedure : (1) past experience, (2) new conditions or changes, (3) an observed order of events. To these terms correspond, in the method of types, (1) the actual social type which is the epitomized result of the social experience and the method of whose determination has been pointed out; (2) the potential situation within which by typal adjustment to changes the social type tends normally to find its equilibrium, and (3) the selective relation between the actual and the potential type, giving us the observed order of·

events according to which the social process must be guided. This selective connection may appear in typal subordination, typal substitution, typal assimilation, or of typal solidarity as the leading phases in the established order of events, but the selective continuity between the actual and the potential is the essential assumption that runs through all social thought in the effort to deal scientifically with changed or changing conditions of existence. " When the Roman jurists applied their experience of Roman citizens to dealings between citizens and aliens, showing by the difference of their actions that they regarded the circumstances as essentially different, they laid the foundation of that great structure which has guided the social progress of Europe. That procedure was an instance of strictly scientific thought. When a poet finds that he has to move a strange new world which his predecessors have not moved; when nevertheless he catches fire from their flashes, arms from their armory, sustentation from their footprints, the procedure by which he applies old experience to new circumstances is nothing greater or less than scientific thought. When the moralist, studying the conditions of society and the ideas of right and wrong which have come down to us from a time when war was the normal state of man and success in war the only chance of survival, evolves from the conditions and ideas which must accompany a time of peace, when the comradeship of equals is the condition of national success; the process by which he does this is scientific thought and nothing else. . . .

The truth which it arrives at is not that which we can ideally contemplate without error, but that which we can act upon without fear; and you cannot fail to see that scientific thought is not an accompaniment or condition of human progress, but human progress itself." *

We have thus defined for us the general outline of the method of types. We have seen that its general method is essentially that of scientific thought. When we proceed by this method in social study wé do substantially though less precisely what the worker and thinker in the exacter sciences do when they study other fields of past experience in connection with future possibilities to bring both under the synthesis of a universal law.

We get for the method of types a measurable degree of definiteness by studying the social process from the side of those natural conditions of personal association in which the integration of types goes on first in the simplest unitary scope of association, then in the separate fields of interests, then in the area of the social system and finally in the domain of the social mind. There remains now the task of finding for the differentiating axioms of the social process that historical content which social organization gives us. For this we have to define the social organization with respect to those fields of scientific thought by which the human mind has sought to organize its associative energies under conceptions peculiar to history.

Logically regarded, history is a series of verified

* Clifford, Lectures and Addresses, pp. 155, 156, 157.

axioms respecting the differentiation of social aggregates from the actual to the potential in the development of social types. In its inner character its process of differentiation from event to event is indicated in the sociological axioms of typicality, normality, institutionality and ideality. But, for the historical motives which these imply we have to refer to those well-known divisions of knowledge in which man has analyzed the processes and products of social organization. And the method of types accepts these results by the methods which each division has found most convenient for its own purposes.

The master motives resulting in the growth and development of social organization are æsthetic and domestic, economic, political and ethical, including the religious motives. By the study of the corresponding sciences we get at the real forces which form the content of the sociological axioms. To give definiteness to the method of types we must make each of these special social sciences as much the subject of study as we should the sciences of natural conditions of personal association. Just as far as these sciences are developed, so far can the method of types go in its effort to show the typical products by the relations which man in association has to nature and history. From these two points of view the method of types must always proceed, if it would utilize the results and understand the primary factors that universally figure in the evolution of types of personality—organic, social, sociological, and ideal. The sciences which treat of so-

cial man as related to nature furnish us with the
conditions on which development in society is necessary.   The sciences which treat of historical
forces of social organization show us under the
pressure of what social purposes and powers the
fact of social development becomes a reality.   The
definition of the joint product of the natural conditions and the historical causes as individuated into
one result—the types of personality—is the task of
this method of interpretation of society.   It is only
by such definition as will show the bearing of natural
and historical factors on the type of personality
that tends to prevail that we can ever give any of
the sciences their proportionate valuation in educational policy.

   Æsthetics, regarded from the standpoint of the
observer impressed with the attractiveness of objects having some kinship with himself, includes the
facts of fellowship or community.   We are fond
of what attracts us by qualities we believe it contains in common with us or as complemental to
ours.   It is this quality in human beings that lies
at the basis of sociality—the selective sense of what
is agreeable to us in others.   It is also this quality
that makes domestic organization.   To like others
is to find that others have awakened in us the
æsthetic sense of the typical.   Æsthetics from the
artist's standpoint deals with the attempt to give
expression to the *ideal* type of social feeling in personality; but from the standpoint of the impressed
observer it is an attempt to give expression to the
organic type of personality by physical acts of asso-

ciation resulting in habitual relationships.* The
one is particular and the other universal in the form
of expression which it gives to the æsthetic impulse
and ideal in social consolidation. But while æsthetics in this more common sense of sensuous sociality enables us to define the typical social individual, and while in its artistic sense it serves to embody to our senses a representation of the ideal,
still it cannot adequately explain the intermediate
stages of the typal evolution between the organic
and the ideal.

For explanation of the social type normal to environment we must go to economics and biology.
For the explanation of the organized tendencies of
society we need to have recourse to politics and
to psychology. But politics as the science of the
State is not inclusive enough to furnish us with the
scope of survey which the sociological point of view
requires. As the science of public policy, permanently expressed in the political constitution of the
social population, its principles and practices coordinate all forms of social system such as the domestic order, the social classes and the numerous
communities under the sovereign aims of the State;
but politics does not give sufficient insight to the
sources of the social organization as we find it in
voluntary associations nor to the natural conditions
of human association in time and place to make its
point of view the exclusive standpoint of sociology.

* Marshall, Principles of Æsthetics, pp. 1-8, and Ch. III.,
especially pp. 81-3. See also Guyau, Non-Religion of the
Future: A Sociological Study, Introduction, II.

Sociology insists on using a more universal category of social coordination than the State. The rise of organizing ideals in the social minds of peoples of mutually exclusive States leaves no option to the sociologist in the effort to find a standpoint potentially more comprehensive and more cosmopolitan than that of the political state.

Ethics alone remains to offer its point of view for comprehensive interpretation of society considered from the twofold or coordinated aspects of natural association and historic social organization. Here again we see that there are ethical as there were economic, political and æsthetic considerations pervading the whole of social life, but there are natural strata of associative relations into which the ideal of the social type has not struck its roots deep enough to serve as the sole law of its interpretation. The function of the ethical is to individuate the social ideal by constraining the tendencies toward the solidarity which it represents to the social consciousness—the typally organized thought and feeling of the social population. The ideal is far too universal a form of expression to account for the association of two strange children on the street, for the equilibrium of social classes in social interests and for the balancing of tendencies in a politically organized social system. But its point of view does enable us to rightly interpret all subjective relations of personality which have arisen to the rank of the social ideal.

This true standpoint of sociology we deem to be that of the type of personality which normally tends

to prevail in the direction of the ideal. In this
point of view we bring together the results of the
foregoing study of the social process both from
the side of natural association and of social organization. If we compare these results we shall see
that the method of types exhibits four distinct aspects from which social development must be considered. It has the aspect of an organic type, of a
type normal to conditions, of a type as coordinated
with a social tendency, and of a type consolidated
with the ideal of the social process.

From the sciences called inorganic and the science of æsthetics we have the physical conditions
and the subjective qualities of the organic type
which determines the question of community of
kind. In these we must look for that logically persistent quality which the sociological point of view
requires. That quality is the *typically human.* The
scientifically measurable degree of adaptation which
biology and economics give enables us to determine the second step in the standpoint of sociology
as that of the *socially normal.* Psychology and politics enable us to define for sociology its third essential standpoint. From them the consciously reciprocal interdependence of functional tendencies is
shown, and the third point of view of sociology is
that of the *tendentially organic.* By philosophy and
ethics we disclose to the social apprehension the
fourth point of view of sociology to be that of the
potentially ideal, in which the possibilities of development are harmoniously imaged in the solidarity
of the tendencies normal to social conditions of

survival under which all known types of human beings appear.   In the typically human we have the
organic type of personality; in the socially normal,
the social type adapted to conditions of survival;
in the tendentially organic, the developmental tendencies of types, or the sociological type; and in the
potentially ideal the ideal possibilities of social solidarity.   Hence this standpoint of the organic type
of personality that normally tends to prevail in the
direction of the ideal type comprehends under these
categories all the phenomena of human association.

I. The sociological point of view is primarily concerned with the typically human.   This involves all
that we call anthropological, ethnological, together
with what we include in the terms civilization and
culture.   In these generic aspects sociology is required to look upon man as that associated portion
of the animal world, which is made up of personal
beings and to which in the totality of the genus we
give the name humanity.   We are concerned with
this fact of a genus integrated with its own kind
and differentiated from other kinds of the animal
world.

The typically human involves what is ethnological.   Ethnology treats of anthropological species
—of the specific races into which on physical and
psychical grounds the race as genus is found to be
differentiated.   As these facts of racial traits are
data which enter fundamentally into the shaping of
the course of social evolution of human types at
every step of history we must include this survey
of ethnical man in the sociological survey, lest we

fail to understand one of the strongest of forces in the development of types of social man.

Only indirectly and in an introductory way has the subject of human sociology anything to do with sub-human association. Comparative sociology must take into account all forms of association among organic beings from the coral colony up to the ideal congregation of the immortals. But for sociology considered as bent upon the service of social policy of human communities, the human is quite sufficient as a field of research. Human sociology is concerned with all that is human but only after the individuals have become, or as they are found in the form of, typically integrated aggregates upon whose general tendencies the community has learned to count as upon a group that has come to some degree of self-consciousness. This excludes the sub-human and the non-typical. Of course no human being is organically non-typical, though we may have survivals and types which appear "before the times are ripe" which we cannot readily classify because we do not value the factors. Yet they are typically human.

2. The sociological point of view is that of the socially normal. From the standpoint of sociology there is no absolute criterion of social normality. But all normality is *relative* to the conditions of association and organization in the community. We have different levels one above the other or different areas of social normality among classes, communities, peoples or races. One who is normal to a certain social status may be abnormal to another

social status in the same organized community. To be normal is in general to be at equilibrium with one's general environment. To be socially normal is to be at equilibrium with one's social environment; and to be at equilibrium with one's social environment is to be differentiated out of a general adjustment to environment into that typal tendency in which one's personal constitution entitles him to find his equilibrium; that is, the balancing of his ratio of individual and social units of personal efficiency with the social tendency in which there is an equivalent ratio in the demands which the natural conditions and the social organization make upon its members.

3. The sociological point of view is that of the tendentially organic. We have in the evolution of types of personality to remember that personality is tenanted in a typal tendency always normally operating in the direction of the potential type. But no such tendency lives wholly unto itself; every tendency is organic in the sense of being reciprocally coordinated with other functional tendencies which go to make up the social organization. These differentiated functions duly coordinated make a set of tendencies by which society secures survival by division of necessary social labor, and attains to development by conserving the tendencies in the direction of the ends which the social mind requires all to conform to, and by permitting all typal tendencies, on condition of this organic conformity, to differentiate themselves as far as the

typal conviction of the social organization will allow.

Within each tendency required for the order and progress of the social organization numerous specific tendencies arise. But all tendencies are nevertheless axiomatic in their origin and aim. They integrate, they differentiate, they assimilate, they idealize types of personality. In the study of typal tendencies we must be sure of the organic function of the social organization and be able to measure the degree of differentiation and assimilation.

4. The standpoint of sociology is also that of the potentially ideal. It is a fatal mistake to think that the potentially ideal is not an object of associative effort in social policy. The normal tendency in the evolution of personality lies in the direction of the ideal, but for most men it is not the goal of the tendency or tendencies in the development of society. The potentially ideal is the ideal which arises from the development of a high degree of sympathetic solidarity in the possible achievements of a people. Social organization of tendencies in a developmental process is only a necessary method of progressing toward the possible ideal in which society believes. By realizing the ideally possible the sociological type becomes the ideal type of the social mind in which real solidarity resides.

The development of man as a member of society depends on the development of these four points of view in social life and policy. And these aspects will be developed as rapidly as the natural conditions of human association and the causal forces of social organization can be systematically coordinated in the evolution of types of character.

The following diagram represents this coordination in mere outline.   On this basis educational

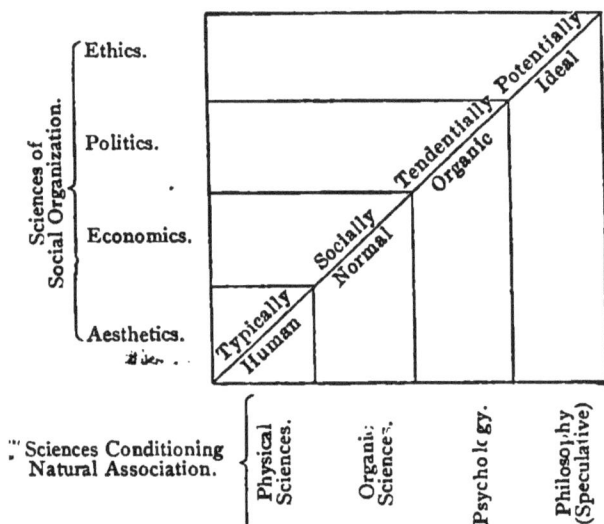

FIG. 16.

values can be reformulated.   Social policy must take into account (1) the facts or conditions of natural association, (2) the forces that belong to social organization, and (3) the coordination of these factors in the individuation of the type of character that normally tends to prevail toward the ideal. The social process being a type-developing process, educational policy must organize knowledge and its uses to that supreme end.

INDEX.

171 ; develops symbolism, 172; of typal quality, 218.

Law, is institutionalized custom or habit, 206 ; logical and scientific, 253–4; definition of, 254 ; hypothetical, 254 ; social development, 258–9; a universal, 261.

Letourneau, on facts of race, 43; on affective motives, 87; on social necessities, 123.

Logical, contradiction, 112 ; forms, 116; the social system is, 117; conception of social sciences, 318.

Loyalty, to type, 109; to the lowly, 133 ; in the social population, 157.

Lotze, on logical method, vii; on meanings of law, 254.

Lubbock, J., on sociality of ants, 43.

Mackenzie, J. S., on subjugation of nature, 289; on ideals, 333.

Maine, H. S., on legal fictions, 113 ; on kinship, 171 ; on property and conventionality, 176.

Malthusian, analysis, 89 ; interpretation, 324.

Marriage, an institution of social needs, 123–4.

Marshall, A. R., on art and social consolidation, 152–3.

Martensen, on the aim of history, 248–9.

Martineau, J., the type, a permanent standard, 41.

Method, of scientific ideal, 228; and aims of progress, 284–92 ; of types, Ch. XVI., 312–46.

Mill, J. S., on theory of types, 46; "state of society," 83; on the logic of social sciences, 316–18.

Mind, role in social development, 45, 283.

Mitchell, A., co-operation of animals, 71.

Morality, natural basis in normality, 177.

Nash, H. S., on social effect of ideals, 157; on idea of personality, 182; on religion in progress, 333.

Nation, older than state, 117; must select or degenerate, 269.

National efficiency, requires nourishment of type, 133–4.

Nationality, modern, exalts social system, 134.

Natural selection, 273–5; and the social consciousness, 279.

Nature, association, a fact of, 12; a source of sociology, 40; nourisher of social man, 52; effect of property on man's relation with, 195–6; eliminates useless types and tendencies, 210; gives organic limits to selection, 273.

Nordau, on degenerate types, 164.

Normal, adaptation, 251

Normality, the second logical axiom, Ch. X., 176; a criterion of adaptation, 186; its requirements, 189–90, 278; in method, 320.

Order, in social evolution, 115; aspect of institutionality, Ch. XI., 192.

Organic, types, 26, 27, 35, 275, 278, 338; tendencies, 114, 117, 344.

Organization, social, iii, 24, 67–70; personality in, 75; connections of, 81–2; of life, 226; sciences of, 346.

Organon, the type is, in human development, 28; potentially normal type is, 33; as sociological type, 37; of social life, 276.

www.ingramcontent.com/pod-product-compliance
Lightning Source LLC
Chambersburg PA
CBHW030914270326
41929CB00008B/694